1 MONTH OF
FREE
READING

at

www.ForgottenBooks.com

By purchasing this book you are eligible for one month membership to ForgottenBooks.com, giving you unlimited access to our entire collection of over 700,000 titles via our web site and mobile apps.

To claim your free month visit:
www.forgottenbooks.com/free2897

ISBN 978-0-265-59879-5
PIBN 10002897

"Till I see my ring, I will not again look upon your face."

Novels from Shakespeare Series

The
Merchant of Venice

TOLD BY
A POPULAR NOVELIST

WITH EIGHT ILLUSTRATIONS
IN COLOR BY
AVERIL BURLEIGH

PHILADELPHIA
THE JOHN C. WINSTON COMPANY
PUBLISHERS

PUBLISHERS' NOTE

In this Series the plays of Shakespeare appear in an altogether new guise.

In his Preface to the "Tales from Shakespeare," Charles Lamb confessed the omission of "many surprising events and turns of fortune, which for their infinite variety could not be contained in this little book, besides a world of sprightly and cheerful characters, the humour of which I was fearful of losing if I attempted to reduce the length of them."

Here, however, in the "Novels from Shakespeare," the limit of length is removed and the plays appear as old time romances in which almost every character keeps his place, and every incident is retained, only the dramatic and poetic setting giving place to the devices of the novelist.

It is hoped that by means of this Series the charm of the stories in Shakespeare's plays will be better appreciated than before, and that through this means a fresh inducement will be created to read the plays themselves and to see them upon the stage.

CHARACTERS IN "THE MERCHANT OF VENICE"

THE DUKE OF VENICE

PORTIA DI NERLINI . . . . . Heiress of Count Pietro

NERISSA . . . . Her maid

BALTHAZAR ⎱
STEPHANO ⎰ . . . . Her two servants

THE PRINCE OF MOROCCO . . Suitor to Portia

BASSANIO RAMBERTI . . . . A young Venetian noble

GRATIANO MARMOTTINA . . . A friend of Bassanio

ANTONIO CAINELLO . . . . . A merchant of Venice

SALANIO ⎱
SALARINO ⎰ . . . . Merchants of Venice

LORENZO FORTUNATO . . . . A friend of Bassanio

SHYLOCK . . . . A Jew

JESSICA . . . . His daughter

TUBAL . . . . A Jew, Shylock's friend

In the novel, the following minor characters who are not represented in the play, are also included:

COUNT PIETRO DI NERLINI . . . . . Portia's father

NICCOLO GRIMANI . . . . A profligate Venetian noble

PAOLO . . . . Antonio's servant

TONI PANOCCHI . . . . Shylock's servant

PETER CHUS . . . . A friend of Shylock

FLORIO . . . . Portia's steward

ANGELO SUTARI ⎱ ⎰ Ruffians hired by Niccolo
GIACOPE ⎰ ⎱ Grimani

MONNA ELENA . . . . Keeper of a wine shop

DR. CERELLO

GASPARD . . . . Messenger from Bassanio

CONTENTS

PAGE

I. A DANGEROUS EXPEDITION 11

II. THE JOY OF SPRING-TIDE 21

III. THE REVELERS 29

IV. ON THE PIAZZA SAN MARCO 37

V. THE HOUSE OF THE JEW 49

VI. THE JEW'S DAUGHTER 62

VII. THE COMING OF A LOVER 71

VIII. THE QUEEN OF MANY SUBJECTS . . . 77

IX. A ROYAL SUITOR 83

X. GRIMANI PROVES IMPORTUNATE 94

XI. A BROKEN OATH 104

XII. TONI OVER-REACHES HIMSELF 109

XIII. LORENZO TELLS HIS PLANS 118

XIV. THE SKELETON AT THE FEAST 126

XV. THE ELOPEMENT 135

XVI. ROBBED! 143

XVII. A VAIN SEARCH 152

XVIII. A TALE OVERHEARD 163

PAGE

XIX. THE AMBUSH 174

XX. THE FAILURE OF PURSUIT 195

XXI. IN THE CHURCH OF SAN MARCO . . . 206

XXII. NERISSA MAKES CONDITIONS 218

XXIII. THE CHOICE 224

XXIV. AN ILL-OMENED MESSENGER 234

XXV. STEPHANO GOES TO PADUA 245

XXVI. THE HOUR OF TRIUMPH 259

XXVII. THE TRIAL 268

XXVIII. BELLARIO'S SUBSTITUTE 278

XXIX. JUSTICE! 295

XXX. THE GUERDON 302

XXXI. THE HOME-COMING 309

XXXII. A SWEET CONFESSION 322

LIST OF ILLUSTRATIONS

"TILL I SEE MY RING, I WILL NOT AGAIN LOOK UPON YOUR FACE" . . . . *frontispiece*

"I WILL COLLECT THE DUCATS AND FOLLOW YOU AS SPEEDILY AS MAY BE" . . . . *to face page* 60

"DO YOU NOT REMEMBER, LADY, A VENETIAN, A YOUNG SOLDIER?" 82

"LOOK TO MY HOUSE—YES, LOOK TO IT WELL" . 114

"TAKE THIS PACKET," SHE CRIED 138

"THE DUKE SHALL GRANT ME JUSTICE" 212

"HERE CHOOSE I. JOY BE THE CONSEQUENCE". 226

"A POUND OF THAT SAME MERCHANT'S FLESH IS YOURS" 292

THE
MERCHANT OF VENICE

CHAPTER I

A DANGEROUS EXPEDITION

"**N**ERISSA!"

"I am here, lady."

The dark-eyed waiting maid came to the side of the couch on which her young mistress lay.

The bond between these two lay deeper than mere service commanded and rendered, for they were foster sisters, and the motherless and only child of the Count di Nerlini clung with tender affection to the girl who had been her childhood's playmate in these pleasant woods and amidst the fair scenes of her home—the Palazzo Nerlini at Belmont, situated close to Padua.

A happy childhood it had been too for Portia, in spite of a certain loneliness which a loving father's care had striven constantly to shield her from; and it was perhaps the memory of that tender guardianship which brought a cloud now to the young girl's face.

"My father is ill," she said, looking towards Nerissa with troubled eyes. "I am certain it is so, though neither he nor the learned leech who traveled hither last week from Padua, are willing to admit it. But oh,

Nerissa, can a daughter's eyes mistake in such a case? There is a weariness which comes over him when he thinks none spy upon his solitude, and he grows thinner too. It is this fear which haunts such sunny hours and makes me tremble. He is all I have, Nerissa, all I have to love, save you, sweet friend."

The maid came closer, kneeling by the other's side, eager with her comfort.

"Surely you mistake," she urged. "Why, my lord your father is even now expecting the company of the noble Marquis di Montferret. There are to be feastings, dancings, masques and hunting in the forest. This cannot be the scheming of a sick man."

"When did my father ever think of self when he hopes to plan for my happiness?" replied Porta di Nerlini passionately. "Oh, I am sick at heart, Nerissa, and there is but one way of comfort. Presently you shall go and bid Balthazar and Stephano meet me at the side postern. I go to the Convent of St. Ursula to pray that my dear father's health may be restored."

Nerissa's black eyes widened in surprise, not unmingled with alarm.

She even ventured to protest.

"It is a solitary road, lady, and full often bandits haunt the woods or lurk upon the hillside. Balthazar and Stephano are trusty knaves, but—but they would scarcely suffice in our defence if—if——"

But her mistress cut short the protest by clapping her hands sharply.

"Go, Nerissa," she commanded, "do as I tell you. I am going to the convent to pray."

Nerissa rose, curtsying obedience. "On foot, lady?" she questioned.

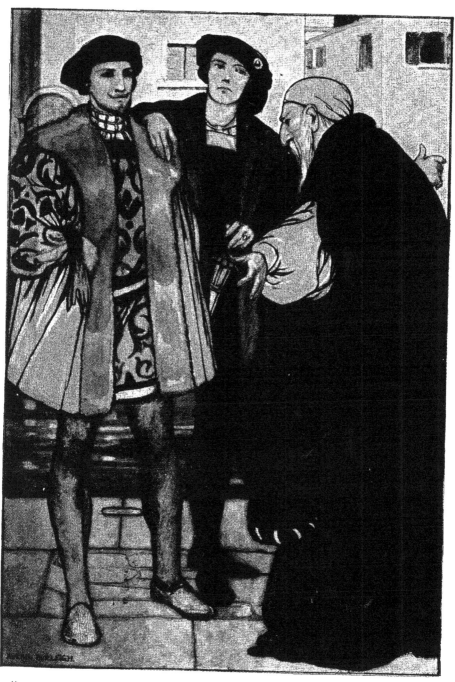

"I will collect the ducats and follow you as speedily as may be."

"Yes, on foot.   Why!   It is not two miles by way
of the pine woods.   Tell the men I shall be ready anon."

Sweet and kindly though she was by nature, di Nerlini's
daughter had early learned the art of ruling.   Tender,
she was at the same time dominant; proud, though
gentle; and on occasion, self-willed.   So Nerissa, hearing unalterable decision in those brief sentences, went
her way reluctantly to give a message whose purport
she inwardly disapproved.

In that sixteenth century many turbulent rogues
haunted the highways of every European country, and
Italy was no exception.   Armed banditti lurked for
the unwary traveler and were ready enough to cut a
throat for the price of a ducat.   But the high-spirited
Portia ignored such dangers in her set purpose to seek
the convent and relief for her fears in the outpouring
of prayers, which she felt would be so much more
efficacious before St. Ursula's shrine than in the dim
solitude of her own oratory.

Rising from her couch she moved slowly across a room
where love had been lavish in its gifts.   Rich hangings
of Eastern silks draped the doorways and windows, the
walls were covered by the costliest arabesques, velvet
couches and quaintly-carved stools were set in artistic
daintiness about the apartment, whilst an inlaid table
of rare mosaics was heaped with fine broideries and
illuminated manuscripts.

Nor was the inner bed-chamber less luxurious.   All
that wealth and art could bestow was here employed to
make fit setting for so rare a jewel—the most treasured
of all Count di Nerlini's possessions.   And fair she was,
this blue-eyed daughter of his, as the long mirror before
which she stood showed her.   Hair the color of bur-

nished gold was piled in soft curls about a queenly head, delicate features showed pride of race, whilst sweeping lashes only half veiled eyes which revealed the blue of slumbering lagoons in the midday sunshine.

In her white robe girt by a crimson girdle she looked like some young goddess come from Olympian heights to bewilder men by a vision of queenly beauty which might set them dreaming of love beyond hope of requital.

Love? Ah! She had heard the word whispered in the sighing of summer breezes amongst yonder dark pine trees, or in the song of the river which babbled of it as it flowed on to the sea—glimpses of which could be seen from the hill-top near. But, as yet, the word had no more meaning than such as dreams are made of, to the young daughter of di Nerlini.

So far, the horizon of life was bounded by her father's sheltering care, and the first shadow had fallen with the fear of his secret sickness.

Nerissa was back by this time, busy in wrapping the long black cloak about her mistress and twining the silken scarf about her bright tresses.

For once the maid was silent, mumchance through anxiety, for she liked not the thought of this expedition which might end so disastrously for all.

Closely wrapped and veiled, both girls stole swiftly down to the side postern, since wilful Portia knew well enough that her father would have forbidden the purchase of prayers at such a price.

Near the door two men in blue liveries awaited. Fine, strapping fellows, quick-eyed and ready-fisted, with daggers in preparation for any creeping footpad. If they were surprised at their lady's command they did not show it, but followed closely along the path which led to the shadow of the pine woods. Beyond these stretched an upward slope, long and toilsome, crowned by the gray Convent of St. Ursula. Here and there a purple fig tree stretched a canopy of broad leaves to screen the traveler from fierce sun rays, or a clump of gnarled mulberries added a picturesque touch to lichen-covered boulders strewing the ground where white Madonna lilies grew straight and tall, tempting Portia to linger and pluck them for a votive offering before a sweet saint's shrine.

Birds sang their canticles of springtide in jubilee overhead—the world was surely a very joyous place this day. Already an anxious daughter felt her fears slip from her, as presently she returned down the hillside, refreshed with earnest prayer, and cheered by buoyant hope which is ever ready to play song-fellow to youth.

It was life—not death—which surrounded Portia di Nerlíni on such a day. Life and the joy of it, leaping in her breast, so that, flinging back the stifling folds of her hood in an ecstasy of delight, she stood for a moment, looking back up the track to where the gray convent stood like some shadowing peace above her.

A cry from Nerissa was echoed by a still louder one from the attendants, who sprang forward with drawn daggers at sight of the men who came at a rush from the dark confines of a cypress grove to their right. Nerissa shrieked, seeing the flash of steel and hearing the croaking shouts of men growing gleeful at the thought of an easy prey.

But Portia did not cry out. She also had her dagger, aye, and was ready to use it too. But alack! opportunity was not afforded to prove the strength of that slim arm of hers, for a hulking ruffian, having spied a lovely uncovered face, had stolen quickly upon her from behind, kicking aside little Nerissa, who clung desperately about his booted legs, whilst he swung her mistress across his shoulder with a laugh and jest which sent all Portia's courage oozing through her finger tips.

"Save me!" she shrieked. "Save me!" and so piteous was the appeal that Balthazar, fighting with his back to the straight stem of a pine tree, screamed aloud, flinging himself blindly upon his mocking adversaries.

, Yet his despair would have availed nothing had not answering cries rung merrily through the woods, and lo! our banditti, with no stomach for reversed odds, went flying helter-skelter back to their lairs, whilst Portia, dropped unceremoniously to earth, lay panting and sobbing in a delirium of terror, till strong arms girt her—more respectfully this time—and a deep, mellow voice bade her take courage since her enemies had fled.

Portia, with tears still heavy on her lashes, looked up to see a tall gallant bowing low before her. A cloak of white taffeta was flung back from his shoulders, whilst the black doublet with its girdle of embossed silver marked him for a noble of Venice.

In face he was handsome enough to attract the attention of any woman, fair complexioned, with close-cropped brown hair, fine features, and gray eyes which told of a merry humor—though for the moment they were filled with a deep concern.

"I would I had come sooner, lady," said he, in that musical voice of his, "and that I had punished the villains who thus molested you more summarily. But I waited, fearing you were hurt."

. The Lady Portia curtsied, rallying her wits as she saw that both Balthazar and Stephano lived, though

not without wounds to show for their pains, whilst little
Nerissa was seated on a boulder near, in the care of a
gallant belonging to this same company of rescuers.

"I am the Lady Portia di Nerlini," she replied, with
a dignity which lost nothing through the dishevelment
of her clothes. "My father's self shall thank you,
Messer, as do I for your opportune succor."

The speech was stiff, but the lady's eyes were kind,
and the little quiver of rosy lips went straight to her
rescuer's heart.

Again he bowed.

"It is a favorable fate indeed, lady," he replied,
"which brought me to your aid, since I, Bassanio Ramberti, with my friend Gratiano Marmottina, ride in
advance of the noble Marquis di Montferret to acquaint
the Count di Nerlini of his coming."

A radiant smile acknowledged the words.

"My father, Messer, shall hold you no less welcome
for having saved his daughter," quoth pretty Portia,
and then, losing desire for conventional phrases, they
fell to chatting more in accord with their youth, whilst
Balthazar's and Stephano's wounds were bound, and
Nerissa more wholly recovered from the shock of so
terrible an adventure.

Thus it happened that the Marquis di Montferret
himself with his suite reached the spot where they
lingered to find his messengers halting over a romantic
adventure.

A stately cavalier was this noble marquis, grizzled and
middle-aged, yet strutting it still with all the pride of
youth. He had heard of the beauty of Nerlini's heiress,
knew something too of the wealth which should some
day be hers—and perhaps herein lay half the reason for

2

his visit to Belmont.   So he listened grudgingly to the
lady's faltering account of his follower's service in so
fair a cause, wishing he had been his own ￬messenger
since gratitude brought such tenderness to blue eyes
and a soft flush to fair, rounded cheeks.   If report had
exaggerated as little concerning the lady's wealth as
about her beauty, here was a prize indeed.

Other messengers were quickly despatched to the
castle, informing the count not only of his guest's
approach but of his daughter's safety.   An addition
which perplexed di Nerlini in no small measure since he
had fancied Portia was resting in her own apartments.

Anxiety, therefore, as well as courtesy brought the old
nobleman forth to welcome the marquis and embrace
his pretty Portia, holding the latter to him with one
circling arm, whilst he listened to a brief description
of the fight in the pine woods.

No wonder his face grew pale, whilst his eyes searched
those of his daughter for explanation to this mystery.

But courtesy to his visitors restrained the questions
he was so eager to put as to what had taken place on
so perilous a journey.

Later, however, when the marquis and his suite had
withdrawn to their apartments to remove the signs of
travel from their persons and prepare for the evening's
entertainment, he sought his daughter, finding her in
her boudoir with Nerissa before her, the latter spreading out a choice of jewels for her lady's wear.

Di Nerlini opened his arms and Portia fled into their
embrace.

"Tell me?" he whispered, smoothing her bright hair
with a hand which trembled slightly, "what took you
so far from home to-day, carissima?"

She looked up at him, yearning in her eyes.

"I went to the convent to pray, noble father," she whispered. "It has been in my heart these many days past that you are sick, though you laugh when I speak of it, not trusting me. And so I went to pray to the good God and His blessed saints to preserve the one who is father, mother, all to me."

His eyes grew very tender, very pitying.

"My little Portia," he replied, "my little daughter, who has been my greatest treasure all these years, it is not lack of trust, dear child, but because I would not have one shadow dim the brightness of your face. As to sickness, why, it is the friend who jogs along side by side with age. We must not fear such a companion, we who watch the sunset in the west. Aye, and were I sure that I could leave my treasure in safe keeping I should not fear the summons, but welcome it as the call of a friend long listened for."

The girl shivered, as though from cold.

"Do not speak so, dear father," she implored. "Death is far away. I prayed to-day that it should be so, and left white lilies on St. Ursula's shrine. The birds sang as I came down the hillside—and their song told of life— and prayer answered."

He kissed her, long and tenderly, his arms folded about her as though he would fain shelter this fair blossom from the very shadow of trouble.

"The saints were truly watching," quoth he, "else had my home been one of mourning indeed, to-night; we will not forget that in our prayers, little daughter. And now I leave you to robe for the festa. A queen with many subjects you will be. A queen."

He watched the flushing face keenly, wondering

whether it were merely youth's delight at the promise of revelry which brought an added sparkle to his child's eyes.

If death were as near his own side as he deemed him to be, it was his one cherished desire to see Portia happily mated first, well knowing how greedy schemers and false suitors would be trooping to the wooing of the lovely heiress of Belmont.

"The saints have her in their keeping," he murmured to himself as he passed down the gallery towards his own apartment; and as he spoke, he stretched his arms wide, feeling very sadly how impotent they were to protect the child he loved so passionately.

CHAPTER II

"NERISSA—my pearls."

And Portia di Nerlini bent her golden head for the waiting-maid to fasten the gleaming rope of jewels round a neck no less white than the gems which lay there soft and shimmering, adding a last touch to the picture which the mirrors reflected.

A queen—no less, in her gown of palest green satin with its wide sleeves hanging loose from the shoulder, showing the dainty undersleeves of white, laced with gold and pearl broideries. The whole dress seemed to blaze with jewels, whilst the high collar of lace, stretched upwards like a great fan, framed the wearer's little proud head with its towering pile of golden curls in which dainty ribbons, flowers and jewels were twined.

Nerissa smiled slyly as she watched her mistress' critical gaze at her own fair reflection.

"The Marquis di Montferret is a very proper gentleman," she observed, with the freedom of a proved confidant.

The lady frowned, rearranging an errant curl.

" 'Tis a pity," continued the maid, "that these nobles of Venice dress in so somber a fashion. Always black, black, black, with naught but the sparkle of a jewel or the silver glinting of a girdle to enliven their attire. For myself I prefer the splendor of my lord marquis."

Portia di Nerlini laughed a little contemptuously.

"Your birds need fine feathering," she scoffed, "to hide other defects. For myself I find a black habit sets off a handsome face to best advantage."

Nerissa's merry eyes twinkled. She was a pretty lass, for her own part, with a nose fashioned for pertness and lips for kisses.

"Certes," said she, "Messer Ramberti is a handsome man, and gay too as I hear."

Portia was round in a flash, playing the mistress with command in her tones.

"Since your tongue's been wagging," she replied, "I'll hear who was your informant."

None so demure as pretty Nerissa at sound of that voice.

"Your pardon, lady," she murmured, her eyes downcast.

"It was by chance that I met the Signior Gratiano—friend to the Signior Ramberti—in the gallery just now. It was he who saved me when those foul brigands nearly murdered me as I lay swooning on the hillside; and—and—meeting me he but stayed to ask if I were recovered."

"Your recovery, girl," retorted her lady severely, "has little to do with a noble Signior's gayety. You shall explain your meaning."

Nerissa hung her head.

"I did but ask him—the Signior Gratiano," she whispered, "if all the Venetian *nobili* were as gallant and courteous as he and his friend; and therewith he told me tales of the gay doings which entertained them in that fair city, which he would have me believe was incomparable upon earth, so that—so that I said I would

I and my mistress might go thither.   Whereupon he
enlarged still further of the merry doings which would
follow our arrival, leaving me persuaded that he and the
Signior Bassanio were very gay gallants."

"And meantime," chided her mistress, "your duty
went lagging.   Out on you for a gossipmonger! And
mind there be no more of it, since this gallant Signior's
gayety may cost you dear."

With which warning the lady went her way down
the long passage leading to the marble staircase and wide
halls below, leaving Nerissa laughing slyly and no whit
humiliated by seeming displeasure.

Had she not noted her mistress's added flush at the
mention of Bassanio Ramberti's name?

There is that touch of romance in the proudest of
natures which claims interest for one who has rendered
gallant service.   And downstairs the music played in
joyous melody, scaring away that haunting shadow
which had stolen hither in the silence and quietude,
brooding there like some unwelcome trespasser to mar
the peace of a sheltered home.

But to-night who so gay as the Lady Portia?   Who
so eager for the dance and merry-making?   She was
the spirit of the springtime, laughing, beautiful, witty,
a reigning queen at whose feet all men knelt in homage.

Yet she grew weary presently, and so stole away out
onto the moonlit balcony, where the scent of orange
blossoms and roses lay sweet and pungent upon the
night air.

By her side was Messer Bassanio **Ramberti,** no less
handsome in his somber suit of black than any other
soldier in the train of my Lord Marquis.   He was at
pains too to prove that the nobles of Venice were not

so dull of wit as of attire.   His eager eyes sought those
of the lady—and she did not find their admiration
distasteful, though she had read the same approving
glances on the face of the Marquis di Montferret himself.

"Tell me of your Venice," she commanded, and
paused, dallying with the pink carnation she held,
listening first to the flooding of melody which a night-
ingale poured forth from a myrtle grove close by.

Then Bassanio spoke, and before her eyes was pictured
a vision of that fair bride of the seas, with her deep
lagoons—fathomless depths of blue waters—from which
rose the stately palaces and fairy bridges spanning the
waters of winding canals, linking each gorgeous color
scheme with that panorama of dreaming loveliness
which was Venice.

The musical voice ceased.   It was no longer of Venice
that the gallant spoke.   He touched a more personal
note, telling how he had come from Arcadia to find
Paradise.   A paradise with but one angel—golden-
crowned.

Music of instruments, music of bird-song, music of
voice, and a pair of gray eyes to complete the spell.
What wonder that Portia di Nerlini smiled, wondering
if this were the threshold of life on which she stood,
and whether the fair mysteries beyond it were to be
read in the kindling glances of gray eyes?

Then came a jarring note.   Her name was called.
She must tread a measure with the noble Marquis di
Montferret, in whose honor this festa was held.   But
she went reluctantly, more conscious now of weariness
as she moved up the great room beside a grizzled
cavalier, whose compliments fell on deaf ears.

Lights flared in their silver sconces, laughter and music

drifted to her from afar—she was tired, quite tired, and this Marquis di Montferret grew wearisome with his extravagant praises of her charms.

She was almost glad when, in the dawn of a new day, she was free to retire to her rooms, where sleepy Nerissa waited, yawning, to unrobe her mistress before retiring to her own couch.

But Bassanio Ramberti did not seek his couch with the dawning; instead, he walked by the banks of a gayly flowing river, watching the sun flame in the east, sending rosy heralds adrift over a primrose sky, whilst in his hand he held a carnation, which having been the gift of a fair lady should be honored even in death. And yet he too sighed, for all the glad awakening of life around, since was not the Lady Portia the only child and heiress of Count Pietro di Nerlini, for whose hand—and heart—the princes of the earth would be seeking?

"But to me," whispered the young man softly, as he halted on the mossy bank, following with somber eyes the foaming trail of the river's current as it swirled past him, "golden tresses are more than golden ducats, and one smile from rosy lips more precious than all the jewels of the world."

Was there mockery in the river-song which echoed his words—seeing that Bassanio Ramberti, being the most reckless of Venice's younger nobles and soldiers, had very constant need of ducats and this world's goods.

Dreamings by moonlight; dreamings in a springtime dawn—they must fade, the one and the other, in full glare of day.

And so it happened, in the ordinary turn of events,

that the Marquis di Montferret, taking a very courteous leave of his host and tender one of his young hostess, rode away from Belmont on his road to Verona, carrying with him two disconsolate gentlemen of Venice, who were each equally convinced that he left his heart behind him in the care of a fair woman, since Messer Gratiano Marmottina had found the maid Nerissa no less attractive than his friend had seen the mistress.

And here lay a truth as old as this gray old world of ours. Since if a man look at a woman in the way of love he cares not at all if she be a queen—and so, far away in the clouds above him—or a kitchen wench, whose hands may be stained by honest toil, and her station so humble that he must abase his pride in stooping to the level of lips in whose sweetness all else, is forgotten.

But when the gay company had gone, the palace of the Count di Nerlini seemed emptier than before its coming, and in dreaming of a handsome gallant who had so romantically entered her life yonder near a whispering cypress grove, the Lady Portia forgot to look for the shadow which before had haunted corridors and galleries, sending her grief-stricken to pray at St. Ursula's shrine in the gray convent on the hill. Yet, had she had eyes to see it, the shadow was still there, stalking grim and unforbidden to pass behind silken hangings and screening tapestries till it reached the side of a man who sat with bent head and saddened eyes, listening to the approach of inexorable feet. It was death who stood in the shadows and would not be denied.

Count Pietro di Nerlini knew that, and with a patient sigh of acquiescence gave up the hope of placing his

cherished treasure in safe keeping ere he went forth
to meet his Emilia, who in giving him that guarded
treasure had herself passed into the Great Beyond.

But the eyes which looked forward into Eternity
grew wise.

Father and mother both had Count Pietro been to
his little Portia, and it was scarcely a week since he
had realized she was a woman grown.

The knowledge had come to him that evening when
he had watched her pass by on the arm of a somberly-
dressed gallant to where the moonlight played upon the
tesselated pavement of a balcony. Wearily he sighed,
as he wrote that which might serve to shield his daughter
from those who would seek not her but her fortune.

"They shall be tried," quoth Count Pietro to himself.
"So that their choice shall prove them and their vows.
If Heaven answers prayer my child's happiness shall
be thus assured."

He smiled then, having finished the careful writing
in which he had been engaged—three slender rolls of
parchment bound and sealed. Rising, he drew back
silken curtains disclosing a shelf on which stood three
caskets. Within each casket he placed a parchment
roll, and turned the key in every lock. Afterwards he
walked back to his seat, with the air of a man who has
finished his task. It was there that, later, a servant
found him, his head resting back against the carved
woodwork of his seat, a pleasant smile upon his noble
features.

The Count Pietro di Nerlini was dead—yet death
had come so peacefully and in such friendly guise that
his daughter could only weep with hushed breath, and
the knowledge that though the lilies were scarcely faded

yet on St. Ursula's shrine her prayers had been answered. It was life she had asked for the father she loved so fondly—and life had been the gift bestowed.

But because the life was that of immortality she could not restrain the tears of a great loneliness, dreading to look out upon a future which appeared so full of difficulties and darkness.·

If only she had someone—besides little Nerissa—to whom she might turn for advice and help! The tears welled in the girl's eyes again at the thought, which, drifting wide of its mark, dwelt half-consciously on a gray-eyed gallant to whom she had given a pink carnation. She wondered whether Bassanio Ramberti in his gay revelings had bestowed a second thought on the donor.

The color dyed her pale cheeks at the suggestion of her heart. Did not the night winds, moaning amongst straight-stemmed cypresses, tell her that Bassanio Ramberti would come no more to Belmont?

CHAPTER III

THE REVELERS

"A TOAST," cried Niccolo Grimani, raising his goblet high so that the white rays of moonlight showed the ruddy color of wine through the delicate tracery of engraving on the glass. "Come, you shall all drink it, my friends; to Portia di Nerlini, the heiress of that Count Pietro whose soul, no doubt, rests in the purifying fires of Purgatory."

And the young noble crossed himself before tossing off the contents of the brimming goblet. He, with three or four friends, amongst whom was Bassanio Ramberti, were seated lounging on a balcony of his stately palazzo in Venice. Small tables, on which were placed wine flasks, goblets and heaped dishes of fruits, stood close to the elbow of each guest, whilst through open casements the sound of gay voices came drifting from an inner room; the rattle of dice and an occasional oath suggesting the occupation of these other visitors to the Palazzo Grimani. It was a fair night, and from the balcony could be seen the deep waters of the lagoon, on which the moonlight played, whilst every palazzo in Venice appeared to be gleaming with many lights. Music of revelers returning from a masque came floating across the waters, and into view glided a train of illuminated barges and gondolas, with rows of colored lamps of every tint and shape slung to the square rods of the awnings, the slim figures of the gondoliers showing

(29)

plainly in their holiday dress of white, with parti-
colored sashes looped up at the sides.

Grimani, leaning over the crimson cushions of the
balcony, cried some gay jest to the master of the masque,
and was answered by laughter and quip as the pleasure-
seekers passed on out of sight.

Niccolo Grimani turned back, smiling to his guests.

"You've drunk my toast?" he questioned.

A comrade yawned, refilling his glass.

"Aye, Nicco mio," he retorted, "and would hear
more of the lady. Is she fair, or rich, that you should
dwell so lovingly on her name?"

"Corpo di Bacco! What a question! But I forgive
you, poor Pietro, since you have been sweltering all the
summer through in Rome, whilst we have dreamed
here in Venice. And what dream could be more fair
than Portia di Nerlini?"

"Ah," retorted the other, "then she is fair?"

"As a goddess—rich also—moreover an orphan."

"Diavolo!" chuckled his friend. "You will send me
a-wooing in earnest."

"Why, that is what we are all doing," mocked
Grimani. "But there are difficulties in the way of winning this lady and her fortune. Have you not heard
the tale?"

Bassanio Ramberti leaned forward. He too had been
away from Venice during the summer months and had
but lately returned. Niccolo's words reminded him of
a spring idyll and how, having saved a very fair lady
from marauding bandits, she had shown him much
favor. Had he not still treasured a faded carnation
given him by Portia di Nerlini? He thought now of
the hour in which that gift had been bestowed—an

hour of sweet dreaming on a moonlit balcony with the warbling of nightingales for music, and the loveliness of a fair lady to gaze upon.

Portia di Nerlini! Golden-haired Portia, a goddess indeed, in her clinging robes of green and white, her perfect face slightly upraised to his so that he might steal a sight of blue eyes, deeper in hue than summer skies, yet alight with a hundred joys.

Had sorrow drowned that joy-light since? He had not heard of the Count di Nerlini's death, but then he had been away, first in Verona, then Rome, his life so crowded by business and pleasure that a brief visit to the palazzo at Belmont had drifted into the background of his thoughts.

But he listened eagerly now, as Niccolo Grimani, cross-legged on his cushioned seat, told his tale.

"Di Nerlini died suddenly," the young man was saying, "leaving great wealth and one fair daughter— our gracious Portia—behind him, as a legacy to the fortunate suitor who should win both. But it appears that, fearing he might not live to choose the husband of his child, Count Pietro devised a scheme which I vow adds zest to the quest of lovelorn swains. Three caskets, one of gold, another of silver, a third of lead, stand for the choice of him who seeks fair Portia. He who chooses that casket which contains the lady's picture wins a rich and lovely bride; but if he chooses wrong he may woo no more, since first he must have vowed that in the event of failure he will never speak word of marriage to her or any other maid again, nor divulge the secret of his choice of casket."

Bassanio caught his breath in a low gasp of amaze.

"And the lady is not plighted yet?" he asked.

"No, by my faith," retorted Grimani. "Till yesterday she was as free as air, though the train of suitors
does not slacken or wane. She is rich—very rich—
amico mio, and as fair and chaste as Diana. To-morrow,
no later, I myself go to stake my chance on those caskets.
You shall drink again to my success—unless indeed you
desire to try your own fortune."

"No wooing for me," mocked another of the little
group.

"I am vowed to a single life and a merry one. Come,
Nicco, let us see how the game goes within?"

All rose, standing there, a somber little group amidst
gay surroundings. Above them an orange-colored awning flapped softly in the night breezes, crimson cushions
lay upon the balcony, whilst pots of flowers added another scheme of soft pink and white. The Venetian
noble had scope for his love of color in everything but
dress, but the laws concerning the latter were rigidly
regulated by a college existing for that purpose.

According to these laws, a noble Venetian must have
eight cloaks, three for masques, one of which was for
the spring festa of the Ascension, when the Doge married the sea. In addition to these they had two of
white taffeta for summer, one of blue cloth for winter,
one of white cloth for great occasions, one of scarlet
cloth for the days of church ceremonial. For the rest
their doublets were uniformly black, girt with a girdle
embossed with silver, open collars, showing the diamond
button of their shirt stock, and round black caps fringed
with wool.

The law had the advantage of thus saving the extravagant from lavish expenditure in dress, though the result
was shown in the costly furnishing of the palaces of
the richer nobles.

The room which the young men entered was a striking example of this love of display. Marble statues, rich hangings, exquisite pictures, showed Niccolo Grimani's tastes, whilst in the center of the apartment a group of some seven men were gathered about a table of wonderful mosaics, intent on their dicing.

The newcomers, greeted by a shout of welcome, were speedily involved in the game, and for the next few hours the play went on, the monotonous rattle of the dice broken by the cries, laughter and oaths of the players, who drank, gambled and jested till far into the night.

They would probably be playing when dawn broke, but one at least could not remain till then. Bassanio Ramberti had entered that room resolved only to watch the hazard. Already broken in fortune by reckless extravagance, he had been haunted for weeks past by the grim shadow of debt. What would the future hold for this gay young soldier? He had asked himself the question and groaned over the answer, since ruin and he were likely enough to be bedfellows ere long. His estates must go, his palace be sold, he himself finding it necessary to seek fortune in the wars which in the sixteenth century were always convulsing some part of Europe.

So he had watched, gloomy-eyed, seeing haggard faces brighten, and gay ones grow glum over the chances of the game; and always at the back of his mind he was thinking of the tale Niccolo Grimani had told just now of how Portia di Nerlini, whose image he still carried in his heart, was alone and orphaned in that fair palazzo of hers, and that her hand—perhaps her heart—was to be won on a hazard before which the issues of this dare-

devil dicing grew pigmy-like and insignificant.   If he
could but go to Belmont!

With a mocking laugh he leaned forward and joined
the game.

If fortune smiled, lining that lean purse of his with
golden ducats, he would start for Belmont without
delay.   His heart beat high with hope—and fortune
seemed to smile.

His pile of ducats grew.   His dream grew nearer
realization. · Then, alas! fortune turned her back upon
his hope.   With paling cheeks and hardening eyes he
played on.   But the dawn had not broken before the
end came—for him.

"My last ducat, friends," he cried glibly, as he rang
down the coin on the table.   "And so—good-night
to all."

He gazed round at the ring of eager faces, flushed by
wine and the excitement of their play.

Niccolo Grimani protested at his words.

"Nay, nay, good Bassanio," he urged.   "You'll not
leave us?   Here, let me be your banker once more."

He held out a silken purse. heavy with ducats, but
Bassanio shook his head.

"I am already too deep in debt," he replied gloomily.
"Nor dare I risk the smiles of a jade who holds me
cheap to-night."

So, bowing, he left them, going slowly down the wide
staircase alone, leaving his friends too immersed in their
gambling to express more than a parting regret at his
departure.

A broken man?   They did not believe it.   To-morrow
their Bassanio would be swaggering on the Piazza with
the best of them.   It was only to-night that his pockets

were empty. Thus, if they thought of him at all, reasoned Bassanio Ramberti's friends, whilst he himself came down the marble steps of the palace, pausing at the water's edge to summon a gondola.

Waiting there, in vain at first, the young man fell to a dreaming which had its haunting of grim nightmare.

Far off in the distance he could hear the murmur of the waters lapping against the girdling sea wall. It drifted across the still lagoon like the droning of bees in summer time, whilst nearer at hand came the rhythmic dipping of oars as the great galleys, rowed by sweating slaves, made their way from Chioggia to Venice with their daily freight of fresh water.

The music of a guitar, played very softly beneath some beauty's balcony, came from a distant canal, accompanied by the mellow notes of a man's song. From where he stood on the steps of the palace Bassanio could hear the impassioned words with which an importunate lover wooed his mistress.

"Voleme ben, che sa ò sempre vostro,
Sine che durerà l'aria del cielo,
Sino che durerà pena e l'ingiostro. . .

Did the lady dream on, deaf to that call of love, or was she standing, white-robed and blushing, her soft cheek pressed against the barring shutter which presently she would open to send some token fluttering down to the singer's feet—or even permit him a swift glimpse of the beauty he desired?

While pen and ink endure, I'll leave thee never;
Love me but well; I will be thine forever.

Bassanio sighed. Alas! his dream of love was over, since, beggared and broken, how could he go to the lady of his hopes—a suitor who would—as it seemed— fill his purse at the expense of hers?

And yet—if he could! Would not the years-to come prove his devotion?

To one of Bassanio Ramberti's optimistic nature hope was a boon companion. He could not brook despair, and already hummed the refrain of that ardent lover's song as he stepped into the gondola whose coming at last rewarded his patience. There was always to-morrow—and Portia di Nerlini was still unplighted.

"If Antonio Cainello will but play his part of ever-ready friend once more," vowed Bassanio, "then will I forswear 'my sins and sail forthwith for Belmont—and the Lady Portia."

He was wondering how he could have let those summer months pass by with so little thought of her. Was it possible she had thought of him? He dared not believe it—though he pressed a dead carnation to his lips as he stood at his chamber window, watching the dawn break in the east.

CHAPTER IV

THE Piazza San Marco was thronged by a holiday crowd. What medley of color was here! Red, yellow, green, blue and pink, a veritable rainbow, embracing every hue and shade, whilst here and there the black dress of a noble gave a sober touch to the jostling throng of gayly-attired citizens and peasants. Here a dark-eyed flower girl did brisk trade with her roses and carnations, whilst at another spot a juggling clown held the crowd. Vendors of fruit and refreshments of all kinds bargained and smiled, readier to-day with a jest than a scowl, whilst gorgeously decked barges and gondolas went gliding by, filled with merrymakers.

It was noontide, and the whole spot was basking in golden light. The Byzantine mosaics of the great church shone like jewels, whilst its pinnacles and spires lifted up their white beauty to the blue heavens, an iris-hued cloud of pigeons circling around the topmost tower, crowned by a platform upon which was a bell—two bronze figures called *i Mori* striking the hour with great hammers.

This tower had been built in 1496 by Coducci of Bergamo, to receive the wondrous clock fashioned three years before by Paolo Rainieri, which, besides marking the hours, the zodiacal signs, the phases of the moon, and the month and day of the year, boasted an ingenious

(37)

piece of mechanism by which, on certain festivals, the
figures of the Magi, preceded by an angel with a trum-
pet, issued from the interior of the clock, passing before
the Madonna, to whom each bowed.

The whole Piazza had been re-paved by order of the
late Doge, Girolamo Priuli, and the Senate had caused
to be removed all the shops of notaries, dentists and
barbers, which had clung round the columns of the
Ducal Palace, together with all the benches, boxes,
chests and cases, which formerly encumbered the colon-
nade of the palace itself.   Workmen were even now
busy over the demolition of the ancient hospital of San
Marco which stood in the same line as the Campanile.
Venice indeed was at the height of her glory, and her
governors and citizens were intent on adding to the
magnificence of her buildings and the strength of her
position.

Not far from the quāys, leaning against a low marble
wall, stood a man, still young, though his closely trimmed
beard and the sober richness of his attire added unduly
to his years.   By his dress he was evidently of the merchant class rather than that of the *nobili*, whilst his
handsome features were dignified by an expression of
grave reserve which deepened now into sadness as he
looked out over the sparkling waters, marking but not
heeding the busy plying of the gondoliers and the gay
chatter of those who stood upon the quays.

Voices at his elbow roused him from a contemplative
mood, to find two friends ready with their greeting.

"Dreaming of your argosies, Messer Antonio?" cried
the younger of the two.   "Such should be my wager,
since never did I hear of bright eyes winning an answering smile from Antonio Cainello!"

"Though tales of suffering never yet found an inattentive listener in him," added the elder, resting his hand in friendly fashion on the young merchant's shoulder.

"But what ails our Antonio that we find him sad?"

Antonio Cainello smiled. "Forsooth I know not why I am so sad," he confessed; "it wearies me indeed to seek. its meaning, so out of place it seems on such a day."

And he looked round at the thronging crowd, with a kindly glance. for a black-eyed child who lagged in the heat, blinking solemnly at him at first, then dimpling as one who sees a friend.

For Messer Salanio had spoken truth when he said that the sorrowing or suffering together with every innocent child found a sympathizer in Antonio Cainello, though beauty might try her arts and crafts in vain.

"A fair day truly," agreed Salarino, placing his hand on his hip, whilst turning to stare at a blue-eyed nymph who had raised the corner of her veil just high enough to show him a pretty, laughing face. "But for myself I do not wonder at your clouded brow. With so much at stake I should tremble every time the wind blew, fearing the wreckage of my wealth and enterprise."

The three were pacing together down the Piazza, heedless of jostling sightseers. Far overhead the great hammers of bronze struck the hour of noon, whilst downward swooped the pigeons in eager circles, searching for crumbs on the pavement below—then upward winging on discovery of an unwelcome crowd.

"I thank my fortune," quoth Antonio clamly, "that my ventures are not all launched in one frail barque, so I have less fear of disaster. I confess it is not my merchandise that makes me sad."

"Why, then," cried Salarino, returning from too bold a quest of the blue-eyed little citizeness, "you are in love."

Antonio shook his head, his dark eyes very serious, so that even the gay Salarino scoffed at his own suggestion. "Not in love, neither," he echoed.

"Then let's say you are sad because you are not merry, and 'twere as easy for you to laugh, leap and say you are merry because you are not sad. Come, Salanio, I'm for the Rialto. Will you accompany us, Messer Antonio?"

"As you will," replied the other, making brave effort to shake off that unnamed despondency, which to Salarino's lighter nature seemed so foolish a thing.

Passing from the Piazza by the street called Merceria, they came upon the no less lively and far busier scene of the Rialto, the emporium of Venetian commerce and meeting place of shopkeepers and traders. Here the people swarmed under the porticos of the market, by the buildings of the Scorpagnino, amongst the benches of the fish market and the baskets and chests of the fruit sellers. Here were grouped chattering throngs of vendors and buyers, in their picturesque dresses, gay-colored handkerchiefs tied over their heads or knotted about their throats, whilst the vivid orange of the pumpkins, scarlet of pomegranates, and purple heaping of grapes, added to the blaze of color. At the landings were moored the boats, laden with vegetables from the islands and mainland, whilst merry laughter and quick rallying of wit told that business was being conducted for the main part in a spirit of good fellowship and mutual satisfaction.

Salarino and Salanio soon moved away, engaging in

eager converse each about his own particular affairs, leaving Antonio Cainello standing as a kindly spectator of a familiar scene, till once more his cloak was plucked by friendly fingers and he turned to find Bassanio Ramberti with his two friends, Gratiano Marmottina and Lorenzo Fortunato beside him. The two latter linked arms as soon as the formal salutation had been exchanged.

"My lord Bassanio," quoth Lorenzo, a merry fellow whose auburn locks and blue eyes had won him many a heart in his time, "since you have found Antonio, we two will leave you; but do not forget that at dinner-time we must meet."

Bassanio nodded. He was looking pale and weary this morning, ill-attuned to the revelry of the holiday, whilst his gray eyes had the anxious look of a man in sore need of counsel.

Antonio Cainello looked at him tenderly. They two were friends, not as the world counts friendship, but owning a closer bond, which in Antonio's case surpassed and out-valued that of any other.

"I have been to your house, Antonio," said Bassanio, holding out his hand, "and they told me I should find you upon the Piazza San Marco, or perchance in the church itself. I am glad I have found you at last."

He turned to look after his late comrades. Still linked arm in arm, the two young men had paused beside the stall of a pretty flower-seller, and were bargaining with sly chaffings for roses.

Perhaps the sight of the flowers reminded Bassanio of his purpose, reluctant though he seemed to name it.

Antonio saw his hesitation and half guessed its cause.

"The Rialto," said he, with a grave smile, "is scarcely the spot for confidences. You shall come home with me, Bassanio, and tell me all your mind."

"I will," cried the other impulsively. "You are my friend, Antonio, and you shall hear a tale which has much of folly in it, something of repentance and very little of hope. You must forgive me that petition is added to it all."

"Is there need of such a question," replied the merchant gently, "between friends?"

It was some way from the Rialto to St. Maria dell' Orto, where stood the house of Antonio Cainello, a house with balconies and curiously arched windows, speaking, even from without, of a wealthy owner of artistic temperament. The ironwork of the balconies was cut into arabesques of the lightest but most intricate designs, the walls themselves were of inlaid marble, whilst along the façade on a level with the second story from the water was an alto-relievo of great antiquity. Leaving the gondola at the steps, Antonio led his companion into the house. Sober richness of furniture, hangings and carpets was noticeable everywhere, seeming well in accord with the self-contained, quiet owner, whose library showed rare taste without any sign of that extravagant luxury which characterized the palazzo of Niccolo Grimani.

"Now," said Antonio quietly, "you shall give me a friend's confidence, Bassanio mio."

He was looking across to where the young noble had flung himself down on a cushioned embrasure of the window, his fair head resting back against a green velvet curtain, the sunlight glinting across his handsome face. And, as he looked, the merchant leaned his elbow on the table at his side, shading his eyes with his hand, as though the sunshine dazzled them; whilst, waiting for his friend to speak, his thoughts flew like winged spirits back through the dead years till memory's vision showed him this Bassanio's twin sister, fair Bianca Ramberti, beautiful, gentle, saintly, who had probably never guessed that her brother's friend, the young merchant from the Rialto, had loved her with that love which, still and silent as hidden pools, possessed a depth which fiercer passion, like mountain torrents, lacked.

So she had passed from the sight of an unknown lover to be shrouded forever from the gaze of men behind the gray walls of a convent.   There she had died, still young, leaving behind her a memory like a track of light leading upwards to the very presence of God.

To Antonio she was as some sweet saint, possessing once and forever the shrine of his heart—that inmost shrine wherein he dared not often look, though, because he knew whose image it contained, his love to Bassanio Ramberti was something more than mere friendship.

Bianca loved Bassanio, consciously, dearly, more closely than any earthly love had bound her.   So, for dear Bianca's sake, Antonio would have died for Bassanio, and for the man himself he cherished deep love, so that he would have been a patient listener to any tale his friend had for his ear.

Yet to Bassanio it was hard to voice this confession of folly.   Born to a rich heritage, he had lived extravagantly, spent lavishly and gambled not infrequently, though as a rule games of skill such as chess or *tarrochi* interested him more than the reckless hazard of dice.

"You know me so well, Antonio," he began, "and have very often told me of my faults, in the way of friendship, so that you will guess which way my folly has led me.   Alas!—how differently we should act if, in our foolishness, we could possess one grain of after-wisdom."

He sighed wearily, whilst, through that dimly lighted room, ghosts passed him by—ghosts of the follies whose reckoning he must pay, mocking and gibing as they stood in swelling array with greedy, outstretched hands.

Was he not debtor to them all? and most of all to this grave, kindly friend, who, from childhood's days, had always been so staunch and true to him?. Mad had he been, and thrice cursed fool to act as he had done.

But the gate of the past is closed to all who would go back along the path—only our acts come stalking forth to bear us company in the future. Seated there, Bassanio saw all that foolish picture of misspent years.

Left young an orphan, he had been dazzled by his own wealth, whilst pride of possession craving for popularity and an unrestrained hunger after enjoyment had launched him on a treacherous sea.

Who so gay as handsome Bassanio Ramberti? Who so reckless, so prodigal, so generous? His masques had been as famous as his feasts, whilst the splendor of his palace was unrivaled.

Thus for a time; then gradual reduction of fortune, less frequent entertainments, more zest in his soldiering, a quickening of that sense of manhood and responsibility, with brief lapses when temptation touched him, as it had done no later than last night.

"Being in debt," said he, "not only to you, Antonio, but to less kindly creditors, I resolved to win a fortune in a night, so that I might be free to sail to Belmont— and the lady of my dreams." •

His voice—hard when he had spoken of his reckless follies—softened at the thought of Portia and an all-too-brief idyll of spring.

"You love?" asked Antonio gently—and, looking

back once more, saw lovely Bianca in golden robes, standing upon the marble steps of her brother's palace, soft veiling framing a face so fair and sweet that the man who had watched her felt he could sooner kneel in prayer than dare to touch the rosy fragrance of her lips. Yet now, after many years, he could grow pitiful over another's tale of love.

"Why, yes," cried Bassanio hotly, "and, fool that I was, rode away, leaving my lady yet unwon. Aye, rode away in Montferret's train, idling at Verona through half a June, then traveling on to Rome to spend months whose golden moments might have been lived in Portia's presence.

"Would it have availed? I dare not ask, since mocking voices call down the wind, 'Lost, lost, lost!'"

"And she is wed?" asked Antonio gently.

Bassanio shook his head, telling in brief the story which Grimani had recounted.

"No day passes," he added, "without suitors presenting themselves at her palace. If I delay, another will win the jewel which I failed to take when it lay beneath my hand."

"Why then delay, poor Bassanio?"

The young man gave a gesture of despair.

"Last night, instead of winning the fortune I sought," he retorted, "I lost what remained of all my patrimony. Niccolo Grimani hath my last ducat, and vows he'll go a-wooing on his own account."

"It is money you lack?" murmured Antonio. He was realizing what request it must be which came so haltingly to Bassanio's lips.

Even as he spoke he saw the deep flush dye the other's cheeks.

It is ill work for pride to play the beggar—and **Bassanio** had the added sting of being already a debtor.

Yet his need was great, his longing suddenly quickened to passion as he thought of the Lady Portia

Even now others, greedy for her fortune, bearing her little love for her sweet self, would be visiting Belmont to try the hazard of their fortunes. Surely the lady's father had been too near death to think discreetly when he set his child's happiness to such a testing.

"Three thousand ducats," muttered Bassanio, "three thousand ducats, so that I may seek my fortune in my lady's eyes?"

Antonio smiled.

This was the same Bassanio as of old. Impetuous, unlearned in fair discretion, impatient now his purpose clamored fully grown within. Gold he needed, for revelry and state; so, setting to his wooing as my Lord Bassanio—though at another man's expense.

Yet, for all his improvidence, the man's nature was so lovable, so full of good intent, needing only the ballast of some great love or grief, that Antonio did not hesitate.

"You know me well, amico mio," he replied, "and understand well enough how my love would serve you. But I too must explain a difficult case. Money for the moment I have little or none. A thousand ducats to-day would be as difficult for me to touch as three. My argosies are all abroad. This is a year of ventures for me—I dare hope a year of wealth. But at present I am poor. These ships of mine sail far over many seas— one to Mexico, another to England, a third to Tripoli, a fourth to the Indies. I have staked my fortune on these ventures since fate could never be so cruel as to make shipwrecks of them all. Yet, let us think of present need, instead of building on future princely fortunes. Three thousand ducats!"

Bassanio's face was pale. He had not anticipated this failure, and suddenly a rosy future grew dark.

"Three thousand ducats—and my hopes of Portia," he said hoarsely. "I cannot go to her as a beggar."

Haughty pride was in arms at the thought. If he went to Belmont at all, he must go equipped as a Venetian soldier and noble.

Antonio raised his hand.

"You shall have them," he replied. "Do not fear. On the Rialto men talk of my argosies, and prophesy wealth for Antonio Cainello. So I have credit in the city. Come, Bassanio, you shall go without delay. Find where money is and so return. Some-rich usurer you are sure to find to take my bond. Ere many hours are passed you shall be furnished with fortune enough to seek fortune."

Bassanio sprang to his feet, his gray eyes kindling with hope once more.

"You promise me this, friend?" he cried. "Santa Maria! Need I have doubted for one moment? And you shall be repaid, Antonio, not only in ducats, but love and gratitude—when fair Portia weds with me."

Antonio looked up at him as he stood, slim, graceful, handsome, in the sunlight which flecked his brown hair and fair complexion. He was so confident, this young lover, thinking nothing of others' failure in his own certainty of success.

To-day the world was rose-lit to Bassanio Ramberti, and his friend was glad that it should be so. For himself he was content to dwell in the shadows, looking back rather than forward, yet neither whining nor complaining because, for love's sake, he must travel the road of life alone.

At least he could find joy and an abiding pleasure in bringing the sunshine he had once coveted for himself into other lives.

"Go," he said, smiling, "find me a creditor, Bassanio. And together we will claim from him ducats which shall pave the golden road to love."

CHAPTER V

"**I**T is a child, Signior; she brings a basket of figs for your acceptance. A poor child, unfit to bring into the presence of your nobility."

Old Paolo spoke contemptuously as though grudging to bring the news at all.

But Antonio Cainello was instant in his reply.

"She shall come and see me," he said, with quiet rebuke in his voice. "Tell her to bring her figs with her, Paolo."

The servant shuffled off, muttering. He loved his master, but was often inclined to grumble at him. Why, indeed, should so wealthy a man live in a house in the Via St. dell' Orto instead of in a palace? And why should he be content with two humble servitors when he might possess a regiment of lackeys?

Had he put these questions to Messer Antonio, the latter would have smiled, replying he was content enough with life. A virtue which Paolo did not share.

He was an eternal grumbler, this old man, and nearly frightened pretty little Gemma to death as she meekly followed him up the stairs with as much awe as though she went to the presence of a king.

But her fears subsided when she found herself face to face with a Signior whose dark eyes were quite as kind as those of old Father Sylvester, to whom she confessed once every month.

4 (49)

"Ah, little one," said Antonio gently, seeing how the child's face flushed and paled, "so you have come to visit me and bring me those beautiful figs? But that is very kind. And will you also tell me your name?"

She advanced slowly towards him, clasping her basket very fast, and looking at him all the time with such big, wondering eyes, that he smiled again in amusement.

"I am Gemma Scappini, lord," she whispered, "and these figs came to us from our cousin who lives near Padua. They are very fine figs."

There was pride in the soft voice, whilst she lifted a broad leaf from the top of the basket to show the luscious fruit beneath.

"But if they were a present from your cousin why do you wish me to have them?" asked the merchant kindly. "Do you not like figs, little Gemma?"

"Oh, yes," said the child, "but these are for you. My father would have brought them himself but he is sick in bed, and he told me to come here and to tell you that always, always we pray for the good Signior Cainello, who saved him from prison and all of us from starvation."

She gave a little eloquent gesture, tears stealing to her brown eyes.

"It was Shylock the Jew who would have put him in prison," she went on, breathlessly. "Do you not remember, Signior? My father borrowed money from him, quite a small sum, but when he came to pay the debt Shylock told him it was much, much more. Oh! so much more that my father could never have paid it, though he wept, entreating the Jew for mercy."

She crossed herself piously, lowering her tones as though she spoke of the devil.

And Antonio Cainello was remembering the incident now; the scene on the Rialto, the sobbing debtor, the implacable Jew, his own anger, and how, having paid the man Scappini's debt, he had spoken to this Shylock as to a dog, lashing him with his tongue. Aye! spitting upon him in his fury because of the man's cruel harshness and greed.

"So," he mused aloud, "Tito Scappini is grateful. A rare quality, little Gemma, a rare quality."

He looked at the child's flower face and shuddered as he thought of what her fate would have been together with that of the rest of Scappini's family had he not been on the Rialto that day.

"Always we~pray for you, Signior," repeated little Gemma, "and I think I shall pray still more now I have seen you, for you are good and kind, like dear Father Sylvester, and I love you."

.She was only a child, bred in poverty and want, but her words were as balm to her listener.

How easy at times it is to win love!

"I thank you, child," said Antonio gently, "for your figs—but still more for your prayers. Will you tell your father so, and say also that I shall come to see him soon, yes, very soon? Will you remember?"

Her brown eyes, soft as velvet, sparkled with delight.

"Oh!" she gasped—but said no more, only standing, a quaint little bright-hued figure, with clasped hands, gazing at the young merchant as though he were some pictured saint.

And Messer Antonio knew that he would find a welcome when he went to the humble home of Tito Scappini.

The trifling incident gave him food for thought after Gemma had gone away, leaving her figs behind her. He had not met so much gratitude before at so small a cost, and it pleased him.

After all, life could be very sweet when spent in serving others' needs.

The smile still lingered around his lips when Bassanio himself came leaping up the stairs, bursting in upon him, radiant as a bridegroom on the wedding morn.

"Come, good Antonio," cried he, "I have found one ready to take your bond. I have promised we shall meet presently in his house. Already my gondola is at the steps. And you——"

"Am ready too," replied Antonio heartily, "but tell me the name of this ready friend who accepts me so instantly as a debtor?"

"A Jew, Antonio," replied Bassanio, laughing gayly, "by name Shylock. A bearded patriarch, with rheumy eye and the soul no doubt of a miser. But he knew the worth of your name, amico mio. 'Bring him hither,' quoth he, 'whilst I prepare the bond.' I am as sure of my ducats as of your friendship, Antonio. It will not be long before I greet my mistress."

And so great was his delight that his friend strove carefully to hide the fact of his dismay at Shylock's name.

Along many a winding canal, under innumerable one-arched bridges, glided Messer Bassanio's gondola, bringing him and his companion to the neighborhood of meaner houses, which, though more or less dilapidated, were not without their beauties of architecture, whilst upon every window-ledge and balcony were set flower pots with their burden of gay blossoms, behind which at times bright faces peeped forth and laughing eyes watched approvingly the two young men resting at ease on the silken seats of the *felzi*—or cabin—which sheltered them from the powerful rays of the sun that glinted on the gilded prow of the graceful gondola and poured relentlessly down on the bent backs of the picturesque gondoliers who nevertheless sang softly at their task, the song being accompanied by the ripple of the water as the boat glided swiftly onwards.

The house of Shylock the Jew stood at a corner and was linked by a bridge to a side street.

A dismal abode, with but one brilliant patch of color in the orange awning over the balcony on which stood a pot of crimson carnations.

As the occupants of the gondola stepped out a figure glided from the shadows above and leaned for the briefest of moments over the side of the parapet—a girlish figure, clothed in a gown of blue and yellow, her long veil bearing the blue badge which proclaimed her a Jewess. As she raised this veil to peep down in hopes of recognizing her father's visitors, she disclosed features of glowing beauty. Black eyes shone sparkling under sweeping lashes, black tresses gave dusky framing to a face whose delicate features were slightly aquiline, and rendered the more attractive by reason of the clear brunette complexion where the red blood showed vividly under the soft, dark skin. A shade of disappointment crossed the eager face, and, as quickly as she had come, the girl glided back into the room behind, unseen by any.

Meanwhile Bassanio and his companion had been admitted by a lean, crafty-faced fellow, shabby of clothing and hungry-eyed, with a trick of rubbing his ear as he spoke, reminiscent perchance of many a tingling cuff. The interior of the house showed signs of wealth, cheek by jowl, so to speak, with the greatest poverty. Dust-laden objects of art adorned walls where the plaster hung broken and crumbling, costly rugs only half hid rotting boards, whilst the atmosphere was close and stifling.

In an apartment of splendid decay sat its owner, Shylock the Jew, at a table of rare, inlaid mosaic, over which were strewn parchments, ink horn and quills. A ray of sunlight shone over his attentuated and shrunken figure robed in long black gabardine, a yellow turban—distinctive badge of the Jews in Italy at this period—set closely over his gray head, a few scant locks escaping to lie in long wisps on his neck and mingle with the patriarchal beard which hung almost to his girdle. Wizen-faced, blear-eyed, was the man, with long, lean fingers, which moved in a constant clawing motion—true index to their owner's mind.

There was something sinister in that hunched little figure which rose at sight of the two who strode so masterfully in upon him, bowing in servile fashion first to one then the other of his guests.

Even Bassanio grew less joyous in such a presence, and, though still swaggering bravely, it was with an air of forced geniality, whilst he looked from the Jew to Antonio Cainello, who stood erect and calm regarding the cringing Shylock with lofty contempt.

"This is the noble Signior Antonio, Jew," quoth he, "come to place his name upon the bond of which we spoke just now."

Shylock ceased his salutations and stood blinking in the unwelcome sunlight, whilst clawing fingers, for lack of aught else, tugged at his long white beard.

"For three thousand ducats," he answered, in shrill, whining tones. "Three thousand ducats on loan to the noble Signior, who herewith signs his bond."

He hobbled back to the table, glad to be in shadow once again.

"Aye," replied Bassanio, since his friend stood silent regarding his future creditor with still contemptuous glances, "for three months, we agreed."

"For three months—well—!" muttered the Jew, with shifty side glances for them both.

"For the which, as I told you, Antonio shall be bound," went on the young noble, impatiently.

But Shylock the Jew was minded to play the tune to his own measure.

"Antonio shall become bound—well," he echoed, purposely obtuse.

Bassanio thrust his hand within his girdle.

"Well," cried he, irritably, "can I have the money on those terms, old man, or must I go elsewhere for it?"

"Softly, softly," urged the Jew. "Three thousand ducats for three months and Antonio here bound?"

He peered into the merchant's immovable countenance, his red-rimmed eyes blinking in the light.

"Your answer?" demanded Bassanio. "Your answer?"

Shylock pressed those restless fingers of his together as though counting; he was very deliberate.

"Antonio is a good man," he murmured, "by which I would have you to understand he is sufficient; yet his means are in supposition. Have I heard truly, Messer, that you have an argosy bound to Tripolis, another to the Indies, a third to Mexico, a fourth to England?"

Antonio bowed his head.

"With other ventures," he replied coldly, "scattered abroad."

Shylock chuckled.   "Your ships are but boards," he commented—as though still weighing considerations of his part; "sailors but men; there be land rats and water rats, water thieves and land thieves; I mean pirates. And then there is the peril of waters, winds and rocks. But, notwithstanding, I think I may take your bond."

Antonio bowed.   "And the ducats?" quoth he.

The Jew turned back to the table, so that his face was hidden from his companions. Perhaps it was as well neither could see the expression of fiendish hate which, twisting his wizened features, stamped them with the devil's image.

"Do you hear, Shylock?" demanded Bassanio, impatiently.   "What of the ducats?"

"The ducats?" echoed the old man. "Yes, yes, I was just debating of my present store. It is a large sum —three thousand ducats. I have not the money by me. But you shall have the gold, fair sir. If I cannot raise it myself the money will be furnished by Aaron Tubal. My friend Tubal—a wealthy Hebrew of my tribe. You shall have the gold, rest you fair there, good Signior."

He had re-adopted the old whining tones, bowing and cringing first to one then the other.

Antonio Cainello regarded him with more and more distaste. Sooner would he have been beholden to any man in Venice than this suave usurer, whom he had seen last screaming threats as he shook the lean body of his unfortunate debtor Tito Scappini.

"Shylock," he said sternly, "for this dear friend's sake I break a custom. Though I do not lend or borrow, yet now I do both. To lend to Bassanio here, I borrow from you—if you will accept my bond."

"Aye, aye—three thousand ducats." Shylock was growing eager. " 'Tis a good round sum. Three thousand for three months—then let me see the rate."

The details of the transaction appeared to absorb him, but all the time his fingers clawed and his rheumy eyes watched the man who stood straight and dignified before him.

And as he watched, a sudden madness seemed to possess the gazer. Uncontrollable anger shook him so that his shriveled figure swayed, as some long-dead mummy might sway in winter tempest. But though he opened his lips many times, no words came from them till he had mastered the passion which had been as some gust of fierce wind blowing across a peaceful lake.

Yet, deep suppressed by iron will, passion echoed like some warning note in his voice as he spoke, half-mocking, whining, yet with a hate which flashed across each sentence as lightnings across midnight skies.

"Signior Antonio," said he, spreading his hands wide and raising his face to that of the young merchant, "many a time and oft have you rated me on the Rialto about my moneys and my usances. How have I borne it? Why, how could I bear it but with a patient shrug? —for sufferance is the badge of all our tribe. You call me—misbeliever, cut-throat, dog, and spit upon my Jewish gabardine—and all because I use that which is my own!

"Well, then, it *now* appears you need my help. You come to me and say, '*Shylock, we would have moneys.*'

You ask me that, you, who another day might have kicked me as a dog from your threshold. But now you come for money. I can aid you—so you come to the despised Jew. Well, what should I say to you? Should I not be justified in asking, 'Hath a dog money? Is it possible a cur can lend three thousand ducats?' Or shall I bend low, humbly whispering as a slave might do, 'Fair sir, you spit on me on Wednesday last. You spurned me such a day; another time you called me— dog. And for these courtesies I'll lend you what you ask.' "

Antonio frowned, still more contemptuous of the old man's barely-veiled hate than of his servility.

"I am as like to call you so again," he retorted grimly. "Aye, and spit upon you again, spurning you too!"

He clenched his hands, recalling deeds which he had heard laid to this man's account, besides those which he had witnessed.

The fellow was vile, remorseless in his breaking of Christians, greedy in his gold lust, which absorbed his whole soul. Antonio thought of poor Scappini and the brown-eyed Gemma and itched to lay his staff about the hateful Jew. Yet he recalled Bassanio's need and went on more calmly.

"If you will lend the money," he added, "let it be lent to him you call your enemy. You will not be the more eager than in other case to exact the penalty should I fail of my bond."

Shylock bowed low, as though he had listened to the kindliest speech, whilst his reply was reproachful in its submissiveness.

"Messer Antonio," he asked, "why do you storm?

I would be friends with you and have your love. Forgetting the shame you have put on me in the past, I am but too eager to do you this service, making the loan of money which you and your friend need, and taking no interest for the same. Is not this honestly spoken? Does it not prove my kindness?"

An expression of blank amazement passed not only over the face of Bassanio, but that of Antonio too. Never had the latter been more astonished. He had been prepared for some exorbitant demand, resigned to pay it for his friend's sake. Shylock's proposal staggered him in its simple generosity.

"Why, this were kindness, indeed," he stammered, surprised out of his usual calm.

Shylock flung wide his arms. "This kindness would I show," he vowed, with suave smiles.

"Come with me to a notary, Messers both. And you, Antonio, shall there seal your single bond. Whilst stay! since a generous mood—unaccustomed you may say—makes me merry, let us in jesting add a clause as I dictate. Now, let me see, how shall it run? If you repay me not on such a day, in such a place, such sum, or sums, as are expressed in the condition, let the forfeit be nominated for an equal pound of your fair flesh, to be cut off and taken in what part of your body I may please."

Antonio laughed dryly. Surely the old man grew towards senility to make so foolish a condition.

Yet he saw nothing more than a feeble jest which was harmless in its way, and might be humored, seeing how in the main these terms advantaged him.

"I am content enough," he replied, "to seal to such a bond, and say there is much kindness in the Jew."

But Bassanio grew glum, having seen the look Shylock had fastened on his friend.

"You shall not seal to such a bond for me," he told Antonio fiercely. "Sooner than you should do so, I'll forego the ducats."

Here Shylock, chuckling still in foolish fashion, raised hands and eyes aloft, whilst the tears of empty mirth rolled down his withered cheeks.

"O Father Abraham!" he groaned, reproachful, yet amused. "What these Christians are! Is it their own hard dealings which make them so mistrustful of others? Nay, Messer Bassanio, tell me this, if indeed your friend broke his day, what should I gain by the exaction of the forfeiture? A pound of man's flesh taken from a man is not so estimable nor profitable as that of beef or mutton. Why, this was but a jest, to buy Signior Antonio's favor. Will you take it, Messer? If not, farewell, but do not wrong my motive, which was innocent of aught but kindliness."

"Yes, Shylock," replied Antonio, speaking more kindly than he had hitherto done to the Jew, "I will seal unto this bond."

The old man rubbed his hands gleefully. He was very pleased to find an ancient enemy regarding him so favorably.

"Good," said he. "Will you go to the notary? You will find Messer Romoni a commendable fellow, an honest knave and a nimble lawyer. You shall tell him of this merry bond, and whilst he prepares it, I will see to my house, collect the ducats and follow you as speedily as may be."

He spoke with the air of one who concludes a bargain favorable to all.

Antonio nodded approvingly. He was glad for Bassanio's sake that the affair should be so speedily settled.

As to Shylock's whimsical condition, he gave it no second thought, and rallied Bassanio, who followed him down to the stationary gondola with puckered brow.

"The Jew will yet turn Christian," cried Antonio, striking his friend softly on the shoulder. "He grows kind, Bassanio."

But the latter shook his head.

"I like not fair terms—and a villain's mind," he retorted. To him this jest of Shylock's rang on a sinister note.

Even now, but for his friend's persuasion, he would have ordered the gondoliers to turn the boat's prow back to his palazzo.

Antonio, however, would have none of such reasonless fears.

Much as he disliked the Jew he could see nothing in this bond but a new-born kindliness which might mean a hard man's conversion.

"And for the rest," he argued, as Bassanio sullenly gave the order which should take them to Jacopo Romoni's, "what should I have to fear, since my ships come home a month before the day?"

So Bassanio, growing more cheerful as he thought of all the rose-lit way which golden ducats would open, bade lingering doubts depart, taking present good and thanking his patron saint for sending him such a friend as Antonio Cainello.

CHAPTER VI

"THE bond is signed," muttered Shylock the Jew—and again, "The bond is signed."

Crouching low in his chair, he fell to gnawing his finger nails, laughing shrilly from time to time as though the devil whispered some sugared jest into his ear.

Almost one could imagine the evening shadows twisting themselves into some towering Satanic shape to hover above the old man, whose evil face was contorted by hate and joy.

"I hate him," he muttered, "not only because he is a Christian and lends out money gratis, bringing down the rate of usage here in Venice, but because for ever he loves to come between me and my lawful gains. Not once only but many times, till those who sit searching the very garbage pause to point at me in scorn. Shylock the Jew! Is that a name for beggar's scorn? And yet that it is so I owe to this fawning Christian— Antonio Cainello!

"By Jacob's staff! Cursed am I and all my tribe if I forgive one who has done me such harm, hates our sacred nation and ever rails on me, my bargains and my well-won thrift, when he spies me upon the Rialto."

To and fro the speaker rocked himself, gloating, cursing, now swollen with rage, now chuckling in evil glee, so that a figure on the threshold paused, staring

(62)

towards him shuddering and afraid. It was the same slight girlish figure which for a moment had leaned from the gray balcony to spy down on Antonio and his friend.

Throwing back her heavy, striped veil, the girl advanced into a room where she looked strangely out of place, her vivid beauty lighting its gloom, as she stood where the dying light caught and encircled her slim figure.

Shylock turned and saw her there.

"Jessica," he grunted. "Ah, girl. Here is news for you. Aaron Tubal and Peter Chus will sup with me to-night; see that all is prepared."

She came a little nearer to his side.

"Those were strangers who came just now," she hazarded, curious as any daughter of Eve. "At least I do not remember to have seen the elder before, though one was like the Lord Bassanio Ramberti."

Her father scowled at her from beneath bent brows.

"And where were you, girl," he raved, "that you should see these Christian dogs? I'll have no such bold trafficking between my daughter and heathen swine."

Jessica flushed, whilst her black lashes hid the mutiny of dark eyes.

Yet she answered meekly, "Nay, father. I did but set my flowers on the balcony, when, hearing voices, I—I leaned forward, thinking you spoke with Toni, but instead it was these strangers, one of whom I have seen and heard named on the Piazza. Toni talked with them as they entered their gondola. I think he had much to say to the younger gallant."

Shylock still scowled.

"Toni is a Christian dog," he muttered, "ungrateful as the rest of mongrel curs. So he leaves my service

for that of this other dog—this Bassanio, who is as likely
to pay him wages as to learn wisdom and discretion.
Yet let him go—the house is well rid of an unthrifty
knave. But see to it that supper be served for these
guests. I set great store on the friendship of Aaron
Tubal, a man of wealth and substance who shall presently wed with you, Jessica."

The girl drew her veil partly over her face, so that
her father's quick eyes should not spy on her growing
pallor, whilst her reply was meek as that of Abraham's
daughters should be.

"At your pleasure, father," said she. "But if Toni
goes and I am wed, who will rule your house?"

"True," grunted the old man. "Tubal must wait,
though he importunes me for you. Did not Jacob wait
many years for Rachel? How said I to my enemy but
now? Sufferance is the badge of all our tribe. So
Tubal, waiting, shall not wait in vain. I'll find me
an honest servant and Aaron shall have his bride.
Whilst, having found my vengenace, I can say 'content.'
Now away, girl; see that Toni in going takes no more
in his bundle than he came with. A curse on all Christians who would rob the Jew!"

He drew a parchment near as he spoke, claw-like
hands busy with the untidy litter of the table, but he
laughed again and again in the hush of that quiet
room, as he thought of a task completed that day.

"The bond is signed," he was muttering as the dark
curtain fell into place behind Jessica's retreating figure.

But he did not know how, in the passage beyond,
his only child leaned against the wall, panting as though
sorely spent, both slender hands pressed against her
bosom to still the throbbing of her heart.

"I," she whispered, whilst the color flamed over her dark face, "to marry Aaron Tubal? The fat, sleek Aaron, whose very presence sets me shuddering. One who gloats over his gold as though it were living souls of men; whose fat sides shake with glee when he has tortured a hard bargain from his fellows. I, Jessica, to wed with such as Tubal, when my whole heart is given in love to fair Lorenzo?"

Her eyes glowed like dark jewels, her breath came fast as purpose kindled in her. She was not Shylock's daughter for nothing, but shrewd of wit and daring as women are when they set their hazard on love.

So she went swiftly in search of Toni the servant, who had seen fit to change his service to-day. A fellow of nimble wit, this wily Venetian, who combined hatred for his master the Jew, and liking for the Jew's daughter, with a yet finer interest in his own advantage.

He saluted Jessica with elaborate politeness, whilst she, being a consummate actress, became voluble with regrets.

"Good Toni," said she, "I do regret your going, yet you are wise. This has been but gloomy service for you. This house is hell, and you, being a merry devil, robbed it of part of its tediousness. So I am sad—though I hear you will serve a generous lord in Bassanio Ramberti."

Toni watched her askance.

"Indeed, lady," quoth he, "I shall have a full supper as well as breakfast. So it will be the changing of lean service for a fat one, though I shall not forget your kindness."

Jessica sighed.

"I would have shown you more, poor lad," she

5

responded, "had it been in my power. However, I make no plaint of my father, though I tell you you are wise to leave him. But, if I have been kind at all, Toni, you'll do me a small service in return?"

"Why, that will I," cried the Venetian, with a ready palm for the ducat his young mistress slipped within it.

"Shall I go in search of the Jew, lady, and tell him my opinion of him? Or would you rather that I told the secrets of his house abroad and so win pity for you in every heart in Venice?"

"Nay, neither one nor other, good Toni, but instead give but this packet, secretly, into the hand of Messer Lorenzo Fortunato, who is a close friend of your new master, and whom you will no doubt see to-night. Do not fail in this as you love golden ducats and the thanks of Shylock's daughter."

She smiled on him so radiantly as she spoke, that, for the first time in his life, Toni gave ducats the lower place in his esteem.

"Messer Lorenzo shall have it," he promised, "though I search Venice through. Addio, lady, a happy fate be yours."

Jessica watched him go, then returned to the performance of those duties on which her father set such store.

"Will he come?" she whispered to herself. "Will he come—Lorenzo, Lorenzo?"

The music of the name set her laughing, as young maids laugh in springtime, when love is in the air.

So, though autumn shadows darkened that gloomy house, Jessica, the dark-eyed Jewess, laughed, because love lighted all her sky with noonday splendor.

It was some two hours later, when to Shylock's house

came guests more welcome and congenial to its master than those who had earlier darkened his doorway.

Jessica, robed in a crimson and orange satin gown, was seated on cushions in a corner of a room lighted by many candles.

Very beautiful did she look, though she took care to bend her dark head low over her embroidery, so that the screening veil should hide her glowing face from the approving gaze of the man who sat on the right hand of her father at a table near.

Aaron Tubal, though not yet thirty-five years old, was fat and unwieldy of body, coarse-featured and sly of expression; craft and greed stamped him for what he was, and though his plump hands lay heavy and inert enough on the table before him, his little dark eyes twinkled restlessly from one object to another, very often resting upon the fair form of Jessica, who had withdrawn as far as possible from his gaze.

She hated him, this fat and oily man, whom her father destined for her husband. With the fierce passion of a Judith she resolved that either she or Tubal himself should die before she suffered his embraces. Then her heart began to sing. Would not Lorenzo be coming to-night? Lorenzo, the joyous! Lorenzo, the handsome Venetian who had stolen her heart the first time he passed in his gondola beneath her balcony, and looked up to espy a glowing beauty leaning half over the side of the old gray parapet. Since then they had spoken together in short, delicious interviews of which Shylock was totally ignorant.

And to-night—

Sweet meditations were broken in upon by Tubal's raucous voice asking a question.

"What bond is this between you and Antonio Cainello? Come, you shall tell me again. A bond between you and Antonio the merchant? By Jacob's staff! it will not be a bond of love."

Shylock laughed, rubbing together restless fingers.

"A bond of love?" he mocked. "Nay, nay, Aaron. You know better than that. Yet it was a merry jest. If this Antonio breaks his day I make my claim. Ha, ha! a foolish claim, friends both. What do you take it to be? Gold, jewels, house, his body to a prison bound? Why, better than all—though it was but a jest. A pound of his fair flesh to be cut off where I desire. A pound of flesh—of Christian flesh. The flesh of Antonio the merchant, who spat upon me, spurned me, called me such names as made that of Shylock the Jew stink on the Rialto; so that I have become a thing of scorn to all. A mock and jest! But even dogs can bite. So you hear the tale of a merry bond. *A pound of flesh.*"

The golden broidery slipped from Jessica's hands, the evil hatred, the terrible triumph which rang shrill as clarion blast in her father's voice made her cold in sudden horror.

Even Tubal and Chus, hard-souled men without bowels of compassion for the most pitiful, paled as they saw the wizened face of their host distorted by its hate.

"Antonio Cainello is a wealthy man," quoth Tubal in his drawling, lazy tones, "and though he ventures all upon the seas this year, his argosies are bound to many ports. I do not think, Shylock, that he will break his bond."

"It shall be my prayer night and day," mouthed the old man, "my constant prayer that destruction comes upon his ships. May storms break them, winds delay them, pirates sink them, so that my vengeance is assured!"

Peter Chus grunted as he drained his goblet.

"A pound of flesh," quoth he. "And Antonio, no doubt, laughed as he signed that bond, little guessing the jest might become earnest."

Shylock chuckled malevolently.

"Nay, he thought I grew kind," he mouthed. "*I* kind, *I* forgiving. *I* to lend money to him without usury. A madman, friends. A fool!—whose folly I pray may cost him the price of his bond. No fear that I shall treat it as a jest that day. Already I whet my knife. It shall be sharp to carve the daintiest meal that ever vengeance supped on. A pound of Christian flesh! Oh, rare meal for a Jewish cur, whose honest gainings have been balked by Christian gibings. A pound of flesh! By Abraham's life, I hate him!"

His knuckles gleamed white as ivory as he brought down skinny fists upon the table, repeating those last words in a frenzy of that rage which long nursing and suppression had rendered virulent. Aaron Tubal, stroking his short black beard, glanced from his aged host to where Jessica had been seated but a few moments before.

Now, however, the pile of cushions was unoccupied, though a heap of shining embroidery lay on a low stool near.

Jessica had fled, unable to endure the horror of that conversation.

Could it indeed be her father who thus gloated over the prospect of so bloody and undeserved a vengeance?

It seemed to the poor girl, as she crouched in the

solitude of her own room, that she could no longer breathe in the tainted atmosphere of that house.

"Lorenzo," she moaned, and stretched wide her beautiful arms as though entreating some all-powerful saint for deliverance from bondage.

CHAPTER VII

A NIGHT in Venice. Such a night as poets write of, with a clear moon riding high in purple skies, reflected again and again in the deep waters of a lagoon or the rippling surface of the canal, up which a number of gondolas had just passed, bearing a party of masquers home to one of the stately palaces whose arched basements were clothed in tender green. Music and laughter, song and the soft splashing of oars, gradually drifting down to one of those perfect silences, broken only by the call of nightingales from their leafy cages, across the *traghetti*.

Did Venice sleep? Did she ever sleep? If so, there echoed the music of waves against the distant sea wall to sing their lullaby to her dreamings.

Then the dream was broken, a hundred fairy lights danced once more over the lagoon as three gondolas, illuminated from bow to stern by colored lamps, showing the rich coverings of embroidered cloths and the still gayer costumes of masquers, glided into view again, vanishing down one of the many canals, though the vibrant echoes of a guitar and the rich notes of a single tenor voice lingered behind for many minutes.

A city of pleasure, this Venice, by night and day. Pleasure seekers were its inhabitants, loving the gorgeous, the picturesque, the romantic, as much as they loved brilliant colorings and the splendor of valiant deeds.   This was the same people, be it remembered, who in the early fifteenth century held carnival for a whole year to celebrate the accession of Foscari to the Dogeship.   Poor Foscari! who thirty-four years later stood alone and deserted on the great staircase, listening to the clanging bells and clamoring shouts which welcomed another Doge.

Yet, for all their love of pleasure, these Venetians were no effeminate voluptuaries, but deified vigor, manliness and strength.   In other countries of the south the worship of the Madonna preponderates over that of Christ.   In Venice it is noticeable that churches, pictures, altars, are chiefly dedicated to Christ and His saints.   Out of sixty churches only five are devoted to the Madonna, and three to female saints.   So when Venice dreamed, we must suppose her dreams were of valor and high deeds of prowess, kindling her ardor and maintaining that spirit of independence and resolute courage which made her position in Europe unique.

Yet no doubt there was room too for softer dreams, those dreams of love which are woven in the woof and thread of every tender romance.

The men and women of Venice, passionate in patriotism, were passionate too in their personal loves.   No night could pass without the music of the serenade floating soft and sweet across lagoon and canal, whilst white hands were ready to push open barring shutters to send a flower or written message to reward the song. But no music of voice or instrument broke the silence around the house of Shylock the Jew.   Yet a shutter was being softly unclosed above, and out onto the balcony stole Jessica, the Jew's daughter, a rose in her dark hair, a tender expectancy in her eager eyes. How fast her heart beat as she looked back towards the gloomy house and then down upon the moonlit waters of the canal!

Would he come? Would he come? And if not—. She clasped her hands in anguish.

If not?

, An hour since her father had called her to bid·farewell to his guests. As she had looked into the eyes of Aaron Tubal she had grown afraid. Had they been talking of her during her absence? Was it possible that this wealthy suitor's importunities had prevailed? If so—and Lorenzo came not—what might her fate be?

In agony of spirit the girl had again retired to her room after bidding her father good-night. But she had been haunted ever since by the memory of Aaron Tubal's sleek smile which had held some hint of possessive right in it as he gazed boldly down into her face. A boat shot out from beneath the single arch of the bridge. He had come! Lorenzo was here. The nightmare of her fears slipped from her, as she leaned over to fling the silken ladder down, first fastening it to the iron-work of the balcony above.

Tall and slender stood the figure of the boat's solitary occupant, with face upraised in the moonlight.

He was good to look at, this merry Lorenzo, fair skinned, auburn locked, with the eyes which had caught the trick of laughter from babyhood and never known the way of tears. He was laughing now, as he stood there in his gay doublet and cloak, since he was not of the *nobili*, and could wear what color it pleased him without the law-giving of grave academies.

To-night his fancy had been for blue and silver, so

that he made a brave figure to play the lover to his dark-eyed houri.

He was beside her before she had had time to breathe a prayer for his safe journey to the balcony, and since moments were. precious he did not stand on ceremony.

Was he not a lover? And was not pretty Jessica kind to him to-night?

So he held her in his arms, whispering passionate vows into a willing ear, whilst overhead sailed a silver moon; chaste Diana, cold in her loveliness, yet patroness to all hot-headed, amorous-hearted lovers the old world over.

"Come," whispered Lorenzo, "will you not come, carissima? Why should we wait? My boat is there, awaiting us. Shall we not set sail to Arcadia to-night?"

He laughed joyously, thrilled by the touch of those scarlet lips which clung so passionately to his. But Jessica hung back, shaking her head.

"No, no," she replied. "I cannot come to-night. Harken! It is my father's voice which calls. He must have heard something—or else I mistook when I thought I heard him retire to his room. Go, Lorenzo, go—but come again, because I love you."

He still held her, unwilling to quit so dear a presence.

"If you will not come to-night," he replied masterfully, "you shall not refuse me again. Listen, carissima. All shall be prepared for our flight, so that we may straightway set sail for Genoa. And you will come, my bride, my wife. You will be mine?"

She shivered a little, as one who grows afraid at the parting of the ways.

To go forth to a new life—a new religion—a new world. Yet in all to find Lorenzo—to taste the sweets of love in all its fullness. Could she tear up the roots, which bound her down into the straight tenets of a Jewish woman's life?

Her lips parted, her dark eyes sparkled. Love was the conqueror. Could she look back to where amongst grim shadows she saw the repellant figure of Aaron Tubal awaiting her with all the pride of possession in his eyes?

"You shall send a letter to me," she said, yielding to a lover's will, "by that Toni who is now Lord Bassanio's servant, but who for years lived here in service to my father. And, in that letter, contrive some plan for me to steal hence when we can be assured of my father's absence. If not—if not—O Lorenzo, I am afraid, for my father would have no mercy did he learn our secret before we were safely wed."

But Lorenzo, merry and confident, laughed at such fears. The Jew's mind was too intent counting his shekels to be given to the secret doings of a daughter whom he supposed to be too deep-grafted in old traditions of race to cast the glances of a wandering eye upon a Gentile.

So, whilst Venice slept, dreaming her splendid dreams of a golden age, these two, Jewess and Gentile, forgetful of racial hatred and an ancient curse, whispered of love together whilst the minutes fled, till warning sounds from within told Jessica that danger might be near.

"Farewell, Lorenzo," she whispered—and again—"farewell, my lord that is to be. I shall await your letter—and the day when I am yours for all time. Farewell, dear lover."

She watched him go, waving his cap to her, so that white moonbeams crowned his ruddy locks, and to the last showed her his laughing eyes.   Then the boat, swift as a swallow, darted beneath the bridge—and he had gone.

Jessica sighed, regretful, poor child, that she had not listened to importunate pleading and fled with him to-night.   Yet that had been folly, since her Jewish dress alone would have helped betray her, and cold horror lay at her heart as she thought of what tragic fate hers would be did her father discover and stop her flight.

No, they must go cautiously in this elopement.   She would disguise herself in page's dress (none saw her blushes as she crept back to her room) and so deaprt from this house which she had termed hell to Toni the servant.

And if this were hell, surely the land to which she fled with Lorenzo would be paradise.   Sleepless she tossed upon her bed, fear and delight possessing her, as first she thought of Aaron Tubal—then of her lover.

To-morrow—the next day—love's messenger would come and she would learn how cunningly the gate of this prison house should be opened for her.

Love and Lorenzo!   No wonder in the turmoil of such thoughts as these Shylock's daughter forgot the story of vengeance against Antonio the merchant, which she had heard her father recount in such gloating triumph to his friends.

CHAPTER VIII

THE QUEEN OF MANY SUBJECTS

"GRACIOUS Signora, a courier has arrived who announces that his master, the Prince of Morocco, and his train, journey to Belmont. I think from what he says the Prince comes as a suitor for your hand."

Portia di Nerlini gave vent to an impatient sigh.

"A suitor, Nerissa?" she complained. "Why, of course he is a suitor—for the hand of my father's heiress. I am rich, child, so rich that a Prince deems my dower worthy of him. But, for the woman? Why! What does she count, excepting as a needful part of a rich bargain?"

There was a bitter note in the young voice as the Lady Portia rose, pacing the room till she stood before the window looking out upon lawns and flowers, which showed a riot of color, gorgeous in beauty, even though autumn breezes shook fading leaves to the ground.

The months succeeding her father's sudden death had changed a gentle girl into a woman grown strong of necessity to fight a lonely battle. In her sweeping sable robes, only relieved by the string of pearls around her white neck and the long veil which fell to the hem of her gown, she looked like some lovely spirit of night, no whit less beautiful than of yore, though the tremulous lips were more firmly set and her blue eyes kindled with a fire which they had lacked in the days of a sheltered

(77)

and irresponsible life. She stood alone—a queen still of many vassals, though her own heart had never yet been subject to one.

Never? Ah! Why did the Lady Portia sigh as her thoughts flew to one who had never ridden back to the Palazzo di Nerlini with all this never-ending train of suitors?

Had she never loved? Autumn breezes sighing amongst tall cypresses, repeated an unanswered question. And now the Prince of Morocco, a dusky potentate from afar, rode hither to test his fortune after the manner of her father's decree.

Those caskets! The very thought of them set her heart beating in terror. Surely Providence itself in answer to her father's many prayers for her happiness, had decreed that none of these greedy suitors should guess right.

Again and again the test had been put, whilst she, eyeing with distaste a possible husband, had sung her thanksgiving very gladly at sight of his crestfallen departure.

But one day—one day—the casket would be chosen containing her portrait, and she, unable to refuse the claim, must yield herself as fate and a dead father had decreed.

Over and over again had she complained of that decree. What wild inspiration of a dying brain had that been which devised so strange a method for her mating?

Could not her father have relied on his daughter's wisdom and discernment rather than leave her destiny to a chance—a trick—an idle guess?

But it was not so that Fra Angelo had seen it. Had

he not told her that she must look upon this dying act as one of heavenly interposition? That was how it seemed to the holy priest. There would be no chance or idle guesswork in this proving of the test, but the seal of Providence in a choice which it had decreed an earthly father might not make.

But Portia, though in moments of exaltation believing the good confessor, had her hours of despair. For behold! the months slipped by, and though suitors by the score came riding to the palazzo, never came he for whom she sought in vain.

"Sing to me, Nerissa," she commanded feverishly, and Nerissa, sympathetic in her mood, took up the lute and sang.

> Yea, thou art fair; I pray the heavens to bless thee,
> For where thy footsteps fall the grass is spread
> In springtide verdure underneath thy tread,
> As though the spring were born but to caress thee.

Did it seem strange to the lady that the maid sang a song of Venice? If so she made no comment, asked no question, though as Nerissa ceased, twanging the strings in mournful melody, Portia's blue eyes had darkened in a tender reverie.

It had been springtime when Bassanio Ramberti rode hither in the train of the Marquis di Montferret, and she minded the friend she had brought with him—the Signior Gratiano, who had confided in pretty Nerissa.

Suddenly she turned, flinging herself back on her couch, beckoning Nerissa to lay aside the lute.

"Oh, me!" she sighed, impatient as one bound who seeks in vain for freedom. "How I hate the word *choose*, for I may neither choose whom I would nor

refuse whom I dislike.   So is the will of the living
daughter curbed by the will of a dead father. Is it not
hard, Nerissa, that I can neither choose nor refuse my
husband?"

Nerissa came and knelt by the couch, twining her
arm around that of her mistress as young girls do in
friendly love—for were they not friends, these two,
bound yet more closely than before?

"I will believe what Fra Angelo says," she declared
encouragingly, "that till the husband of your choice
comes the right casket will never be chosen.   Tell me,
dear lady—he has not yet come—and gone?"

Portia shook her head emphatically.

"There has not been one," she declared, "but I dote
on his very absence.   Think, then, Nerissa, what manner
of wooers there have been.   Name them, and I will tell
you how I regarded their suit."

Laughter chased the shadows from her eyes, a dimple
played roguishly in her smooth cheek.   She had not
been a woman had she not found delight in the torments
of lovers who had a first mind for her fortune and but
a second for herself.

Nerissa, glad to see a stormy mood depart, and to
while away a time of suspense before the arrival of an
unwelcome visitor, made haste to obey.   Kneeling
back, she pressed finger after finger in slow counting,
keeping a small, merry face uplifted to that of her
mistress.

"First there was the Neapolitan prince," said she,
her lips a-quiver with smiles.

Portia's chin tilted in disdain.

"A colt," she averred, "who could talk of nothing
but his horse.   His chief commendation seemed that
he could shoe him himself."

"Then," went on Nerissa, "there was the County Palatine."

"Who did nothing but frown, as who would say,'*and if you will not have me, beware!*' What will he be, Nerissa, when he is old, being so full of sadness in his youth? I had rather be married to a death's head with a bone in his mouth, than to either of these!"

Nerissa shook her head, pursing wry lips, as some silk vendor who hears his merchandise disparaged, yet knows the truth of the verdict.

"What say you to the French lord, Monsieur le Bon?" she inquired.

Her mistress shrugged comely shoulders.

"In truth I know it is a sin to be a mocker," said she, "but if I should marry him I should marry twenty husbands—and every one a braggart."

"Then there was the Duke of Saxony's nephew. How like you him, lady?"

"Very vilely in the morning, when he is sober, and most vilely in the afternoon, when he is drunk; when he is best, he is a little worse than a man; and when he is worst, he is little better than a beast; an' the worst fall that ever fell, I hope I shall make shift to go without him. I will do anything, Nerissa, ere I will be married to a sponge."

Nerissa was silent. Lovers had come, riding hither gayly, riding away sadly, as those she had enumerated; so many that she had no count for names or titles. Surely the good father confessor was right in saying that Providence had guided such in their choice, since her lady looked so aversely on all.

Then suddenly she spoke again, this time with eyes averted.

"Do you not remember, lady, in your father's time, a Venetian, a young soldier, who came hither in company of the Marquis di Montferret?"

This time the Lady Portia did not scoff and her answer was low pitched.

"Why, yes—it was Bassanio Ramberti, as I think he was named."

"True, dear mistress, and—and he, of all men that my foolish eyes have looked on, seemed best deserving a fair lady."

A thrush lilted a high, sweet melody in the garden, swaying its slender body on a slim acacia twig.

Portia was looking towards the bird, her blue eyes tender with memory.

"I remember him well," she whispered. "And I remember him worthy of thy praise. Yet he has not come a-wooing to Belmont, Nerissa. Did he come— did he come——"

The silken curtains before the door were sharply withdrawn. A page had come to announce the arrival of the Prince of Morocco.

"Do you not remember, lady, a Venetian, a young soldier?"

CHAPTER IX

A ROYAL SUITOR

THE long dinner drew to its close. The Lady Portia, weary these many hours, because of secret fear straining at her heart as she surveyed the dusky countenance of an honored guest, raised the goblet of wine to her lips, essaying a faint smile.

For this prince, dark-complexioned and swarthy as he was, possessed a noble air, proving himself a very gallant gentleman. Here was no mountebank or brainless fool, he had no shadow of melancholy, nor boisterous wit heightened by deep potations. And, throughout the meal, had shown such courtly consideration and gentle courtesy that Portia could have found neither quip nor gibe in her heart for him.

Yet, as a *husband!* She shuddered, turning to encounter the Prince's dark eyes fixed on her.

"Lady," he said, bowing gracefully, "I think you know my purpose in coming here. Rumor, traveling swift-winged to my country, told of the peerless beauty of the lady of Belmont, also of the strange condition which was imposed on every suitor for her hand. Do you blame me that I came?"

She colored rosily. Courteous, princely, refined, though this petitioner for her favor might be, she had been zealous to note how his appraising eyes had scanned the costly rooms of the Palazzo, marking the gold and silver which adorned the table, the signs of luxury and

(83) ·

wealth which were so visible around.   She had even
fancied he had looked longer at the beauteous pearls
which hung about her neck than at the white arch of
the throat above it.

So her own eyes hardened as she listened to words
which were more formal than eloquent, expressing
sentiments of the lips rather than the heart.

Aye! He had heard of the *wealth* of the Lady of
Belmont—before her beauty.   Could a woman be deceived?   It was the woman, grown strong and wise
before her time, who answered, rather than the tender
girl who had given a pink carnation to the lover of a
day.

"It is true," she said, "my father has imposed a
strange condition with my hand.   In another room,
Lord Prince, stand three caskets, one gold, one silver,
one of lead; within one and one only lies my portrait.
Who chooses that chooses me, and I, obedient to my
dead father's will, am ready to go with that man to
church, and be thenceforth his loving wife.   But unless
my suitor abides by that condition I have no word save
that of dismissal for him."

The Prince smiled with a happy confidence which
seemed to mock at failure.   Unaccustomed to opposi-
tion to his will, he was convinced that an easy success
lay now before him.   The victories of a lifetime are ill
preparation for defeat.

So he looked on Portia di Nerlini, the richest heiress
in Italy, as one already destined to be his bride; saw
her fair and desirable in that pale, blue-eyed beauty
of hers, which was in such direct opposite to his own
swarthy complexion, and felt his ardor leaping in the
hot flame of a sudden passion.   He had come to win a

wealthy wife, he now desired to gain this fair woman
for his own; yet the dominant note in his fast-beating
heart was the greed of the possessor, with little admix-
ture of a lover's worship and humility. So he answered
lightly to the lady's warning:

"By this scimitar I vow I would out-brave the most
daring heart on earth to win you, loveliest. Tell me
what other conditions are imposed with this choice on
which my whole fate hangs?"

His dark eyes, burning in their gaze, seemed to scorch
her, so that for all her courage she trembled. Was it
possible that only the caskets lay between her and the
desire of this masterful and dusky potentate from far
Morocco?

She tried to daunt him.

"It is my father's command," she replied gravely.
"You must first take solemn oath before your choice,
that if you fail you must remain dumb as to which
casket you unlocked, and moreover vow never to woo
another woman in way of marriage. Whilst from this
palazzo you ride forth at once, never seeking me again."

The Prince was silent. Here were hard conditions!
Should he take vow of celibacy did this lady fail him?
Yet she should not fail him. Had he not always stood
victor of every field, either in love or war?

Again he looked at Portia and felt his pulses leaping
in furious longing, saw the red blood creep under her
lily-pale skin, noted the crowning glory of her golden
hair but half-concealed by her long veil, marked the
rounded curves of the white neck whose beauty showed
in contrast to the dull black of her mourning robes.

Could he ride away from Belmont, because he dared
take no risk in winning such a prize?

That other suitors had done so, fearing the issue of so strange a trial, he knew well enough. But he would mot follow their example.

"I accept all conditions," said he quietly, "and will take the oath."

But Portia, feeling a suffocating sense of fear, seeing how a dark hand clutched convulsively about the jeweled hilt of a scimitar, rose hastily from the table.

"You shall take the oath, Lord Prince," said she, striving after that calm dignity it was so hard to assume. "And presently, either choose and straightway go hence, or choose and stay to celebrate our nuptials."

Then, with a deep curtsy, she withdrew, bidding her steward summon her train, so that in the usual state they might proceed to the room of trial.

In the meantime she fled alone up the marble stairs to seek her room.

She could not endure the coming ordeal till in solitude she had rallied failing courage and steadied trembling nerves.

Only a tender moonlight filled the room, showing the gleaming marble of the mantelpiece and the rich hangings of the bed.

Portia flung herself down beside a low, carved chair, stretching wrung hands out over the cushioned seat whilst she buried her face in the curved hollow of white arms from which the long, hanging sleeves fell back. It was a moment of weakness, of abandon, of utter loneliness, in which life appeared wholly impossible to this young girl, whose high position left her to be the prey of every fortune hunter.

Deep sobs shook her, rending her very heart. Fate stood above her, grim, inexorable. The thought that this dark-visaged Prince might win her was terrible, and yet if he failed, what remained? Other suitors would come, as covetous, and perhaps less courteous. Others, who would accept her father's fanciful conditions, and who, alas! could not *all* be losers.

Only a miracle seemed to have saved her thus far from a husband who openly sought not her but hers.

It would be the same to-morrow—the next day—till at last the inevitable happened, and she must give herself to a rightful claimant.

A rightful claimant! Ah! but not *he*. Not the man with whom she had stood in the marble-paved loggia listening to the warble of nightingales, drinking in all the ecstasy of springtide.

Involuntarily she raised her bowed head so that the moonbeams played on her tear-stained, lovely face, so pale and sorrow-stricken.

"Bassanio!" she murmured softly. "Oh, my love, my love! Yet no love of mine. Bassanio! Nay, he hears me not. He will never return to Belmont. Never! He has forgotten me. Yet how tenderly he spoke with me that night long since. And I, a child, thought his eyes spoke love. Love Bassanio! Oh, what a dream—Bassanio—husband. Shame on me, shame! To feel my heart ache so sadly for a man who has forgotten me. He'll never come again. Perhaps he is already wed. No, I'll not believe it. Did he not look up and back as he rode away, pressing my flower to his lips? Moonlight may deceive—but the sun shone on the day in which he rode away—carrying my heart with him. Oh, shame again that I should say such things—or even dream them. Yet, I have dreamed of him. And always in my dreams his eyes were kind.

Bassanio!—love, will you never look so again upon Portia?"

She fell to moaning, her empty arms widespread, yielding herself to a passion, which, being impossible of fulfilment, beat itself out in tears, as you have seen the wild waves flung back from cold, hard rocks in showers of glistening spray.

He would not come to Belmont. And, because of that, her soul despaired, thinking of these others who were come and who would be coming.

Not her—but hers. Yet, had Bassanio ridden hither, she felt it would have been a lover who claimed admittance.

With hands fast locked she prayed—such wordless prayers as were but dumb cries launched into space, yet winging faintly upwards.

And had she framed those prayers in living phrases each would have echoed the same name. Bassanio! Yet what had Heaven to do with the weary aching of a maiden's heart?

She grew bitter with the thought, then prayed again, feeling a shadowed peace lay soothing balm within her breast.

Did Heaven heed indeed? Did a mightier power gird her round than she had dreamed of? Was it possible she did not stand to do battle with Fate alone?

A bird sang out in the darkness, and her whole being thrilled in a new-born strength.

Behold, in a curtained sky, the stars shone forth, their far-off light searching her troubled heart.

She would no longer despair, since Heaven lay nearer than the stars, whose message told of hope.

Rising to her feet she summoned Nerissa, who came,

startled to find her mistress here when she had fancied her still at the banquet.

"Tell Florio I am ready," said the lady very quietly. "Bid him acquaint the Prince of Morocco. I await my train to join His Highness."

And for once Nerissa said no word of comfort or inquiry, though she brought rosewater to bathe her mistress' tear-stained face, setting a crumpled veil in order without comment.

For she knew that the hour of solitude which the Lady Portia had spent here in a darkened room was sacred for all time.

Through folding doors, held back by bowing servants, the Prince of Morocco led the Lady Portia to a dais-like seat, with gilded back and arms, covered in crimson velvet. Behind them walked their respective trains, eager, expectant, thrilled with all the excitement attendant on such a hazard.

The Prince bowed low before the lady, whilst, in turning, his keen, dark eyes swept round the room. A room replete with luxury. Priceless paintings adorned the walls, tables and cabinets inlaid with porphyry and serpentine or rare mosaics furnished the apartment, whilst at the farther end costly curtains of softest silk of interwoven colors were even now being drawn aside by the Lady Portia's servants, displaying three caskets ranged along a gilded table, which stood back against the wall.

Three caskets! One of gold, one of silver, one of lead, richly embossed in scroll-like patterns.

Three caskets! And on them lay the hazard of this strange wooing.

A proud, magnificent and very confident figure, the

Prince advanced, without undue haste, and with a dignity which could not fail to impress the spectators who were grouped around the room.

The Lady Portia herself sat grasping the gilt sides of her chair, her lovely face drained of all color, yet composed and calm.

The Prince came to a halt near the table, scanning the caskets, whilst in deep, meditative tones he read aloud the inscription on each.

"Who chooseth me, shall gain what many men desire," was the legend borne by the golden casket.

"Who chooseth me, shall get as much as he deserves," was inscribed on that of silver, whilst the leaden casket bore the enigmatical words—

"Who chooseth me, must give and hazard all he hath."

Portia di Nerlini drew a deep breath.

"If you choose the one containing my picture, Prince, I am yours," said she, and seemed to herself that she rang her own death-knell.

But the Prince was in no hurry to risk his hazard, thus keeping the lady on the rack of torment.

"Some god direct my judgment," he muttered. "Let me read these inscriptions again. What says this leaden casket? *"Who chooseth me, must give and hazard all he hath.'* Must give—for what? For lead! hazard for lead? This casket threatens. When men hazard all they do it for great advantage. I do not choose to give or hazard aught for lead.

"Then this silver casket with her virgin hue—*'Who chooseth me, shall get as much as he deserves.'* "

"As much as I deserve! Pause here, Morocco. Why, do I not deserve this lady? Am I not worthy? By birth, in fortune, graces, qualities of breeding, but more than all these, in love itself, I do deserve her. But before I choose let me see once more this saying graved in gold: '*Who chooseth me, shall gain what many men desire.*' Why, that's this lady! All the world desires her. From the four corners of the earth they come to kiss this shrine. For far and near the tale of her wealth and beauty rings. And in one of these caskets her heavenly picture lies hidden. Is it likely lead contains her? It were damnation to think so base a thought! Or shall I believe her hid in silver being ten times under-valued to pure gold? Never so rich a gem was set in worse than gold. Give me the key, lady, here do I choose, whatever of fortune that choice holds for me."

A soft flush had risen to Portia di Nerlini's cheeks; bending forward she handed the Prince a tiny key.

"Take it," she whispered, "and if my form lies there, I am yours."

All craned forward, a deep hush pervaded the room. Men and women caught back their breath in expectancy as they listened to the soft click of a turning lock.

Then, pale for all his confidence, the Prince stooped over the open casket, and lifted out a small picture with dependent scroll.

He reeled a little and his swart face grew livid.

"O hell!" he muttered, "what choice is this? A carrion death to mock and gibe at me. My choice! A fateful one which rings its own knell to the doom of despair!"

Unfolding the scroll, he read its contents aloud:

All that glitters is not gold,
Often have you heard that told;
Many a man his life hath sold
But my outside to behold,

Gilded tombs do worms infold.
Had you been as wise as bold,
Young in limbs, in judgment old,
Your answer had not been inscrol'd:
Fare you well; your suit is cold.

With haggard face and downcast eyes which dared
not meet the pitying gaze of the lady, the young Prince
approached Portia di Nerlini.

It was his first defeat—and a very bitter one. Yet,
even in that despair which high hopes made the darker
he neither forgot his solemn oath nor the fact that he
was a Prince.

With deep obeisance he bowed before her whom he
had thought to make his bride and from whom he was
now vowed to part forever.

"Lady," said he, "I accept my fate and hasten to
obey the conditions imposed on failure. Thus losers
part. Yet I neither swore to forget the Lady of Belmont
nor in those memories, bitter-sweet, shall I forget to
pray for her happiness."

Portia held out her hand, very gracious and womanly
in pity for so noble a suitor, yet it was as well perhaps,
that, as the Prince pressed those white fingers to his
lips, he did not raise his head to see the look of infinite
relief and thankfulness which was mirrored in the lady's
blue eyes.

In stately dignity he withdrew, princely in defeat,
whilst Portia, the strain of that fateful hour over, dismissed her servants and retired to her room, weeping for
pure perversity since, now her passionate prayers were
answered and an unwelcome wooer gone, Bassanio was
no nearer. Ah! Bassanio! Tears blurred her vision, sobs
choked her voice. What would the end of all this tur-

moil be? Would she live to regret the day when the Prince of Morocco, a very courtly gentleman, rode away to make room for a less worthy but more fortunate suitor?

The silken curtains were drawn aside, and Nerissa, eager and flushed, stood before her mistress.

"Gracious Signora," she cried, "a courier stands without, bidding me acquaint you of the coming of his master—a noble of Venice."

Portia sprang to her feet, transformed on the instant from weeping Niobe to Aurora, goddess of a summer's dawn.

The color rose crimsoning her fair face; her eyes sparkled with a hundred fires.

"From Venice?" she echoed, softly clapping her hands. "Then speed you, speed you, girl, and bid the messenger ride back to tell his lord that Portia di Nerlini bids him welcome. Aye! welcome as—as all from Venice must be at Belmont."

She was laughing joyously as the curtains fell with swish of silken draperies into place behind the vanishing form of Nerissa.

CHAPTER X

GRIMANI PROVES IMPORTUNATE

"FROM *Venice!*"
What magic in those words. For who should ride from Venice to Belmont but the Lord Bassanio Ramberti?

"Bring me my robe of white silk," commanded Portia briefly, "with the golden girdle. I will welcome this —this new suitor in other attire than dreary black. I've heard it said that the people of Venice have a kindly eye for gay coloring. You shall bring me my chain of turquoise, Nerissa, and bind my hair with the garland of roses. Quick, girl, quick! Are you here only to regard your own saucy face in the mirror? Nay, little Nerissa, I would not be harsh—and Messer Gratiano is a citizen of gallant bearing."

"I thought him so, too, Mistress," whispered Nerissa, and blushed in all the pleasant delight of anticipation.

But alas, for dreams which had been too hastily woven by desire.

When the Lady of Belmont, gracious and radiant in her jeweled attire, came down the marble stairs, it was to find a stranger bowing before her welcome.

In sooth he wore the sober black of the Venetian *nobili* with its silver girdle and jeweled shirt collar—but this was not Bassanio Ramberti, fair-haired and gray-eyed, but a slender, dark-eyed gallant, with short beard and masterful bearing, who gave the name of Niccolo

(94)

Grimani, as though that title would carry weight in any court of state as well as that of beauty.

With difficulty the disappointed lady hid her chagrin, bidding the Signior Grimani welcome, but excusing herself under the plea of weariness from tarrying for his entertainment.

The hour was late, and all day she had been engaged with affairs of importance. Would the noble Signior accept her hospitality at the hands of her steward? And to-morrow she should hope to have the pleasure of playing her own part of hostess.

Niccolo Grimani, looking at the fair vision on the step above him, doubted that same excuse, since no weariness was visible in the lovely face or bright eyes, though he had been quick to notice the bitter disappointment which had crossed the lady's features at sight of him.

And the knowledge that she had hoped to welcome another cavalier piqued his vanity.

At the same time his answer was honey-sweet, as he accepted so simple a reason, whilst he twined a flowery compliment in the hopes of his morrow. It is to be doubted whether Portia di Nerlini so much as heard the tale of his aspirations; was she not mourning over the quenching of her own?

Bassanio had not come! He never would come! And to-morrow must witness a fresh ordeal in this stranger's choice of caskets. Very wearily she hoped he would be daunted by the harshness of the conditions and ride away—as she would all these too greedy suitors would ride away—but one; the one who should be her lover—the man she loved.

Nerissa, no less cast down than her mistress, helped

the latter to unrobe. She too found life a dreary wilderness to-night—because the Lord Bassanio had had a friend, one Messer Gratiano, who might have ridden hither in his train.

"Will he come?" quoth the little maid to herself. "Will he come?" And a dimple flashed in the smoothness of a pink cheek which Messer Gratiano had been bold enough to caress. Remembering that stolen kiss, and the whisper of a lover's vows, Nerissa laughed softly to herself as she crept away to her own room.

"He will come!" she told herself. "He will come!" and bridged those long months 'twixt spring and autumn with a woman's patient faith.

But then Nerissa, having naught but her own beauty to tempt man's desire, had not the fear which clamored at her mistress' heart. No suitors rode to Belmont to sue for little Nerissa's hand and wealth.

The Lady Portia slept late after many wakeful hours, so that Nerissa, weary of waiting for her summons, ran out into the sunshine to gather roses for her mistress' table.

Autumn roses, crimson and white, palest pink and deep yellow, held in clustering fragrance in two small hands.

It was at a turn in the path on her way back to the palazzo that Niccolo Grimani met her, Niccolo Grimani swaggering it in his walk as if he were already lord of all this fair domain. His restless black eyes sparkled at sight of Nerissa, and had he had his will he would have stolen a kiss. But Nerissa's pretty face reflected no gleam of coquetry, and thinking of all the mistress might be worth to him, Grimani was discreet in his greeting of the maid.

"Why, prettiest," quoth he, "yours is a sweet task, for a sweeter lady. Would you could carry all my vows in the fragrance of yon bouquet, so that fair Portia might think kindly of me in her dreams!"

Nerissa pursed rosy lips in dubious fashion. Instinct did not teach her to love this mincing cavalier, even though he came from Venice.

"The flowers, Signior," she replied, "are fragrant only for a day—maybe your vows would be as enduring."

Grimani only laughed.

"Roses," he answered, "are best guarded by their thorns. Yet I'll call a pretty maid by no such hard names; but you shall tell me your other, so that we may be friends?"

"I am called Nerissa," said the girl, half yielding to his overtures, "and I am in haste to return to my mistress."

"I wonder not," laughed Grimani, "since if one could claim the right to be beside her who would remain away? But let me walk with you, prettiest, whilst you tell me what whimsical devil put it into the late Signior di Nerlini's head to impose such conditions with his daughter's hand."

Nerissa peeped slyly from over her screen of roses, and there was laughter in her eyes.

"You have heard the conditions, Messer?" she questioned. "And are not minded to run away as many suitors have done, fearing the oath of celibacy which follows failure?"

Grimani shrugged his shoulders, spreading out his hands in the sunshine.

"Why, truth," he answered, "the ancient Florio, who plays the steward here in the palazzo, acquainted me

with the first, second and thirdly of this mighty oath—
to all of which I cried 'Amen.' Since, if I lose Portia,
I shall not think of mating with her inferiors."

"Why, you talk as if you love my mistress, sir," said
Nerissa, but there was mockery in her tones, since she
set small store on this noble cavalier's honesty.

"You shall tell her so and speak no less than truth,
Nerissa," he urged. "Whilst, if your heart is tender
for love, you'll help me in this. If—as I suspect—you
know the secret of these three thrice cursed or thrice
blessed caskets, you can help your mistress to much
happiness."

Nerissa darted him a swift glance of suspicion.

"Why," she replied demurely, "if I were as sure of
her happiness as of your desire, Signior, I would obey
your request, since both should be golden. As it is,
you must know me for an honest maid who would not
perjure herself for a king's ransom."

Grimani flushed darkly. He had been wondering in
his mind what bribe would best steal the girl's secret—
but Nerissa's scorn showed him the truth only too
plainly. In fear of having made a false step, he laughed
aloud.

"I did but jest, child," said he, "to try your truth,
which I see is all that a good mistress deserves. Here,
take this purse of ducats to buy a trinket against your
wedding day."

But Nerissa, indignant at his deception, refused the
bait.

"The jewel may grow tarnished," she retorted, "before
that time—at least, that will be my prayer if all suitors
come in your guise to Belmont, Signior; since I have
vowed to remain maid till my mistress be called wife."

Grimani frowned.

"Come, I'm your friend, Nerissa," he urged. "As to your vow, prepare to break it before the day has sped, since Fate being kind, the Lady Portia weds with me before another dawn."

He spoke that prophecy to empty air, since Nerissa had fled within doors to answer her lady's summons, though she took care to say no word of how Niccolo Grimani had met her in the gardens and tried to bribe her into the betrayal of a beloved mistress.

There was to be no donning of white and gold to-day, no rose garland for golden locks. The Lady Portia's mood was a heavy one, and there were dark rims about her eyes which told of wakeful hours.

"The Signior Grimani waits to bid me farewell?" she questioned Nerissa languidly, as she stood attired in trailing sable garments looking out over lawns and woods from her casement window.

The waiting-maid shook her head. "Nay, lady," she replied, "he has elected to remain, taking his oath and chance with the caskets."

"He has heard all the conditions?"

"Yes, lady."

Portia clasped her hands. "Ah me, ah mè!" she moaned. "When will this end? What tragedy does life hold for the daughter of Pietro di Nerlini? I believe I shall end in taking the veil and thus being rid of all such importunate suitors."

"Nay, sweet Signora," urged Nerissa, "be not downcast. Did not Fra Angelo himself declare that there is more in this choosing than mere chance? Let us add our prayers to those my lord your father must have prayed; and so hope that Heaven's blessing is safely

locked within one of those caskets which shall be opened
by the hand of love."

Portia smiled.

"You are a good comforter, little Nerissa," she replied.
"And if this is true, why, *this* gentleman from Venice
will not open the casket which reveals a bride."

And Nerissa understood well enough whose task it
should be to turn the key in the lock, which opened for
her mistress the road to happiness.

Meantime, Niccolo Grimani was awaiting his lady
with much impatience. He was not flattered at sight
of her mourning robes, though he ignored the fact as
also that of heavy eyes and pale cheeks.

"San Marco!" cried he, kissing Portia's hand with
extravagant devotion, "they are hard conditions which
are imposed, lady, with this choice, but I count them
mere thistle-down in looking at the reward."

"It is as well," she answered coldly, "to count the
consequences of failure. Think well, Signior. Is it
worth the risk of vowing perpetual celibacy in the
event of a wrong choice?"

"Why," laughed Grimani gayly, "I have been vowing vows ever since I came to Belmont, donna mia,
and the most constant is that there is only one bride
in the world for me, and in losing her the rest may go
hang, though the fairest of January's brides* besought
my favor on her knees."

Portia di Nerlini gave a gesture of impatience.

"Since you are so resolved, Messer," she retorted,
"we waste time in delay. You shall make your choice
straightway after taking the necessary oath."

* The brides of Venice were all married on the 31st of January.

Grimani obeyed, uttering the solemn form with a glibness which smacked of levity very different from the Prince of Morocco's stately fervor.

Indeed, contrasting the two men, Portia felt she could have forgiven the dusky darkness of the Moor's complexion sooner than the mocking laughter of this Venetian noble's eyes, which stung her to anger, rendering her deaf to the compliments he was so quick to turn in her praises.

Entering the apartment, where screening curtains hid the caskets of election, she motioned to her attendants to disclose the gilded table with its momentous freight. Then, seating herself in the chair she usually occupied during the ordeal, she beckoned to Grimani, who stepped quickly forward, the smile still on his face as though he listened to the priestly blessing pronounced on his marriage rite.

Gold, silver and lead! He scanned them all, reading their inscriptions, though with none of the hesitation shown by his predecessor of yesterday. Nor did he use arguments in his choice. Resting his hand on the silver casket, he re-read the inscription aloud in merry tones: " *'Who chooseth me, shall get as much as he deserves.'*"

"Why, I will assume desert, lady—and grow modest thereafter suing for your favor. Give me a key for this and instantly unlock my fortunes here."

There was so little hesitation in the lady's acquiescence that a less vain man might have paused

But not so Grimani! He was confident enough, as he unlocked the silver chest and drew from it a small portrait with scroll of parchment dependent.

He stared at the picture and the smile left his lips, so that Nerissa hid her face in her sleeve, so provoked was she to mirth at the glumness displayed by this fine gentleman from Venice, who had himself proved so bitter a disappointment.

"What!" cried Grimani angrily. "What's here? The portrait of a blinking idiot, presenting me a schedule? How much unlike to Portia! How much unlike my hopes and deservings! *'Who chooseth me shall have as much as he deserves!'* Did I deserve no more than a fool's head? Is that my prize? Are my deserts no better?"

He glared accusingly at the lady, whose calmness the more inflamed his anger.

"To offend and judge are distinct offices and of opposed natures," she retorted. "What says your legend, Signior?"

With obvious irritation the young nobleman unrolled the scroll, reading aloud the contents:

> The fire seven times tried this;
> Seven times tried that judgment is,
> That did never choose amiss:
> Some there be that shadows kiss;
> Such have but a shadow's bliss:
> There be fools alive, I wis,
> Silvered o'er; and so was this.
> Take what wife you will to wed,
> I will ever be your head:
> So begone, sir, you are sped.

Crushing the parchment in his hand Grimani tossed it aside, striding back across the room till he stood before Portia, his brow sullen, his eyes defiant. "Lady," quoth he, "this is but a jest. Why should we play the part of folly? I came hither to woo, and by the sword of St. Mark! you afforded me more than gracious welcome.   Then what effect hath this juggling in parting us?   I vow——"

The lady rose, stately and indignant, with flashing eyes and an air which told of final judgment.

"Yes, Signior," she retorted, "you *have* vowed—here in my very presence to abye the consequences of your choice.   You also vowed to straightway leave this place, should you fail to obtain the prize you sought. I will help you to the keeping of your oath.   Farewell, Signior."

"Nay," cried Grimani desperately, trying to catch at the trailing end of her long sleeve as she passed him. "It is not to be endured.   Can passion shrivel at such a mockery?   I tell you, fairest Portia, I will not be so dismissed.   I have come to Belmont to woo a bride——"

"And, Messer, no doubt to find a fortune," retorted Portia, in severe rebuke.   "Both are denied you, therefore it is better to say farewell, remembering your honor and your oath, since in forgetting them you will not win one who has learned to thank her dead father for a wise decree."

She left him with these words of cold disdain, followed by her train.   Grimani stared after her slender, black-robed figure in glowering anger, as though mindful at first to follow her with importunate pleadings.   Then, thinking better of this, he turned on his heel, calling his followers to him, and thus leaving the palazzo— though not to return in the direction of the ferry which traded with Venice.

CHAPTER XI

A SOFT breeze blew the perfume of flowers and scented shrubs across the wide lawns and shady paths of the Palazzo di Nerlini.

Bees droned lazily at their honey-making and the rhythmic plashing of a fountain added pleasant music to surrounding harmony.

The Lady Portia had stolen forth alone, glad for once to escape even from the companionship of Nerissa. She was in the mood for day-dreaming, and the perfection of that autumn noonday was in accord with her desire.

The jarring note lay in her own thoughts, from which, alas! she could not turn herself.

Were not these gardens empty? Was not the sunshine as cold as her own heart, lacking the one presence which should fill all life with warmth and beauty? With clasped hands and bent head she paced to and fro, pausing to linger by the fountain where an exquisite group of nymphs, chiseled in purest marble, emptied their alabaster vases in a constant stream of sparkling waters into a basin of green porphyry

Birds poured forth their songs from the spreading branches of the trees around. It was a spot for sweet dreams and tender reveries. Portia leaned her hand against the side of the shallow basin, gazing down into the clear water which mirrored her face.

"Will he come? Will he come?" sang a thrush from

the myrtle grove near. "Never—Never—Never,"· echoed the linnet from a rosebush, whose crimson blossoms fell softly into the waters of the fountain.

"Why should I remember one who forgets me?" asked Portia di Nerlini to herself, with growing bitterness.

And the world was without beauty for her to-day, since there was not even Nerissa to speak words of comfort, and the linnet kept on its sweet, monotonous refrain of "Never—never—never."

But the thrush had flown away, startled because of the man who came creeping between the myrtles, till he stood behind the Lady of Belmont, looking down into the water which mirrored the two faces now side by side.

Portia gave a startled cry, turning hastily to find Niccolo Grimani bowing, cap in hand, before her. Fear soon was succeeded by anger in the lady's breast.

"Did not you take solemn oath to leave Belmont should you fail in your choice?" she asked haughtily. "I took you for a noble of Venice, Signior."

Grimani laughed, not in the least abashed by so scathing a rebuke.

"You must not blame my unfaith so much as your own beauty, lady," he declared. "Surely, His Holiness the Pope himself would absolve me did he know my temptation. And, if you are a woman, as I deem you, you will not condemn one whose love leads him by a contrary road to that along which honor would have whipped me."

"A Nerlini," she answered coldly, "places honor above love."

"I vow," laughed Grimani, "that in all Venice no

name shall be so honored or so beloved as that of Portia Grimani."

Wrath, blazing in blue eyes, should have warned him that his masterfulness was unwelcome; but Grimani had his own notions as to how women were best conquered—for in a successful career he had not met a Portia di Nerlini.

"Shall I summon my attendants, Messer, or will you withdraw at my command?" she asked.

He made an eloquent gesture of protest.

"All other commands save that shall be obeyed," he told her, with most unpleasing fervor. "But you demand the impossible. Have other suitors ridden away? I vow Venice breeds no such luke-warm lovers —as I will prove to you."

Portia's pose was disdainful.

"Venice woos wealth, I'm told," said she. "I do not doubt you are her son—though—I have known others—more noble—who swear by San Marco—and hold their honor higher than mere greed."

His face flushed.

"I will not go without your promise," he replied stubbornly. "Why should you have sent my messenger back with such words of welcome as fired my passion— only to bid me cold farewell following a mere tricking of choice?"

"You know know my father's will, Messer Grimani," said the lady, moving away, "and by that will I have sworn to abide. Now, since you forget both oath and obligation, I wish you farewell."

Grimani watched her with brooding eyes, saw how the sunlight kissed her golden locks and showed the beauty of a face still childish in its soft contour, but that of a woman in its resolute pride. How graceful she was, slender as a willow, supple in every rounded limb and delicate curve of her beautiful body. And rich too! After all, that was the crowning goal and good for Niccolo Grimani, whose profligate life and gambling habits had brought him from easy wealth to within dangerous reach of bankruptcy.

Yet to detain the lady now was impossible, since Nerissa, having spied her mistress' dilemma from a balcony of the palazzo, had sent Florio the steward to inquire her pleasure.

At sight of the old man Portia's face brightened, and she moved towards him though still remaining within earshot of Grimani.

"Florio," said she, "you shall presently return with me to the palazzo and, having summoned a suitable escort, shall take me with Nerissa to the Convent of St. Ursula, where I intend to spend some weeks in close repose of my father's soul."

That such prayers had been offered before, she did not choose to add. All she desired was to convince the man who stood gloomily scowling under the shadows of the myrtle grove that she had found a plan to outwit him and prevent once and for all a repetition of his importunate wooing.

Yet no wonder Florio listened to the order in some perplexity, or that Nerissa presently heard it with avowed regret; for what if the Lord Bassanio with Gratiano Marmottina came riding hither to Belmont in their absence? But when the maid hinted of such a possibility to her mistress the latter only shook her head.

"They will never come, never, never, never," she averred.

It had been the lament of the linnet in the garden yonder, as it swayed on a rose spray, sending a shower of crimson petals fluttering down into the marble basin of the fountain. It was the dirge which sounded in the ears of the Lady Portia as she rode behind Florio on her way to the Convent of St. Ursula, where, in escaping from a Niccolo Grimani, she bade farewell to the hope of welcoming Bassanio Ramberti to her home.

CHAPTER XII

TONI OVER-REACHES HIMSELF

"FROM my Lord Bassanio, master, bidding you to supper. I wait the answer."

Shylock the Jew raised his blear eyes to the speaker, a scowling fury twisting his harsh features. But at sight of Toni's expressionless face his mood changed, and he stretched out claw-like fingers to clutch at the yellow badge he wore upon the breast of his gabardine—that badge, insignia, with the yellow turban, of a despised race, which, driven from Venice by the Republic some years before, had been recalled of necessity to set up pawnshops and re-establish its trade of usury.

The touch of that badge seemed to inspire fresh fury into the old man, so that he sat, shaking and mouthing as one in a palsy, glaring in inarticulate rage at the man who had till lately been his own servant.

"May Abraham's curse be on his head!" squealed Shylock at last. "To sup with him? To smell pork! To sit down with unwashed Gentiles! But stop! why did he ask me? What was his purpose? Does he wish to be friends with the Jew—to borrow moneys on his own account, forgetting how highly Aaron Tubal rates his interest? Answer me, villain!"

Toni shifted from one foot to the other, thoughtfully rubbing the knee of his long, parti-colored hose.

"I was but bidden bring the letter," he replied sul-

lenly, "and return with your answer.   My Lord Bassanio holds a feast to-night, followed by a masque.
All his friends are invited to supper no later than five
o'clock—afterwards, it is said, the masquers take the
Signior in his ship as far as the coast, whither he goes
to woo the Lady of Belmont."

The Jew fell to chuckling.   "He asks his *friends*,"
he mocked.   "Is Shylock friend to Bassanio Ramberti?
Is he his enemy?   Well, if I were his enemy I would go
and feed upon him, wasting his borrowed prodigality.
Yes, I will go.   You shall give him that answer, knave.
Go, tell him Shylock the Jew with cringing mien and
humble heart will come to take the crumbs which fall
beneath that table of wealthy substance.   That is the
dog's place, as Messer Antonio will tell him.   So I will
come—aye, come."

His red-rimmed eyes grew cunning in their malice.
Hate stared forth from beneath penthouse brows, his
lips frothed as in a madness of desired vengeance.

"Go!" he snarled.   "What! you linger?   Do you
regret my service, boy?   There is lean faring perchance
in a marble palace, whilst here you did but eat, sleep,
snore and rend apparel out."

Toni glanced cautiously over his shoulder.

"Nay," he muttered, creeping nearer to the Jew's
chair, "but I would purchase your favor, master.
News is worth money at times, excellency, as the householder might have said had he known of the thief's
purpose."

The words were significant, accompanied too by a sly
wink, as the man peered about to make sure there was
no listener near.

Shylock blinked shrewdly at the mysterious speaker.

"What's this?" he croaked. "A plot to rob the Jew?" He began to grow excited at the very thought, rising and plucking Toni by the doublet.

The Venetian edged away, trying to soothe him.

"Nay, nay," he urged deprecatingly, "though *had* there been, it would have been worth money. Say you not so?"

But Shylock, alarmed at the fellow's obvious innuendos, had the would-be traitor by the shoulder, and was shaking him with surprising vigor.

"Out, rogue!" he shrieked in crescendo tones. "I'll have you before the Senate with this tale. Thieves! A plot to rob the Jew! Why, if there are thieves, be sure you, as a most trusty knave, knowing my house and its ways, are in the swim. A thievish accomplice! A very proper rogue—who——"

In spite of Toni's frantic struggles, and the fact that he was by far the bigger and more powerful man, the frenzied patriarch would have dragged his victim to the door had not the latter been opened and Jessica entered. With her striped veil* flung back over a dress of yellow taffeta, and a crimson carnation in her raven locks, she was the picture of youthful beauty, so that more than ever Toni the greedy fell to whimpering, conscience-stricken in his part of traitor to a kind mistress. But Jessica paid no heed to his maudlin tears save to draw her conclusion.

"Why, father," she cried, "what grieves you in this fashion? It is not with our wine or at our cost that the Gentile's servant is drunk. Why should you take

---

* The dress of a Jewess was distinguished by two blue stripes on veil and cloak.

Bassanio's part and beat the man for a fault which no doubt comes of his master's lavishness?"

Shylock paused, whilst Toni, quick to act on so excellent a hint, and in deadly fear of the Jew's purpose in extorting full confession of what his words had hinted, began to play his part of inebriate with sufficient skill to be convincing.

Suddenly released from a throttling grip, he staggered back against the wall, protesting volubly that he had stolen nothing—not so much as a thimbleful of wine from anyone. Then artfully he explained how Signior Bassanio's wine flasks had been so nearly empty that not the strictest priest could give him penance for the sin of finishing so small a measure.

He spoke clearly—as he had before—full of sly hints and artful winks, weaving such rigmaroles that even his late master became convinced that Jessica was right and this matter of thieves but a mare's nest conjured up by a wine-fevered imagination. Yet he proved him with question upon question, putting a word to trip the fuddled Toni here and another there—Jewish wit against Venetian, and the latter won merely because Shylock deemed the fellow a dullard who would not have had the craft to ramble so aimlessly by intention.

And all the time Jessica stood by, a vivid beauty in that dingy room whose costly furnishings were overlaid by dust and dirt, and mocked both Toni and her father, crying that breath was wasted upon one whose tongue ran on after his wit had been clogged with liquor.

"Yet you shall tell Bassanio I sup with him to-night," screamed Shylock at last, taking the servant by the ear and bellowing into it as though he were deaf instead of merely drunken. "And for that matter, thou swiveling

sot, I will be my own messenger. Yes, my own messenger, and the death's head at the feast. What!
There are to be masques there? Will Signior Antonio
wear the fool's cap or the ass' head whilst drinking
friendship with the Jew? Oh! A merry evening it
will be! A merry evening when Bassanio bids Shylock
to supper."

He rubbed shriveled palms together, gloating as
though he touched gold instead of the shadow of that
revenge he cherished in his evil heart. Jessica was
leading Toni to the door, and though the latter dragged
reluctantly behind, arguing in the fashion of a wine-
fuddled man, he was right glad presently to find the door
closed between himself and his late master.

In the passage Jessica turned on him in a flash, her
black eyes accusing, whilst the hot color flamed in her
cheeks.

"So this is how you show gratitude for kindness,"
she whispered. "You would sell our secret, barter the
letter with which Lorenzo entrusted you. Oh, vile
one, I am minded to let Bassanio hear of this."

Toni turned pale. He had indeed hoped to play a
double and profitable game by letting Shylock know
of the intrigue between his daughter and a Christian,
whilst at the same time contriving to hide his own part
of betrayal.

Shylock's anxiety on behalf of his ducats had brought
matters to a very different issue, and Toni trembled,
fearing the loss of easy and profitable service. Previous
knowledge of Jessica's shrewdness warned him that it
was useless to attempt to deceive her again; so, throwing
himself on his knees, he whined out a tale of debt and
desperate straits which alone had induced the thought

8

of playing a double *rôle*.   Jessica listened impatiently.

"My father will be coming down," she said, "and his ears are quick to hear secrets.   Give me Signior Lorenzo's letter and begone.   But take heed you play no scurvy tricks again or I shall advertise Messer Bassanio of your treachery."

Toni made haste to deliver the letter which the girl read, her eyes sparkling, her red lips parted in an ecstasy, as she unrolled the parchment to the end.

"Yes," she whispered, "I will not refuse.   Could I do so, seeing what is at stake?   O Lorenzo, Lorenzo, keep truth with me.   Can I trust a Gentile?   Why, I myself shall soon be Christian too.   Lorenzo's wife. What dreams fulfilled!   I'll stake my soul on it, since if I do not go, my father will certainly wed me to Tubal, and I would die before being bride to such as he."

Very deliberately she laid her hand on Toni's arm, fixing her large, soft eyes upon him.

"Tell Signior Lorenzo," she commanded, "that Jessica will be waiting.   If he sings I shall answer—and there is no moon to-night.   Be faithful in giving this mssage, Toni, and you shall not be the poorer for it."

Toni stooped to kiss her hand.

"Forgive?" he whispered.   "Lady, you shame me. I confess it was an ugly greed which prompted my tongue.   But your kindness has put such check on it as I vow will keep it from all unseemly wagging in future. I'll go straight to Signior Lorenzo with your message and may the devil have the picking of my bones if I forget one word of it."

And so earnestly did he speak that Jessica, smiling, believed him.

"Look to my house—yes, look to it well."

"Besides," thought the pretty Jewess, as she fastened the door behind Toni, "he will have no further opportunity for betrayal, since no sooner has my father gone than Lorenzo will be coming. Ah! My heart! What an enterprise! I must prepare too for that coming—don my page's garb; nor—nor will I go empty-handed to this new lord and love. Do I not know how to find a dowry in my father's room? I think it is possible! What sin is it in me to be ashamed to be my father's child! But though I am a daughter to his blood, I am not to his manners. And he would wed me to Aaron Tubal, knowing I hate him. Why then! I'll think no more of my own sin but of a father's injustice and cruelty. Ah, to-night! To-night! Lorenzo, love, keep tryst, for your Jessica will have no one but you to love and guard her."

"Jessica! Jessica!"

It was her father's raucous voice calling to her impatiently from above.

"Jessica! What, girl, has that sot gone?"

"Yes, father."

She climbed the stairs, standing upon the threshold of his room.

"I am bid forth to supper, Jessica," he mumbled grudgingly. "There are my keys. Look to my house—yes, look to it well. I am right loath to go. There is some ill brewing against me since last night; I dreamed of money bags."

He tugged at his long beard, undetermined, irresolute, whilst Jessica, outwardly calm, was fevered inwardly with suspense and fear. If her father did *not* go forth as Lorenzo had schemed, how fared her project of escape?

"I am loath to go," reiterated Shylock. "Yet there is reason for it. They say there'll be a masque. Fools!, Braggarts! Thus they squander the money hard thrift has obtained. And, whilst they feast their appetites, I shall be feasting too, seeing how nimbly all works to their undoing. Antonio will be there, curse him! But I would see Antonio—how I hate him! As for my house—hear me, Jessica. Lock up my doors, and when you hear the drum, and the vile squeaking of the wry-necked fife, see you do not go clambering up to the casements or thrusting your head out to gaze on these Christian fools with varnished faces and foolish gauds. I'll not let the sound of shallow foppery enter my house. By Jacob's staff! I swear I'm in no mood for feasting! But I'll go. Antonio will be there. I think he heard ill news on the Rialto to-day, if rumor does not lie. Take heed, Jessica, think of all I have bidden you remember. Perhaps I will return immediately. Do as I bid you. Shut the doors after you. Fast bind, fast find."

He repeated the proverb again and again as he slowly descended the stairs.

There was a curious reluctance on his part to leave the house that night. Perhaps a premonition kindled by the ill omen of a dream, to which Jews attach so much importance, and also a lurking suspicion that Toni might not have been so drunk as he seemed when he hinted that thieves might have a fancy for despoiling a rich Jew.

But against these vague misgivings was set the stronger desire to come face to face with his bitter enemy, gloating to see how with careful skill the meshes of his wide net of vengeance were being drawn closer.

He almost forgot his insatiable thirst for gain in dwelling on the pains and torture which he prayed he might be able to inflict on the young Venetian merchant, Antonio Cainello.

CHAPTER XIII

"SO—check! Messer Antonio, I am the winner!"
And Lorenzo Fortunato leaped to his feet,
laughing gayly, whilst his quick movement
scattered the costly chess men from the board about
the balcony.

In the west the sun flared towards its setting, bathing
the waters of lagoons and canals with crimson glory,
rose-tinting the white marble of the palaces and stately
buildings which seemed to have risen at the command
of some Fay Morgana out of the ocean itself; a city
without fields or pastures, hills, valleys, roads or pleasant
woods—but a gleaming panorama of white and gold—
marble walls, gilded domes, with blue sky above, blue
ocean below and the gorgeous contrast of crimson and
orange, violet and scarlet of awnings, flags and flowers,
which bedecked walls and balconies, as well as the gayly-
caparisoned gondolas, which glided swan-like across the
deep lagoons and beneath the fairy spanning of innumerable bridges.

On the Gothic balcony, projecting over the salt waters
that washed the foundations of one of the lesser palazzi,
sat Antonio Cainello and young Lorenzo, awaiting the
coming of their host, Bassanio Ramberti.

Opposite to them rose other houses, and on the wooden
platform crowning one of these a woman leaned forward,
watching the handsome Lorenzo with smiling eyes.

Her companion sat near, a large cat upon her lap, whilst over her loose combing-cloth of white silk were spread the tawny masses of her dyed hair which had just been freed from the *solana*—a straw hat without a crown, over whose brim the hair of the Venetian ladies was duly drawn during the inevitable process of dyeing. So necessary was this part of the toilet deemed that wooden platforms were erected on the roofs of nearly every house for the females of the family to repair to do dye their locks and dry them in the sun.

Lorenzo, looking up, saw the watchful beauty and blew her the airiest of kisses.

"It is Donna Caterina," he observed lazily to Antonio. "She is a very pretty woman, but I do not admire her red hair. It is a pity she is at such pains to dye it; it would be much prettier left alone. How foolish some women are."

Antonio smiled gravely.

This gay-hearted young man was rather a favorite of his, and indeed everyone seemed to like Fortunato— who was well named, since he always managed to fall on his feet without undue trouble or scheming on his own part. A handsome face, kind heart and winning tongue are no bad equipment in life, as our Lorenzo had found.

He was in the merriest of moods this evening, and sat cross-legged, a guitar in his hands, which he twanged now and again as though only half inclined to awake melody.

And though presently he raised laughing eyes to Donna Caterina, he was thinking of pretty Jessica, whose message had been duly delivered by the chastened Toni.

Yes, certainly, raven locks with the blue-black gloss of a bird's wing on them were far more beautiful than dull red tresses—though of course little Caterina's skin was of the whitest, whilst that of Jessica was dark—but such a darkness! The red glow of sunset reminded him of it. And then her eyes!

Lorenzo twanged his guitar again, singing passionately beneath his breath.

> Belina sei e'l ciel te benedissa,
> Che in dove che ti passi l'erba nasse!

Then he broke off, laughing, flushing a little too as he caught the gaze of Messer Antonio's grave eyes fixed on his.

"Would you like another game of chess, amico?" he asked, laying aside the guitar and beginning to pick up the chess men.

Antonio shook his head.

"You have already discomfited me too entirely," he replied.

Lorenzo shrugged his shoulders. "I could be nothing else than a winner to-night," he retorted. "Ah! here comes our Bassanio, looking as concerned over his dinner as though he were the whole Council of Ten."

Antonio rose, moving towards the open casement. Bassanio had entered the room within, in solemn converse with his *sigisbeo*. Every Venetian householder of the higher classes retained one of these indispensable factotums who undertook the arrangement of all domestic details. Dinner parties, masques, the management of the establishment, all were the concern of the *sigisbeo*, who was something more than the ordinary steward, and who indeed was at times accorded the greatest responsibilities; for where there were ladies of the household, he would be expected to act as their chaperon to parties, the theater, church or promenade, failing other cavalieri.

Bassanio spied Antonio and, dismissing the *sigisbeo* with a few brief words, hastened towards his friend.

"Ah, amico," said he, "I should have come before. Has Gratiano arrived yet? I have his petition to accompany me presently to Belmont."

And he laughed very softly, as a lover who, after long waiting, hopes to see his mistress.

"Will she welcome me?" he murmured. "Antonio, if you could guess what madness thrills my soul when I think of this lady! My only wonder is that I could have endured life all these months without a sight of her. How I am on fire to behold her, to touch her hand, to gaze into her eyes. And to-night I sail to Belmont. Do you wonder that I am mute for very lack of words to coin my gratitude to you to whom I owe this happiness? My friend Antonio!"

The two grasped hands warmly—was there need of words after all? But Antonio could have sighed, since a sadder spirit warned him of the grief poor Bassanio would sustain should that ordeal of choice fall contrary to hopes which ran riot in an hour of passion.

Lorenzo's merry voice calling to them from the balcony without was a pleasant distraction for Antonio. Here were two whose moods were one, so that he himself might stand aside in the shadows, rejoicing in the happiness of others, praying for its continuance. The wooden platform opposite was empty. Donna Caterina and her friend had retired—perhaps the former was disappointed that the handsome gallant on the balcony had not finished a song which she never doubted was addressed to her.

"Lorenzo is merry to-night," explained Antonio, smiling, as the three young men stood, in the growing dusk, on the balcony.

Lorenzo showed white teeth in a gay laugh.

"How can I be otherwise," he questioned, "since the hour for adventure draws near?"

Bassanio looked at him questioningly.

"You speak of the masque?" he asked.

Lorenzo shook his head.

"Of *a* masque—why, yes," he retorted; "but not of yours, amico. Shall I be masked? Most certainly. And will pretty Jessica be masked? I think so. At least, she warned me that I should not know her. But I vow that is impossible, since there is only one Jessica in all the world, though you may have your Elenas, your Caterinas and your Genevras by the score."

"I do not altogether take your meaning," quoth Bassanio, with a wry grimace, "though I think you speak of the Jew's daughter."

Lorenzo flung wide his arms.

"The Jew's daughter!" he rhapsodized. "The Jew's jewel. His pearl above price. But do you not remember, amico, how you sent the Jew's servant—who is now your own—one Toni, a shrewd devil with a twisted mouth—to invite Shylock himself to your entertainment? So now I have a clear field for my enterprise, which is no more nor less than to run away with pretty Jessica?"

He dropped his voice discreetly, and neither he nor Bassanio noticed how Antonio flinched at hearing how Shylock the Jew was to take part in Bassanio's festivities.

But a light of understanding had come into Bassanio Ramberti's eyes.

"I do remember," said he, "that I did you this service of asking Shylock to supper, whilst you, as you told me, *serenaded* his daughter."

Lorenzo laughed. "Belina sei e'l ciel te benedissa," he sang beneath his breath. "Oh, I shall serenade her, Bassanio, with so sweet a lure that she will follow me as Orpheus' wife was lured from Hades itself. And I think I've smelled sulphur in the Jew's house! So my sweet lady will venture forth, and we shall tell over our fair loves together when safely 'scaped from hell and Master Satan Shylock."

"I believe you honest, Lorenzo," quoth Bassanio more gravely than his wont, "but I'll have your word that you mean to marry this maid, whose praises I have heard sung as often as I've listened to curses on her father."

"At Genoa," replied Lorenzo, with frank sincerity, "I wed Jessica, the Jew's daughter. You have my oath on it, Bassanio. Indeed, the priest who knows my mind and need will wait to do us this service. The lady— though offspring from ignoble root—is worthy to rank with the highest in the land by reason of her own sweet graciousness."

Bassanio held out his hand, smiling very kindly.

"I well believe it," he said heartily, "and pray St. Julian's blessings on you and your dear love. Why! we are comrades in this, good friend Lorenzo, and speed the same course—though the ship which carries you and your bride to happiness but sends me on my way in search of that same blessing."

"A brief delay if my wishes wing your journey," replied Lorenzo affectionately. "I would I could remain to drink to your prospering, Bassanio, but I must meet the friends who are aiding me to-night, and lay our plans with closest caution and care; for one needs to keep every sense alert when playing a game of craft with Master Jew. You'll make him welcome here for my sake? Set his goblet brimming and his tongue wagging of gain to be found for the seeking. Picture an Eldorado of fat money bags, dazzle his vision with golden ducats, and so entice him to linger in such an atmosphere of gilded wealth—for every minute will be speeding my happiness nearer to consummation."

Bassanio fetched a mocking sigh as he assented to the request. Glancing towards Antonio he was made aware that two friendships plucked him contrary ways—though the merchant's face was averted, nor did he give hint of how the evening's pleasure would be marred by his enemy's presence.

"You have my help in this, Lorenzo," Bassanio said, "seeking it in a happy hour, since Cupid sings aloft in my good ship's rigging, and I have no fear but that the merry boy will stand my friend in guiding my choice to fair Portia's hand and heart. So we'll take it for granted that love stands crowned for you and me, and herewith I give you and your gentle wife that is to be, ready invitation to Belmont, should you and she, straying beyond reach of the old Jew's vengeance and thus exiled from Venice, find yourselves homeless. You'll come— and find your own happiness reflected on the faces of two others, fortunate in the favor of the gods."

"Why, that's kind of you," replied Lorenzo grate- fully, as he flicked the petal of a fallen flower from his short cloak of blue velvet. "And in my own name and that of my wife which is to be, I answer that we shall certainly come to Belmont in our happy wanderings, if only to discover others as blessed as ourselves.   Who finds this world a dreary wilderness is but a moping night-bird bereft of his wing feathers.   For myself, friends, it seems the gladdest place that could be pictured. So farewell—to meet in yet merrier mood, with tales to tell!   St. Julian's shade!   What tales!   Of Hades' 'scaped, paradise gained, and a whole army of money-grabbing, Jew-nosed Beelzebubs put to flight.   Whilst, for reward—a wife—a pearl—a queen, in whose kingdom happiness abides."

Bassanio laughed, being no sceptic to draw another picture of wedded bliss, but rather a fellow worshipper at Hymen's shrine, where the one woman sat for adoration.

But Antonio stood back in the shadows, left alone upon the balcony for the moment, whilst arm in arm Bassanio and Lorenzo descended to the street, which led close by the palazzo to one of the smaller canals, where Lorenzo's friends awaited him.

"At Belmont," was Bassanio's gay word of parting. "I think it should be a' happy meeting, Lorenzo."

He had not a doubt or dread as he reclimbed the stairs to join Antonio.

CHAPTER XIV

L AUGHTER, toasting, jest and song echoed through the apartment where Bassanio Ramberti made merry with his friends.

All knew the tale of whither his ship was sailing that night. All knew the story of Portia di Nerlini's wealth, her beauty and the hard conditions attached to the winning of both.

Few indeed of the guests declared they would be willing to put their fortunes to such a chance or vow perpetual celibacy for the sake of a possible winning of fair bride and dower. Bassanio listened to their raillery unmoved, ready to answer every quip, and to vow himself a hopeless victim to the spell of a lady's eyes. As for her wealth, why, he had a use for it, he was prepared to admit. And, as he spoke, glanced down the long board to where Shylock's yellow turban showed conspicuously amongst his seated guests.

No one to witness such a scene would have guessed that the youthful host was hopelessly involved in debt. Mario, the *sigisbeo*, had done his work well. Gleaming silver, glittering crystal, beautiful flowers adorned the tables, as well as those wondrous sugar centerpieces which at this time invariably graced a feast. The clear candy was artistically moulded to represent animals, figures, a woodland scene, dancing nymphs or a group of Cupids dragging Aurora's chariot.

Wealth and luxury were lavishly displayed, so that Shylock the Jew, taking careful note, mocked in his beard at the prodigality of these Christians.

Antonio, watching his new-made creditor from the opposite side of the table, knew himself wrong in one respect. Whatever had induced the usurer to lend him moneys without equivalent interest, it was assuredly not kindness of heart. The old Jew's eyes were cold as those of a dead fish, and every time he opened his mouth to put food into it, it seemed that he breathed curses around.

"Why comes not our Gratiano?" cried Bassanio from the head of the table. "He promised to be here early. Indeed, it is the stranger since he was very urgent in the matter of accompanying me to Belmont."

"What," cried a youth, raising his goblet, "you take a rival, Bassanio? Would Gratiano also be setting his value on a casket's decree? San Marco! Our maids of Venice would need to wear mourning for a very Catholic gallant turned by solemn oath to drear celibacy."

"The maids of Venice may wear the willow for Gratiano," replied Bassanio, "since his heart is lost."

"Lost!" echoed another, resting his elbows on the table and wagging his head. "Why, if so, I warrant there will be half a dozen offers to supply the vacuum. He need not search farther than his native Venice, even if his own heart be locked in a casket or a lady's money bags."

Bassanio frowned. "Gratiano has nothing to do with caskets," he retorted. "Do you fancy there is but one woman in Italy—one pair of bright eyes at Belmont? But you shall ask Gratiano himself, since here he comes, wearing so gloomy a brow that I shall believe he has hired his own gondola, tried his own fortune and failed dismally in his quest."

All eyes were turned towards the young man who came striding into the room.

Unlike his usual cheery self, Gratiano was dull of countenance, and he tugged at the long chain around his neck in nervous impatience.

Behind him came the bowing *sigisbeo*, who—whilst Gratiano paused to exchange greeting with a comrade who caught at his cloak in passing—hastened to his master's side.

Bassanio listened to the news-bearer with clouding brow.

"Why! This is very contrary to our wishes," he cried. "Friends all, the elements are against our reveling. Mario here informs me that the wind has risen and that there can be no masque to-night. But we'll not say that because we're tricked of pleasure it eludes us. The masque, Messires, is postponed, not countermanded. With St. Julian's blessings it shall be the merrier for a bride or two. What say you, Gratiano?"

And he struck his friend lightly on the shoulder, trying to hide his own disappointment.

Gratiano shook his head.

"I also bring news," he replied, "which is no better than Mario's. The winds should be as feminine as Fate herself. And Fate as feminine as the Lady Portia di Nerlini, if all that is feminine spells caprice."

Bassanio's face became blank.

"What do you mean?" he cried—then a swift fear seized him. "The casket has been chosen," he muttered, "and Portia has been won?"

It had been his dread ever since Niccolo Grimani first

told him of Pietro di Nerlini's death and the curious fashion of his will.

"If she has been won," retorted Gratiano gloomily, "it is not by man, but by Holy Mother Church, though Nicolisi, who gave me the news, could not say whether the lady had entered the Convent of St. Ursula as a novice in preparation for holy vows, or only in retreat to pray for her dead father's soul. Be that as it may, I know she has taken her maid Nerissa with her, and the Palazzo di Nerlini is closed against all comers."

Murmurs of surprise, regret, even pity, ran round the table. Bassanio Ramberti was a general favorite, not only amongst the younger *nobili*, but with the rich merchants of his own age, many of whom sat now about the board, their gay clothing in contrast with the black habiliments of the nobles. But Bassanio stood silent, in part relieved from his first fear that Portia was lost to him forever, being won by some prior claimant. It seemed impossible that the lady, whom he remembered only on a day of unclouded youth and sunshine, should voluntarily bury herself for the rest of her life in a convent cell.

No, this was, as Gratiano suggested, but a temporary retreat. He would yet seek, woo and win her in a golden hour.

Yet the postponement was hard enough to bear, clogged as it was by many difficulties and anxieties, which would shape themselves into definite forms of threatening as he came to dwell on them.

For the present he must not forget his obligation to assembled friends, or the fact that he was master of a feast, the extravagance of which impressed him now as he saw the yawning of many dismal days and weeks between himself and that happy fortune whose crown was Portia di Nerlini. With an effort he returned to his entertainment, failing to notice the animation which had kindled on old Shylock's face, the glee with which the Jew had listened to Gratiano's intelligence and the malice of his glance directed from his host towards Antonio Cainello, whose sympathy for his friend was apparent to all.

The gayety of the feast had vanished. The bubbling, eager joy of their host, so full of true merriment, had gone, to be replaced by something forced and labored.

Bassanio laughed, but the sound rang hollow, not hiding altogether the aching heart which disappointment brought. High hope had been blighted and the shadow of its death haunted the eyes which tried for sake of courtesy to smile at the limping jests which passed from mouth to mouth with poor attempts to rekindle a quenched flame.

At last the strain was over. Guests, ready enough now to hasten their departure, bade their host good-night, each adding his hope that the lady would yet be won with small delay.

"Bare walls are but ill exchanged for gilded mirrors," declared one gallant, encouragingly, "and so fair a lady will weary for a lover's whispers in place of a confessor's drone."

"I shall hope so," replied Bassanio, with his ready smile, "and hold myself prepared to take the confessor's part."

"Though she will not be telling you of her sins," laughed his friend, "but, if she loves you, will declare yours to be the fault that you came not sooner."

The careless words stabbed their listener. Had not

that been the reproach of his own heart? How could he have let those golden months of summer pass him by in Verona and Rome, when he might have been pleading his cause into kindly ears at Belmont?

They had all gone at last, that troop of merry friends, grown grave in sympathy with their host's sore heart. He had been so confident in his hopes. Yet his ship would be at anchor to-night down there by the quays, nor take a lover across those ruffling waters to the side of his longed-for mistress. Amongst the last to go was Shylock the Jew, who had waited, ready to hear the news which brought discomfiture to these his enemies, who feasted him on luxuries bought with his own money— to be redeemed at his own price. His red-rimmed eyes peered cunningly up into Bassanio's grave face and, as he thanked him for his hospitality, marked the contempt which for an instant shone in the gray eyes looking down upon him.

So Bassanio, in inviting him here, had not believed in a Jew's kindness!

Then wherefore had he asked him? To borrow more ducats? Well, he would refuse the loan! Yes, he would refuse it. Was not Antonio bound already—Antonio, who was his enemy?

But as the old usurer limped home, well content with the news he had gleaned at Ramberti's feast, he wondered yet again *why* he had been asked. Not for love—and not for business. In bidding him good-night, Bassanio had made no mention of a loan—had failed to draw him aside with suave request and liberal promises of interest. Why, then, had he asked him to feast? Shylock the Jew clawed at his long beard as he stood, like some grim bird of prey, waiting for a boatman with whom to bargain for a cheap passage home.

"The Jew returns to an empty house," quoth Bassanio, standing beside Antonio on the marble steps, awaiting the coming of the merchant's gondola; "that is to say, if Lorenzo's star shines in a happier hour than my own."

Antonio Cainello laid an affectionate hand on his friend's shoulder.

"Nay," he urged, "do not wear so heavy a brow, Bassanio.   At least the lady is not already plighted. Nor do I believe she has entered the convent excepting as a retreat from importunate suitors.   Soon she will return home, and you shall go and try to win her to more confidence and trust.   If prayers are heard in Heaven I am sure your happiness is assured.   Daily I petition for that same gift for you.   A gift above all others which Heaven can dower us poor mortals with—a woman's love."

Bassanio laughed rather bitterly.

"You speak warmly of woman's love, amico," he declared, "yet a moment before you convince me you have never sought it, else you had not spoken so dispassionately of delay.   Oh, this delay!   It maddens me, Antonio.   I, who had dreamed that before another sun rose, I should be seeing the glory of my lady's eyes. I, who had hoped not to listen again to the songs of wakening birds before I heard the music of her voice. You smile!   A lover's rhapsodies, you say.   Yet you're young too, Antonio, though grave beyond your years. Is it because you have gone too empty of a love which sets the gravest back to the follies of his childhood? Oh, to be young and love!   To love and possess!   But your ears are dull to such a yearning.   Shall I ever jest with you, Antonio, because you have committed the folly of loving a woman?   But I do not think I would jest either.   Love is too sweetly sacred for such gibings. We worship at its shrine, not knowing half the mystery of its powers.   That is to love.   But you do not understand, Antonio."

Antonio did not reply.   Even, and above all, to this dear and treasured friend he could not tell the secret which convent walls had closed round, and death had sealed with its mystic touch.   Yet, gazing upwards to the dark vault of the heavens, he saw a star shine—saw it through a mist of sudden tears.

Did he not understand the vain yearning of an aching, passionate heart?   Had he never cried that voiceless, inarticulate cry of love and desire which might never reach mortal ears?

And was it possible that his love, deathless in its essence, purified of carnal taint, should one day find realization in another world?   Would Bianca Ramberti, that sweet and lovely saint who had looked his heart away, listen in tender harmony of soul to the tale of a great love, untold on earth but repeated at length on an eternal shore?

Bassanio talked on, heedless of his friend's abstraction, assuredly never guessing its reason.   So he spoke only of himself—and Portia.   Of his love—and of her beauty. Of hopes, of fears, of doubt and joy, knowing that he spoke to one of whose sympathy he was certain.   Could it be otherwise?   Was not this Antonio his proven friend—his best and dearest friend, confidant, brother— who had ever the listening ear, the tender heart and the generous purse for him?

Warmly the two men clasped hands as the gilded gondola glided down the canal towards the steps.

"Farewell, Antonio."

"Farewell, Bassanio."

Far off came the echo of a serenade.

The moon was rising in the east—shedding soft, effulgent light upon the waters so lately lashed by contrary winds.

The brief storm was over—but Bassanio's ship would not sail to-night.

"But for him, Heaven willing, there will be a to-morrow," thought Antonio, as he seated himself on the cushioned seat of his gondola. "A to-morrow on earth—of love's fulfilment."

He wrapped his cloak more closely round him. "Bianca mia," he whispered. "Ah, Bianca—for you am not I ready to wait through an eternity? But, for one smile, love, my love—who yet was never mine—but Heaven's. A gift perhaps to be given back again—in the great dawning."

He raised his face with a patient smile.

This was the man whom Bassanio Ramberti, in his hot, impetuous youth, had vowed could never have loved.

CHAPTER XV

THE ELOPEMENT

THE night was dark. Clouds drifted across the sky. The waters of the lagoon were whipped into tiny wavelets by a freshening breeze.

Down a narrow street hurried three figures, cloaked and masked. They halted presently beneath an archway, checked by their taller comrade.

"Wait for me here," whispered Lorenzo eagerly. "Watch carefully. I do not trust that Jew. He has gone to Bassanio's, but he may return at any moment, too soon for my purpose. So, good friends, watch for me, and if at any future time you play the thieves for wives, I'll wait as long for you."

He stepped into a small boat, moored under shadow of a bridge, in waiting for him, and pushed off towards the winding curve of the canal.

"Bring the warning if any approach," he cried back to where his friends, Salarino and Salanio, stood with their cloaks wrapped closely about them as protection against the strengthening breeze which was destined to put an end to Bassanio's masque.

The two young men laughed softly, waved their affirmative reply, and began to pace slowly up and down the narrow street bordering the canal. They had been pleased enough to lend ready ears to Lorenzo's persuasions and give their assistance in carrying out any scheme to the discomfiture of Shylock the Jew, who was very unpopular amongst Venetian citizens; for,

(135)

whilst the latter used him from necessity, they hated him for his heathen extortions, since Tito Scappini, the poor fisherman whom Antonio the merchant had befriended, was not the only one to have found Shylock a cruel taskmaster.   So Messers Salarino and Salanio, swaggering it up and down the pathway that dark night, laughed softly as they whispered together that not only the Rialto, but all Venice would be ringing to-morrow with the story òf how the pretty Jewess had run away with Lorenzo Fortunato.

Lorenzo had found the funereal looking house at the corner darkened and silent.   In fact, so much darkness was perplexing, since without a glimmer of moonlight he could not even see the bridge on the right.   What if Jessica, recalling that she was Abraham's daughter even whilst forgetting that Shylock was her more immediate and less worthy parent, had resolved against wedding a Christian?

The young man sighed.   He was quite as impetuous as Bassanio, and really had fallen deeply in love with pretty Jessica.   Being as improvident as men of such natures usually are, he had not troubled to think so much of money or how he was prepared for the expenses of matrimony.   All that mattered to him was that he wanted Jessica.   Aye, and meant to have her too, with the more determination since he could not win her as any other maiden of his choice might have been won. He had rested his oars and, taking up the lute, which lay at the bottom of the boat, began to sing the song with which Venetian swains addressed their mistresses.

> Yea, thou art fair, I pray the heavens to bless thee,
> For where thy footsteps fall the grass is spread
> In springtide vendure underneath thy tread,
> As though the spring were born but to caress thee.

The clear, full notes of his tenor voice rang upwards passionately, whilst with eager eyes he watched the darkened balcony above.

Yet it was from within the house that the answer came, sweet, but low-pitched, with deep thrills of emotion.

> 'Tis Nane brave and Nane fair
> That's walking in yon field;
> And where he treads the grasses there
> Bow down to him and yield.
> They bow to greet his dearest feet,
> And make him low obeisance.
> The loving heart, it is its part
> To watch and wait in patience!

And, as Lorenzo listened to the words which blushing maids had sung, for centuries through, behind sheltering casements, he laughed aloud and sprang up in his boat, watching how a flicker of light danced hither and thither above, showing the outline of the grim old house and the abutting balcony, out upon which stepped the slender figure of a page, holding a lighted torch aloft in his left hand.

A page! But what a page! The dark green cloak, closely fitting doublet and hose, only served to mark more distinctly every grace and beauty of the figure, whilst beneath the feathered cap a face showed, lit up by the smoking torchlight; a face of dark, glowing beauty, a black curl astray over a low, broad forehead, accentuating the beauty of the black eyes with their drooping lashes.

"Jessica!" cried Lorenzo softly. "Carissima—how I love you! Come quickly, for every moment is an eternity before I clasp you in my arms."

"You have come to take me away?" she whispered,

reluctant in her dallying now that the crucial moment had arrived.

"Why else am I here?" he demanded. "Our gondola awaits us close to the Palazzo di Dolfini. We sail for Genoa to-night. The morning sees you my loving bride."

"Your loving bride indeed," she whispered, bending low over the parapet so that the torchlight fell on her lover's upturned, handsome face. "For whom love I so much? And now, who knows but you, Lorenzo, whether I am your love?"

He stretched yearning arms towards her.

"Heaven and your woman's heart should be witness to that," he retorted. "But do not delay, Jessica. You trust me?"

For the briefest of moments she hesitated. Was it wonder, poor child, since she had been born and bred in the atmosphere of suspicion?

Yet not for long did she delay. Was she not indeed looking upon a lover's face? Fair, gay, handsome, the very soul of her passionate dreams, whilst in the shadows from which she had come forth, lurked the threatening forms of her father and Aaron Tubal. Aaron Tubal! How she hated and feared that man; his craft, his cunning, above all his appraising of her, his mocking air of possessiveness from which she drew back shuddering and afraid.

So she laughed, bending lower over the balcony. Had not her loving heart watched and waited in patience? She had decided to launch forth now upon their new life, trusting blindly and solely to the man who held out his arms to her from below.

Thus she laughed, the swift blushes dyeing her cheeks, her eyes mischievous in their coquetry.

"Take this packet," she cried.

"Take this packet," she cried, "it is worth the pains. A casket of jewels, Lorenzo, which, being possessed of my father's keys, I took for dowry. Ah! you have it? And now the ladder. Yes, I will come this way, leaving the doors and casements barred and bolted against my father's return. See, I put out the torch, and—and I am glad it is night, Lorenzo, so that you cannot see your little page—for indeed I am ashamed of my exchange. Would not Cupid himself blush to see me transformed to a boy?"

A soft laugh answered her, and soon strong arms were about her, passionate lips pressed hers, and Jessica forgot all doubts, diffidence and fears in her lover's embrace.

Half laughing, half crying in her ecstasy, she allowed him to place her on the cushioned seat, whilst with rapid strokes Lorenzo shot the little craft out into the middle of the canal.

Till they had left Venice behind them, till indeed this Jewish maid was his lawful wife, their peril would be great, since Shylock was not the man to be robbed without seeking restitution with clamoring insistence.

And there were the jewels which Jessica had spoken of. She spoke of them again, a little breathlessly, though triumphing in her bold deed.

"I have ducats here," she told Lorenzo, with the glee of a naughty child who has escaped from some hard bondage, taking toll from his captor at the same time; "but the jewels are the most valuable. There are many jewels—some were my mother's. They are mine, my right, Lorenzo; and for the rest, I take them as dowry. You are pleased, dear Lorenzo?"

He laughed exultantly.

"Why!" he cried, "we shall be rich, carissima, instead of poor. Is not that well? Indeed, I thought of nothing but the wealth of our love; but you have been more thrifty of soul. So, with this dowry, sweet, we'll go to Genoa, thence to Verona, perhaps to Rome. Gay will we be and joyous, since love gilds all—the love which leaps and dances in our veins. My bride, my Jessica, am not I wholly yours—as you are mine? But I vow these jewels shall add to our merry-making. San Marco! What will your father say when he knows the truth? But we'll not think of him. Are you his daughter? Nay, you are my wife. That bond's enough for both. You shall tell me so presently, Jessica—but now, see where those figures stand waiting for us? Do not start, sweet, for these are friends."

She clung to him in such a maze of fears and joy that she scarcely heard his whispers.

"Friends!" she echoed. "I thought one was Aaron. Oh! My heart suffocates me with dread. If it should be Aaron Tubal! And if not, if they be indeed your friends, Lorenzo—oh! I shall die of shame to be seen by them, in this immodest dress—and only cloak enough to hide my blushes in."

"Nay, if you will, we'll play an innocent deception which shall deceive no one and nothing but your fears," replied Lorenzo. "Ha, my friends, I crave your patience for my long delay, but this dear page of mine was long in finding what he needed most; was it not your courage, boy? But now we'll not delay, since night draws away, and if Shylock does not attend good Bassanio's masque, he'll be thinking of home and his bed."

Salarino laughed. A pendant lamp, swinging from a hook in a doorway, had shown him the page's face—he was certainly a pretty boy and worth waiting for; but young Salanio looked away, noting in kindly sympathy how Lorenzo's companion shrank to his side in shy confusion, so that Lorenzo was quick to place a circling arm about his slim waist. The Jew would decidedly be a poorer man on his return home that night—and Salanio had it in his heart to envy the thief who was carrying off so fair a prize.

Lorenzo chattered gayly as the four made their way by tortuous paths towards the spot where, close to the arched basements of the ducal palace of the Dolfini, a gondola with attendant gondoliers was waiting for them.

The wind had dropped, overhead the stars shone, though the moon had not yet risen.

The sound of the water, softly lapping the basements of the great palace, which rose white and gleaming through the darkness, was all that broke a long minute's hush, as the four figures emerged from a side street and stood beckoning the drowsy gondolier.

But Lorenzo's arm girt Jessica very closely. He knew she needed its protection sorely now, as she watched the approaching gondola gliding forward like a silent figure of Fate.

She was so young, had lived, like all the women of her race, so secluded a life, that no wonder she trembled as she turned her back on the only existence she had ever known, and went forth to a new one with the man she loved.

And Lorenzo Fortunato, bending low to look into the lovely flower-like face, half hidden against his arm, felt a new sense of responsibility, of protective manhood and loyal devotion born within him. The old, volatile Lorenzo, the jesting, merry-making, idling Lorenzo, of the Piazza San Marco and every wine shop in Venice, must die to-night since this fair child who was scarcely woman yet had given herself to his care.

"Jessica mia," he murmured passionately. "Ah, carissima—how I love you!"

She smiled back at him, a tremulous smile of confidence.

"I love you too, Lorenzo," she answered, too low for either of their companions to hear. "I trust you."

The gondola was at their feet. The murmur of waters was in their ears. Behold a starlit way to Genoa—and happiness.

"I love you," Lorenzo had said, and gentle Jessica had made the same answer.

Was not that sweet assurance enough to launch forth with to the new life?

On the quay near stood those who had played the patient watchers in the night's romance; each was smiling to himself as he watched the dark shadow of the gondola vanish into the deeper gloom of the night.

"She is very beautiful," said Salarino softly. "I think our friend Lorenzo has found a treasure in the Hebrew's house."

"It remains," quoth Salanio in reply, "to see how ancient Shylock takes the theft of it. For myself, I believe he would have grieved more if Lorenzo had stolen one of his money bags."

The speaker did not know how Jessica had brought her husband a dowry as well as her own fair self.

CHAPTER XVI

ROBBED!

"**J**ESSICA! Ho there! Jessica!"
Shylock's voice grew rasping in his indignation.
It was one thing to bid his daughter bar door
and casements against possible burglars or too hilarious
masquers, but quite another when that daughter, no
doubt grown sleepy over her vigil, remained deaf to her
father's summons.

Again Shylock, belaboring the stout door, screamed
loudly for admittance.

No answer was vouchsafed, though presently a white
ray of moonlight, falling softly athwart the dark face
of the house, showed its infuriated owner an open casement leading out onto the balcony, whilst surely there
was something ominous in the sight of an extinguished
torch laid at an angle across the parapet.

"Jessica!" he yelled, kicking and smiting the un-
yielding door in his rage. "May Abraham's curse fall
upon the girl if she has played me false! Jessica, I
say!"

Lower down the street, on the opposite side, a casement was being opened by fumbling fingers, and a man's
head wrapped in a nightcap was thrust forth. Seeing
who it was whose noisy home-coming had disturbed his
slumbers, this man fell to cursing the whole twelve
tribes of Israel in no measured tones. Not that Shylock
heeded him. He was used to curses, and took revenge

(143)

on them by extorting the last coin in payment of debts, heedless of prayers or entreaties.

"Jessica!" he yelled. "Ho! Jessica!"

His fears were growing; it was impossible that his daughter could be sleeping through this din, since the casement of her bedroom was open.

"Why!" screamed he of the nightcap, wagging a mocking head from the upper window. "You may squeal till crack of doom for that black-eyed slut, since with my own eyes I saw her not two hours since descend from that balcony into the arms of Lorenzo Fortunato."

And with that he slammed to the casement, retiring back to his bed, secretly chuckling as he thought of the stark horror on the face of the old man who had become dumb with paralyzing fear and fury.

Jessica gone! Jessica fled with a Gentile! Shylock reeled, almost falling back into the canal in his terror.

Did he not only too well remember that he had entrusted his daughter with his keys?

But the man in the nightcap was able to sleep again undisturbed by cries upon an unresponsive daughter. What use to call for Jessica, since Jessica had gone? With trembling limbs and fast-beating heart the old Jew crossed the bridge, going hastily on his way in search of that assistance which he knew unloving neighbors would refuse him.

It was at Aaron Tubal's door that he first knocked, calling so loudly that Aaron came stumbling down in frowsy night attire to demand whether his ancient friend had been robbed of a fortune.

When he heard that it was merely a daughter, the younger Jew's swart face grew black. He had wished for Jessica, had bargained indeed with her father for a speedy marriage.   Himself a wealthy man, he had a covetous eye for Shylock's hoarded gold, whilst, over and above this first consideration, he admired Jessica's beauty.   Yes, he desired her for his wife, he intended to have her.   Already he had made all necessary arrangements for the reception of his bride, and Shylock's midnight news came upon him as an unpleasant shock.

Yet he did not altogether believe it.   Jessica was but a child, brought up in the seclusion of her father's house.   She would never have dared venture on so bold a step, or, if she had, she could speedily be brought back.   The probability of a Venetian of Lorenzo's standing marrying the daughter of a Jewish usurer did not enter his calculations.

Hastily putting on his gabardine over his night attire and thrusting down his yellow bonnet over the dirty nightcap which adorned his head, he came shuffling after the impatient Shylock, together with a blinking servant who brought tools for breaking the lock of the door.   Shylock gave no explanation of the night's events, he could speak no word, think of nothing till he had entered his house and satisfied himself that his gold and jewels were safe.

Tubal muttered in his beard as he followed the elder man's hurrying footsteps.   He was angry at being disturbed, still angrier at its cause.   He would take payment for this from pretty Jessica later on when she had the honor to be his obedient wife.   Meantime they reached Shylock's house, and the work of forcing an entry was commenced.

Several casements were opened by now, and watchers more curious than sleepy peered out, beginning to jest and mock as they saw what was happening.   The man who had witnessed the elopement had roused again, and soon raised a laugh by his tale.

Shylock and Tubal, inwardly raging at the coarse jesting and levity which this trouble had aroused, urged on the servant to hasten in forcing the lock. Alas! there were the bolts to be reckoned with, and Shylock fell to tearing his beard in a frenzy of impatience, as he danced up and down on his steps, screaming and reviling at the slowness of the fellow who sweated at his toil and grumbled that it was so ill-requited.

As for Tubal, he stood with folded arms, patiently awaiting the chance of entry.

More casements were opened, laughter and chattering voices drifted the length of the canal.

What! A rare jest this! Jessica, the black-eyed Jewess, had eloped with Lorenzo Fortunato—and probably taken her father's money bags with her.

Shylock foamed at the mouth as he heard his own deep fears voiced in ribald lightness.

The great door, unhinged at last, fell back and Shylock, with Tubal at his heels, vanished into the darkness beyond.

This was disappointing to the spectators, some of whom shut their casements and returned to bed, whilst others lolled lazily out, chatting, surmising, speculating, as they saw lights gleaming from the corner house which a few moments before had been in darkness.

The moon had risen now, though the rays only partially penetrated that narrow alley. Here and there a ladder of light was flung across the canal, but the rest was still in shadow.

Then suddenly a piercing shriek rang out from the Jew's house, a shriek so agonized, so intensely suffering, that men and women crossed themselves, whilst the latter whispered in awed accents, "Is it possible she is dead? The young Jewess with the black eyes?" And more than one mother remembered little kindnesses shown by Jessica to their children. But the man in the nightcap laughed raucously.

"More like she has stolen his money—the baggage!" he said. "Not that I blame her, since the old villain owes her more than she could take for the wrong of fathering her."

And, as it happened, Nicolosi was right in his prophecy, since, at the moment he uttered it, an old man lay, half swooning, before his ransacked drawers. His worst fears had been realized. Jessica had robbed him—not only of his gold, but the jewels which he hoarded with such jealous care in this inner cupboard.

Shylock had scarcely been able to climb the stairs in his terror of anxiety, had barely tottered across the room, to strike tinder and flint and light the candle which instantly showed him what he had vowed he could not see.

Alas! What use to say it was impossible? What use to argue that this was a nightmare from which he would awake, sweating but relieved to find it but a dream? This was no dream, but sober, ugly truth, shown him in two empty drawers, which had been left overturned on the floor.

His ducats had gone! Worse still, his jewels had gone! There was the bitterness of death in that wailing cry which reached Tubal's ears as he followed the elder man into the room where Shylock now lay prone upon the ground.

So it was true! Lorenzo had the girl—and the jewels.

Tubal's face grew blacker than before, as he stood cursing
—not only the man—but the girl whom he had hoped
to make his wife.

She had gone! Fled this very night. Gone!

Tubal seized the prostrate Shylock by his shoulder,
dragging him up. His little eyes gleamed evilly and his
thick lips seemed swollen by his rage.

"Come," he cried huskily, "we must find Jessica—
overtake her and this Christian lover. Get back the
girl—and the jewels."

The words infused new life into the despairing
Shylock.

Old and withered as he was, his shrunken form seemed
to dilate with new vigor, his claw-like fingers clutched
and grasped at the empty air.

"You are right," he articulated with difficulty,
"quite right, Aaron. We will find her, we will bring
the jewels back."

"And the girl," suggested Tubal, gnawing at his nails.
"We will bring back the girl."

"And the jewels," repeated Shylock, wringing his
hands, whilst his voice rose in a wailing crescendo.
"The jewels and my daughter. My ducats too! Fled
with a Christian. My curse on her if we do not find
them. Come, Tubal, we'll rouse the Duke. Without
an instant's delay we'll rouse the Duke. There's plotting
in this—the devil's plotting. Oh, woe is me! My
ducats. In two sealed bags, Aaron. The ducats I've
toiled for, contrived for, planned for. My ducats, my
jewels—and my daughter! But the Duke shall help
me find them."

He smote his head, beat his clenched fists against
his breast, and then, closely followed by Tubal, hastened

out and away across the bridge in the direction of the
ducal palace, watched by gibing neighbors, who mocked
at his distress, crying out that he would have to run
faster if he wanted to overtake his daughter's tripping
footsteps.

But Shylock paid no heed, being deaf to all but his
own piteous cries.

"My daughter! Oh, my ducats! Fled with a Christian! Oh, my Christian ducats! Justice! The law!
My ducats, my jewels, my daughter! Find the girl—
she has the jewels on her!"

So, up the narrow streets and by the winding water-
ways he and his companion came at length to the Ducal
Palace, where the Duke of Venice, Niccolo da Ponte,
was about to retire to rest after the entertaining of
various distinguished guests from Italy and Spain, who
at the time were on a state visit to the city.

This Niccolo da Ponte, during his seven years of office
as Doge or Duke of the Venetian Republic, had proved
himself a just and broad-minded man, whose chief interest was centered in the welfare of his people. Under
his beneficent rule the proud motto of the republic,
"Bread in the market place—Justice in the palace,"
was more than ever established.

Venice indeed was at the height of that golden age
of prosperity which drew upon her the eyes and envy of
all Europe.

Magnificent entertainments, splendid palaces, luxury
and revelings of all kinds, showed her visitors a glimpse
of that wealth which her nobles and citizens so lavishly
expended.

The Ducal Palace was but one amongst her gorgeous
buildings. Enclosed on three sides by Gothic arcades,

the fourth abutted directly upon the southern face of St.. Mark's Church with charming effect. The beautiful bronze well-heads or "pozzi" lent a singularly attractive appearance to the open courtyard, from which the palace itself was entered by the Scala dei Giganti, one of the most beautiful external staircases in the world, decorated with exquisite bas-reliefs in marble, and crowned by Sansovini's "Mars and Neptune," between which colossal statues the coronation of the Doges took place.

One of the strangest features of this magnificent building was the famous letter box known as the "Lion's Mouth," which opened from without, so that any statements, petitions, denunciations and appeals, might be thrown into it, the contents of the great box daily read *in camera* by the assembled Inquisitors of the Republic.

But Shylock the Jew would not be contented by presenting his petition for justice in so roundabout a manner. His need was urgent, and he urged it so hotly that even the soldiers of the Duke's guard were impressed by his frantic manner, though perhaps it was Aaron Tubal's quiet distribution of ducats which succeeded in winging the feet of a willing messenger to the Duke. Weary as he was, Niccolo da Ponte was not the man to hear the appeal for justice in vain.

Lesser nobles might and did mock at the demand of a Jew usurer, and speak lightly of his daughter's honor. But the Duke silenced them with grave rebuke.

No doubt his daughter was as dear to the Jew as she would have been to a Christian parent. Yet, when da Ponte had listened to old Shylock's hysterical denunciation, he was perhaps less convinced as to this.

True, Shylock—and Tubal too—urged the necessity for the immediate restoration of the missing Jessica;

but so interspersed was the father's demand with allusions to his lost jewels and ducats that many of the Duke's servants were openly laughing before the appeal was concluded.

To judge by Shylock's grief, it would seem he ranked his losses thus—jewels—ducats—and, more remotely—, his daughter. Yet, since the finding of the last was necessary in the recovery of the two former, the old Jew clamored volubly that this Lorenzo Fortunato, a thieving vagabond, a greedy villain and designing knave, should be searched for, arrested and kept in durance till all Shylock's belongings were restored.

Many of the nobles urged on the Duke that this matter must wait till morning, roughly bidding Shylock return and present his petition in due form next day, railing at him for his importunity. But da Ponte silenced his friends gravely.

"We must do what we can," quoth he, "lest the wrong this Fortunato hath done become irremediable by our delay. Peace, Shylock," he added, turning to the still whimpering Jew, "and if your daughter—your ducats—and your jewels still be in Venice you shall have speedy restoration of your own."

Shylock bowed, cringing and servile, in his thanks, yet his blear eyes were wicked in their hate as he followed the train of the Duke toward the quays, and he cursed again and again not only Lorenzo but his daughter.

CHAPTER XVII

A VAIN SEARCH

"MY Lord Bassanio's ship?" quoth the Duke, as he stood on the quays, his nobles gathered in a semicircle near him, whilst Shylock and Tubal, a grim pair of night-birds seen in that white moonlight, stood apart, side by side, muttering together.

"Bassanio Ramberti, if it please Your Grace," quoth Gratiano Marmottina, who, wandering along the deserted Piazza, out-at-elbows with a world which placed convent walls between him and his Nerissa, had come upon that strangely animated group about the quays. "Ramberti is my friend. We should have sailed to-night for Belmont had I not been advertised before of a bootless quest. So, though the ship was chartered, we have not gone, which explains her presence here."

Shylock spat on the ground, repeating a name with venom.

"Bassanio Ramberti! Bassanio Ramberti!" he muttered, and remembered how Toni Panocchi, having left his service for that of the young Venetian noble, had come to summon him to supper at Bassanio's house.

Yes, and more than that! For had not Toni, whether drunk or sober, fool, knave or honest patch, hinted at some plot to rob the Jew? *To rob the Jew!*

Why, here stood the plot revealed. Bassanio, Antonio and Lorenzo, all friends in love to each other. All enemies of hate towards him. How nimbly came the conclusion. Lorenzo loved Jessica, coveted her father's wealth, planned to steal both, was aided and abetted by reckless Bassanio, prompted perhaps by the grave young merchant, who, more than all, had shown dislike and contempt of Shylock.

So Bassanio summoned the Jew to supper, not for love nor for the purpose of increasing his debts with him, but so that in this way Shylock's house should be left unguarded, open for a thief to entér and steal its treasure.

This was the secret Toni Panocchi would have revealed at a price, but for his late master's violent reception of his hints and Jessica's crafty interposition.

Thus the Jew had been tricked, deceived, robbed. He, the wise Jew, who had spent his life in tricking, robbing and deceiving others.

No wonder the old man, raising his arms aloft, called upon Heaven to give him his vengeance.

The Duke, appalled, watched the rigid figure in its rough gabardine, the yellow badge of shame upon its breast, the yellow turban fallen back from scanty locks, showing the bald peak of the head, the sagging flesh of the neck, only partly hidden by the patriarchal beard upon which great clots of foam lay in token of the old man's frenzied state.

"Curse them!" moaned Shylock. "The curse of Israel upon these Gentile dogs! My ducats lost! My jewels—lost! My daughter—lost!"

"Nay," replied the Duke severely, "ducats and jewels can be replaced, Jew. For them you should not lament in the same fashion as for your daughter. It is for her we will give command this town should be searched, unless indeed we hear these naughty lovers have escaped beyond our reach."

It was at this moment, and before either Shylock or Tubal could reply, that a young man in the rich dress of a merchant stepped forward, bowing to the Duke.

"My name, Your Grace, is Angelo Salarino," said he with deep respect, "a merchant of Venice. As I and my friend Salanio returned earlier this evening from a comrade's house we saw Lorenzo Fortunato, who is well known to us both, hurrying towards the quays."

"You saw him!" screamed Shylock. "You saw the villain? By Aaron's rod! Had I but been there! And the girl? You saw Jessica? You saw my daughter? Woe is me!—belike with the jewels on her, the ducats snugly hidden in the folds of her gown."

"Nay," retorted Salarino amiably. "Lorenzo s companion wore no gown, but instead the hose and doublet of a boy. A very comely youth, as I remarked to Salanio. Black-eyed, black-haired, ruddy of complexion, with nose slightly aquiline and pouting, ruby lips. A comely youth, who in other guise would have made a comelier maid."

"It was she!" shrieked the old Jew, wildly gesticulating. "It was Jessica—my daughter Jessica, wantoning in page's garb. But where did they go? What did they do? You shall tell me, fair sir, at once. Where are my jewels? My——"

"Of your jewels I know nothing," replied Salarino coldly, "but I would tell the Duke"—he bowed to the perplexed ruler—"that Lorenzo and his companion departed in a gondola—I think for Genoa, from stray words I caught as they hurried past."

The Duke drew a sigh of some relief.

He had done all that justice required, and might now return to the Palace and his rest with a satisfied con-

science. Nor did Shylock's frenzied despair awake pity
in him any more than in his train. There was something
entirely sordid in the Jew's reiterated laments after his
money and jewels, beside which the claims of natural
affection appeared to sink into insignificance.

So, after a few courteous words of thanks to Angelo
Salarino for his information, which had saved the necessity for a useless search, the Duke returned to the Palace,
coldly telling Shylock that should Lorenzo return to
Venice justice should be done.

An empty promise, which neither Shylock nor Tubal
heeded. Here was the end of their hopes; at any rate
for immediate restitution, and Tubal's swart features
convulsed in anger as he thought of the wife he had
lost and the golden dowry which should have been hers.
They would have followed Salarino to question him more
closely as to the hour he had seen the lovers embark,
but the young man had been quick to slip away after
giving his information, and not a sign of him could they
see.

But Shylock, plucking at his companion's loose sleeve,
thrust his wrinkled face close to Tubal's gloomy one.

"There is revenge," he muttered, "and there are those
in Venice who helped Lorenzo in this plot. Come, Tubal,
we'll learn the truth of this, and discover the best way
to rack the meddlers in it; for which purpose I'll go to
Bassanio Ramberti's—and in your company. What do
you say, Aaron? Shall we forever cringe beneath the
lash and go begging for justice? I vow by all the prophets
that there are some in Venice still who shall smart for
bringing shame upon my house."

Tubal bowed his head gravely.

"I will go with you," said he, "and afterwards take
ship for Genoa in search of Jessica."

The speaker's jaw set in rigid determination. He too longed for revenge—and he hated the man who had robbed him of a bride.

Bassanio Ramberti did not prove so easily accessible as the Duke of Venice. Perhaps he may have guessed well enough what business these importunate Hebrews had with him, for though he was not yet abed and very wakeful, he refused Shylock's petition, and the latter's resentment had time to grow to almost overmastering passion during the long hours before dawn deepened into day. Tubal was not talkative either as he sat in an upper room of Shylock's house beside his host, listening to the constantly reiterated tale of the old man's losses, his despair at his daughter's treachery, and his resolve to wreak vengeance not only upon her abductor but upon those whom he suspected of participating in the plot.

"Bassanio Ramberti shall pay," Shylock snarled. "By the prophets! he shall pay! I'll strip him, beggar him, torture him. Aye, for I can torture him—through his friend."

"You mean Antonio Cainello, the merchant?"

Shylock writhed as though in physical pain.

"The curse of Israel upon him!" he mouthed. "How I hate him! The cringing Christian, who lends without asking for repayment and lashes me with his tongue everytime I appear on the Rialto. How I hear him laugh! 'What? The Jew robbed? An excellent jest to tickle ears withal! His daughter stolen? Why, the house of the Jew is honored.' But wait, Tubal, wait. If my prayers are heard I'll have revenge. How prosper those Christian argosies? I heard welcome news of one. Shipwrecked on the Goodwins, I am told. That's a fair beginning. May every contrary wind so blow on his enterprises! But let Antonio look to himself. Should he break his bond! We jested, Tubal—a merry jest. No interest would I take for my moneys—only—in jest, mark you—a pound of his fair flesh, to be cut off where I would. A pound of flesh. Of what value is that to any? I tell you none save as rich guerdon to revenge."

Aaron Tubal rose. "The Duke would not permit the taking of such a bond," he replied. "But come, the sun rises high; let us steal away before these swine around awake from their sleep and look forth to taunt and gibe at us. If you would seek Bassanio—well! Seek him now, for I would fain be on my way to Genoa."

"To Genoa," muttered Shylock. "Yes, good Aaron, follow to Genoa, threaten, rage, denounce that villain—and if you bring not Jessica again, do not fail to claim the ducats and jewels—two sealed bags of double ducats, Aaron. Oh! The vile wretches!"

He was mouthing and cursing all the way to Bassanio's house, parting with his friend near the Via Suvano, since Tubal was too impatient to delay longer in his pursuit of the fugitives. Of his purpose when he had overtaken them the younger Jew said little—but there was a lurking passion in his dark eyes which boded no good for the gay young bridegroom Lorenzo when they two should meet.

Bassanio Ramberti lay at ease upon a silken couch when Shylock was brought into his presence; a small table with chocolate served in priceless cups was set between himself and his companion, Antonio Cainello. Bassanio was pale and heavy-eyed. Anxieties indeed oppressed the young noble, treading fast upon the heels of disappointment. In his impulsive enthusiasm he had pictured himself the husband of Portia di Nerlini, the happiest of men in the fulfilment of his love—and also the freest from care, since her great wealth would free him forever from the sordid and unaccustomed chains of poverty.

Gratiano's unwelcome news of the lady's retreat to a convent came as a crushing blow, and already he had heard the news confirmed by a friend of Niccolo Grimani's, who averred that the latter had returned to Venice in a fury at being balked of his hopes.

Had he dreamed of such an untoward happening as fair Portia's evasion of importunate suitors, Bassanio would certainly not have lavished his money on last night's feast; and he was explaining to Antonio his intention to live frugally in closest retirement for the present, and thus save money enough for his venture to Belmont at a later date, when Shylock was announced. The old man might have been a pitiable object with his disordered gabardine, torn bonnet and disheveled locks, had his features not been twisted in so fixed a hate as he looked from one to other of the young men, who, lounging in luxurious ease, regarded him with the calm contempt of those who gaze at some lower creation.

"Well, Jew," quoth Bassanio—for Shylock's words failed him—"what do you seek?   Ducats, jewels— or a daughter?   I vow by the bones of St. Mark you'll find none of the three in the Palazzo Ramberti."

And he yawned, fingering his long gold chain with one hand, whilst with the other he raised his cup of chocolate to his lips.

Shylock stretched out claw-like fingers gropingly, with the gesture of a blind man.

"It was the man Toni who brought your letter," he gasped.   "He was my servant, illustrious sir, before he was yours. Let me speak with him that I may know whether that wanton, my daughter, had any previous dealing with Lorenzo?"

"Nay, by the saints!" protested Bassanio, "you shall not call a fair lady ill names, old man. For myself, I look upon it as a state of grace that she should wish to become Christian and marry an honest lover."

Shylock's face convulsed, but he had come with a purpose, so forbore to lash out in cursing and reviling.

"As for Toni," went on Bassanio, "he shall come hither at your pleasure," and he clapped his hands, summoning his servant and dismissing him in search of the whilom messenger. Pending the latter's arrival, Bassanio and Antonio sipped their chocolate, talking together idly, apparently heedless of the shrunken figure in its tumbled garments which stood in sinister outline against a curtain of crimson velvet.

But Shylock, watching his enemies from beneath furtive brows, felt his lust for vengeance burn like a devouring flame in his heart. Bassanio Ramberti he contemned—it was Antonio the merchant whom he hated with all the ungovernable passion of his nature; such a hatred which, in such a man, would dog a foe untiringly through a lifetime in the hope of striking him down at last. And whilst he fumed and raged, waiting there in the splendid apartment of a bankrupt, its owner was jesting merrily over the impotence of the magistrates to curtail the reckless extravagance of the women of Venice in their dress—a matter which had been perplexing the Senate for the last eighty years, having now reached a culminating point, since, in defiance of the law, fine ladies would prank themselves in silks and broideries, silver and gold tissues, velvets wrought with finest needlework, so that a considerable fortune might be lavished on one gown.

The door opened and Toni, shifty-eyed as ever, entered. He bowed humbly to his new master, ignored the old and demanded to know what the illustrious Signior wished with him.

"Why, nothing but your service, good Toni," laughed Bassanio. "However, Master Jew Shylock here would learn whether pretty Jessica his daughter had long acquaintance with the Signior Lorenzo."

Toni's black eyes twinkled as he turned to the old man with an air of patronage and defiance.

"Why, for that matter," quoth he, "my mistress would listen to a serenade with as much pleasure as any maid in Venice; and, since a man must live on something better than the refuse of a Jew's larder, I was ready to take the lady's letters to her lover at the price of a ducat."

Shylock gnashed his teeth.

The impudence of this man, who had been his obedient servant for years, galled him to a fury.

"You took letters, villain," he squealed, "to this Christian, and the woman paid you with my ducats? Oh! What wickedness is this! What punishment you deserve for such sin, ingratitude, vileness!"

"Why, as for ingratitude," grinned Toni, "I think Jessica will thank me for the virtuous aid I gave in helping her to a Christian husband. You'll live to be converted yet, worship, and will reward poor Toni as he deserves."

He bowed as he spoke, slipping away before Shylock in his rage could hurl himself upon him, as the old man seemed likely to do, so great was his frenzy.

"Thus, Shylock," quoth Bassanio, in more concil-
iatory tones, "you see that your daughter has but
followed the way of her heart and that Lorenzo only
stole what was his already. Therefore cease to bemoan,
but thank Heaven for your child's happiness."

Had the speaker held torch to tow the blaze could
not have been more instant.

Shylock's anger was white-hot now. His enemies
were these two who sat calm and unmoved before him,
though it was Antonio Cainello, who idly played with
his gilt pomander, against whom his more bitter hatred
was kindled.

The lofty disdain of the young merchant's dark
eyes, his air of proud superiority galled the old Jew to
madness.

"So, Bassánio Ramberti," he mouthed, speaking to
Bassanio, with his eyes on Antonio, "I discover the
truth of this plot. You knew of Lorenzo's passion
for my daughter—his greedy lust for my wealth. Therefore you bade me to the feast furnished by my ducats,
for the purpose of making Lorenzo's theft possible,
whilst you welcomed me as your guest. You knew my
house was being entered and despoiled of its treasure.
And this is reward for my kindness! *This* my reward
for granting Antonio here moneys without interest so
that you might both plot for my ruin! O Christian
virtue! O generous youth! Will the Jew take vengeance, think you? Or will he lie in the dust, groveling
for you to spurn him again? Another kick, illustrious
one—do not spare your spitting. A Jew! Well, well.
I know the tale now—I shall read it again presently.
Think of that, Antonio. I shall not forget this pretty
tale, which I do not doubt *your* brain conceived. O

11

my masters! Justice—and the Jew—justice—and the Jew. I think this time he'll be served if there be justice in heaven."

Antonio Cainello looked thoughtfully after the old man's retreating figure, a moment grave, the next smiling. Why or wherefore should he fear the idle railings of a crazed miser? Long before his own debt to Shylock the Jew had to be paid his argosies would be returning safe to port. It was true the cruel Goodwins had sucked much profit into their voracious depths— but his returns were many—his wealth assured.

Lightly he tapped Bassanio's shoulder.

"The sun shines," said he; "let us go to the Piazza, —and forget the vile Jew, whose greed is well repaid. For myself I am glad pretty Jessica is freed from such a father."

And Bassanio, rousing from a melancholy which present disappointment rendered an easy humor, took his friend's arm and sallied out into the sunshine.

CHAPTER XVIII

L ONG weeks, dragging out halting length, passed
slowly by.

Portia di Nerlini still kept her convent cell,
and Nerissa, often yawning over her beads, kept her
company, whilst many would-be suitors made fruitless
pilgrimage to the palazzo amongst the pine woods.

To Bassanio Ramberti, sick with hope deferred, it
seemed that he was destined never to see his fair lady
again, and in these days he did not cease to reproach
himself for the delay of those summer months, when a
hundred gayeties and diversions weaned his thoughts
from the vision of sweet Portia's charms.

He was in truth out-at-elbows with the world as he
lounged along the Piazza San Marco, where a flock of
pigeons circled iris-hued about the gilded dome, and
sunlight fell in golden splendor upon the marble pave-
-ment.

A fair lady clattered by on her high clogs, or *chop-
pines* as they were called, having need to take the arm
of an attendant cavalier to assist her, whilst two cavalieri
walked close behind, one carrying her fan, another her
cloak, though from time to time one or other would
approach the veiled beauty to address some jest in a
whisper to her.

Soft peals of laughter, the ripple of a lute's strings,
the splashing of water as the gilded gondolas glided by,

(163)

the shrill cries of the fruit and flower vendors, all merged into one great harmony, rising and falling on the sunlit air, though there was a chill in the atmosphere now which made it necessary to draw cloaks closely, and be glad that the laws of a grave college permitted the doublets of the *nobili* to be lined with squirrel fur in winter.

The wife of a wealthy citizen, her face covered by a black veil, stood bargaining for fruit with a shrewd Neapolitan seller—her voice rose in crescendo notes as Bassanio passed her by, and the jarring sound made the young man quicken his steps till he paused close to the opening of the Merceria, from which two or three narrower streets and canals branched off from the main way leading to the Rialto.

As he halted, debating whether he should go in search of his friend Antonio, who no doubt would be on the Rialto inquiring if there were any news of his merchandise, two men stepped forth from a doorway close by, even brushing past him as they walked up the narrower street, which led to the lower quarters of the town.

They wore, one a doublet of green, the other of crimson, with parti-colored hose and short velvet cloaks. Evidently they were not of the *nobili*—yet Bassanio fancied the face of the shorter and stouter man was familiar to him.

Ah, yes!—he recalled seeing it now at the palazzo of Niccolo Grimani. The fellow had diced with him on more than one occasion—though Bassanio did not claim either acquaintance or friendship with the man whom he had instinctively disliked. But he remembered his name—one Angelo Sutari, whose reputation was far less angelic than his name.

As they passed, evidently not paying heed to him, Bassanio's attention was pricked by sound of a name— *Portia di Nerlini.*

The very mention of that lady was enough to thrill his heart and quicken his ears.

What had such men to do with the Lady Portia? Always impulsive, Bassanio determined to answer that question for himself, and instantly set about following the men at a discreet distance down the street. They were evidently in high good spirits, laughing and chatting, snapping their fingers, whilst every now and again Angelo would troll forth a snatch of some love ditty.

It struck Bassanio that they had been drinking quite sufficient to rob them of complete discretion, so, since at this distance it was impossible to hear the drift of their conversation, he approached nearer.

"Come, amico," cried the merry Angelo, taking his comrade by the arm and thus, in his lurching, saving himself from slipping into the canal, "we must discuss this matter privately; for if so much as a whisper of it came abroad we should incur the vengeance of our gloomy Niccolo, who has been thinking of nothing since his return from Belmont, but the winning of the lady and her fortune."

A small wine shop stood near, a woman in the doorway, bold-eyed, handsome, with fat arms akimbo. Monna Elena was reckoned a great beauty in Venice, where the fashion prevailed of admiration for big, plump women, and her good looks had brought fame to the "Creeping Vine," where evidently Angelo Sutari was no stranger.

Bassanio, however, was not favored with so ready a welcome, and the young noble found diplomacy run rather against the grain since it embraced the necessity for-stealing a kiss from the heavily-coy Monna Elena, and vowing that he was so completely dazzled by her charms that he needed a flask of her best wine instantly.

Here was likely to be a good customer as well as a handsome one. Though Messer Angelo was free with his kisses, his ducats were few, certainly not extending to the purchase of the best wine! So Monna Elena beamed good-humoredly upon the noble cavalier who so much admired her, and invited him to climb the stair to the open roof, where creeping vines and gay flowers provided the inn with the right to its name and customers with a pleasant resting place after a busy day's work.

Bassanio was not slow in complying with this invitation, and seated himself before a tiny table in a corner, before glancing round in discovery of the men whose conversation had begun to interest him so very greatly.

From behind a screen of vine leaves he spied a pair of legs clad in parti-colored hose protruding, whilst before the bower stood a slim edition of Monna Elena—a black-eyed, saucy little maid who, having brought the illustrious Signiors their wine, stayed to jest with them, till a movement on the part of one of them which threatened the stealing of a kiss, sent her away laughing, since was she not betrothed to handsome Nane the fisherman, for whom alone the sweetness of her lips was reserved? Evidently the gay cavalier did not know that there was anyone else on the roof—for Sutari, leaning forward with hasty scanning, had failed to perceive the figure in black doublet and hose seated well back in the corner, behind flowering shrubs set in large pots.

"Now this is much better," Bassanio heard Sutari say. "We can here talk as freely as we choose, my little Giacope, without fear of eavesdroppers—or the anger of Niccolo. Ohimé, what a man that is! He is in love, Giacope mio—in love with a lady's fortune—and I am told it is a very pretty one."

"Basta!" retorted the other. "But if you are talking of di Nerlini's daughter, I thought it was ordained by her old fool of a father that only he who chose a certain casket should win her. And our Grimani was not successful there."

"No," laughed Sutari, helping himself to wine with much clinking of glass, which betrayed an unsteady hand, "he failed there. But what matter? Grimani is in love, Giacope—and what lover ever stopped short at a first failure?"

His companion swore profanely. "All the same," he replied, "this failure is final, if gossip says truly; for those who essay the choice of casket have to vow to leave their suit forever if they choose amiss."

"Would it be the first vow which a lover has broken?" questioned Sutari, with the melodramatic fervor of a man who has been drinking freely. "I wager you when the lady is Niccolo's bride she will only read loss of faith as ecstasy of love."

"But will she consent to be his bride?" argued the sceptical Giacope. "I heard on good authority that the Lady Portia had retired to a convent to escape from such importunate lovers as our friend Niccolo."

"Per Bacco!" chuckled Sutari, again helping himself to wine. "That is just the kernel of the nut we are to help crack. Here is a lover in despair at his mistress' coldness. She is very cold—Giacope—but the fortune

is a splendid one.   As for our despairing lover, he is
driven to madness—and also to debt, as we very well
know.   There is only one who can cure his madness and
satisfy his creditors—the Lady Portia.   You will admit,
Giacope, that the need is desperate."

"Will the lady so regard it?"

"Diavolo!   That is Niccolo's business.   He hath a
persuasive tongue with the women, amico—and he will
need all the persuasion of his wit if he is to have a
peaceful life."

"Come, you speak in riddles," growled Giacope
irritably.   "Cease your bibbing, Angelo, and tell me the
story plainly.   I understand Grimani is anxious to buy
our services in some enterprise concerning the Lady
Portia di Nerlini."

"Precisely," hiccoughed Sutari.   "I was explaining;
but be not impatient.   There are ducats coming to
line our pouches, amico, and I am ready to admit
frankly that though I would do much for friendship, I
would do more for ducats.   Now Niccolo Grimani is my
friend—he also has ducats to offer—for friendship.   We
will go with him on Friday, Giacope, even though it is a
bad day for luck.   What say you?   We'll be ready to
serve a friend at a good price, especially when everything is on the side of reward with no attendant risk."

He hummed the snatch of a song, and Bassanio
craned forward; the latter would not for the world have
lost a word of this momentous conversation, to the
hearing of which he devoutly reflected that the saints
themselves must have guided him.

Be that as it may, certainly neither of Niccolo
Grimani's hirelings suspected that a third was partic-
ipant in that pleasant tête-à-tête on the roof of the
"Climbing Vine."

"I'm with you if there are ducats in the business," quoth Sutari's comrade, with an oath. "Tell me more of this profitable adventure, my Angelo?"

Sutari yawned. Presently the wine would be making him sleepy, but he was communciative for the present and answered this time more definitely.

"On Friday," said he, "our love-sick, ducat-seeking Niccolo will be setting sail for Belmont, since a servant he has contrived to bribe into his confidence has sent to tell him that preparations are being made at the palazzo for the return of their lady on that day. It seems she has had enough of praying and fasting, so would try a change of feasting and love-testing again. By our Lady! she should be content. What a bridal that will be, Gia mio. What a wooing too! There will be the three of us, and, whilst Niccolo is persuading the lady of his passion, we shall deal with the escort. Two lusty knaves as I understand, who cannot be bribed and therefore must be content with a pricking. You and I will be there to wait on them. Afterwards we shall ride to a certain castello amongst the hills, where there will be a priest waiting to bless our Niccolo's enterprise and persuade the lady that she cannot do better for the sake of her own fair name than bestow the reward of herself and her fortune on so bold and ardent a lover. After that all will be feasting, love-making and renown for the noble Grimani and his adorable lady, who, if she love romance as every maid should do, will not like her husband any the less for his oath-breaking and masterfulness."

And again Sutari broke into song.

Bassanio set down an empty glass and felt the chill of winter smite him, for all the sunshine's warmth.

What devil's work was this?   He would never have believed it of a noble of Venice, though he knew something of Grimani's loose notions of honor, and the reckless mode of his living.   Yet he would not have credited this shame of one whose hand he himself had clasped in way of friendship, had he not heard of it with his own ears.   Yet with his horror came also a sense of triumph and elation.

This had been no chance meeting, but the opportunity sent to him by Heaven itself to frustrate the purpose of villains in wronging a noble lady.

A fire of enthusiasm flamed with indignation, so that Bassanio could have laughed aloud, knowing himself the champion going forth to battle in a cause which, perchance, bright-winged Love himself might crown.

How strange it was that he should be the one to interpose a second time in defence of Portia di Nerlini!   Yet, as his lips set in grim determination, he knew this would be something very different to the scaring of a few weak-stomached bandits, whose purpose was limited to the theft of a trinket or a purse of ducats.

To begin with, it was necessary for his purpose that the men babbling under the vines close by should not know of his presence;   and since there was risk now in every moment's delay, he rose cautiously, creeping towards the staircase with the stealthy tread of some prowling cat, halting now and again to listen to Sutari's droning gabble of what revelries he should indulge in when Grimani's golden ducats lined his pouch.

Step by step Bassanio neared his goal, breathing more freely as the space narrowed between himself and safety.   Then, with a gasp, he stopped short, seeing the way barred by Monna Elena's bulky form.

It was a moment of suspense, in which Bassanio almost lost his presence of mind, since it was evident the woman was about to address him with some demand as to his needs. Her mouth indeed was already open for her speech when Bassanio, recovering himself, laid his finger on his lips, springing at one nimble bound to her side, when he began to draw her back down the narrow staircase.

"Mother of Heaven!" panted Monna Elena, arriving more precipitately than her wont at the foot of the steps. "What jest is this, Clarissimo?"

She gave Bassanio the title coined by the proudest nobles of Venice as peculiarly their rightful and sole title.

Bassanio urged her still further into the shop.

"Hist!" he whispered, in a tragic voice. "Those men up there are my enemies, Monna."

She clucked her tongue knowingly.

"Diavolo!" she murmured. "It is true that Angelo is a rascal of a fellow, though he pays many compliments."

"The most villainous of mankind could not fail to pay his homage to such beauty as yours, Monna," vowed Bassanio, very positively. "Since he has eyes in his head he could not help telling you of your charms, which is a tale of simple truth and no compliment. But, on the other hand, this Angelo Sutari is the agent— or shall we say tool?—of a certain noble Signior, whose daughter I chanced to admire too boldly. It was but the case of a raised veil and a tribute to fair beauty such as any cavalier would have paid; but you know the way of us nobles of Venice, bella donna, and so there is a vendetta which I find exceedingly troublesome. This is why I do not wish to let those Signiors upstairs know I have been here."

Monna Elena was still smiling over the pleasant manner of the new customer's speech, which he moreover gilded with an extra ducat, entirely winning her favor.

"I understand," she declared, setting her fat arms akimbo and nodding again and again. "And neither of those who drink together up there shall know that so much as a mouse has kept them company. As for that pert Ginevra, I will promise her such a thrashing if she breathes a word of it as shall keep her mute as a dead herring. Farewell, Clarissimo—you will remember the way to the 'Creeping Vine,' and be sure no enemies shall know of your coming hither!"

Bassanio assured the full-blown beauty that it would be impossible for him ever to forget the dwelling place of so much virture and loveliness, and thereupon took his departure, in too great haste, this time, to steal the kiss which Monna Elena was waiting to bestow on him. The woman came to the door, watching his retreating figure with lowered lids over heavy, slumbrous eyes.

"He is a very handsome cavalier," she commented, "and bestows ducats like a prince. I wonder who he is?—But that I shall soon discover since he is sure to come again. Ohimé! I had better go and find that little cat Ginevra and remind her that a thrashing follows hard on a babbling tongue."

And away waddled Monna Elena, to find to her wrath that the wicked Ginevra was taking advantage of her mother's preoccupation to exchange love whispers on her own account with handsome Nane, who stood up in his boat, so that he could just comfortably encircle the waist of the girl perched on the wall near.

It was really a pity that so pretty an idyll should be spoiled—but Monna Elena was a hasty-tempered woman when her will was crossed, so pretty Ginevra got her beating after all—and Nane had decamped in such haste from fear of his future mother-in-law's anger that his poor little sweatheart had to bear all the punishment for the stolen half-hour of bliss, with no one to comfort her. It was very hard indeed—but from Ginevra's unhappiness one good consequence resulted. Neither she nor Monna Elena thought again of the handsome new customer who ordered the best wine and paid its price three times over in golden ducats and kisses.

CHAPTER XIX

"SO you and Gratiano sail for Belmont to-night?" asked Antonio. "Why, that is only right, amico, and yet my mind misgives me since you are only two and we know not how many bravos Grimani has hired to his service in the pursuance of this foul scheme."

Bassanio flushed. He did not grow less impulsive with love afire in his veins, and the tale he had told his friend was as impetuous as himself.

"Why, as to that," he retorted, "this Sutari named three as their number, since the Lady Portia deems two servants escort enough, seeing the short distance from convent to palazzo and the rigor that the banditti have been dealt with of late months."

"The lady is ill advised," replied Antonio. "Would it not be better to warn her of her danger ere she starts on so perilous a journey, my Bassanio? Should ill chance befall your plans I should grieve to dwell on her fate."

It was the counsel of common sense, not inflamed by romance or the desire to render signal service to a fair lady in her distress.

"For that matter," replied Bassanio, "we shall out-number these villains by one, so we will not reckon with mishap. Nor will I carry a tale to a lady's ears which smacks of the senseless babble of the wine shop. Unless

(174)

proven, could I swear away the honor of a noble of Venice with no other reason than what seems but the idle chatter of two sots?"

"Yet you attach such weight to this same chatter that you sail for Belmont to-night to lie in wait for rogues, who, being no rogues, will not be there?"

Bassanio gave an impatient laugh.

"Argue on, O rare philosopher," said he. "Cold argument and I can never be attune—though I love the arguer. But can a lover stand to weigh most carefully each reason and event, whilst his lady *may* be in peril of her life? A lover, poor Antonio, will not say, 'this tale, not being proven, is no certainty, so I will wait at ease lest I have to laugh at myself for a hot-headed fool'; but rather will cry, 'I cannot endure to waste a moment for fear of what this whisper breeds. My lady *may* be safe—yet will I be at hand lest the shadow of some danger cross her path.' "

Antonio slowly stroked his beard, keeping his eyes veiled.

"I'll say no more, Bassanio," he said, "for I see you love this lady very truly, since even a cold philosopher may read such passion aright though he has never felt it consume him. So you and Gratiano will sail for Belmont, and may fair winds, good hopes and a successful suit speed you to happiness."

The young noble grasped his friend's hand in an affectionate clasp, unwonted tears standing in his eyes. "I must go," he replied. "I think I shall be happy, since love sings blithely in my heart. Yet my joy will not be complete till I return and listen to your welcome. Tell me, Antonio—for at times my heart misgives me that your friendship costs too dear—have your argosies arrived yet in port? I own I shall be glad to hear your debt to the Jew is paid."

A faint shadow crossed the merchant's brow, though he smiled.

"Each or any day may I expect to hear of their arrival," he answered. "And it is possible that they are long delayed. Do not hasten your return on my account, Bassanio. Long before you have wooed and won your Portia I shall be as much out of the Jew's debt as he is out of my mind. For the rest, take heed, and employ both wit and caution in dealing with Niccolo Grimani, since the latter proves himself a rival of the baser sort, who would win by a shameful trick what fate has denied him."

The entrance of Gratiano—something after the blustering of an easterly gale—checked further confidences, and brought the smile in good earnest to Antonio's grave lips.

Poor Gratiano! His indignation was of a very truculent sort; boding ill for his enemies when he should meet them. Yet his excitement had a tinge of pleasant anticipation in it no less than Bassanio's, since in thwarting knaves they were likely to win favor in the eyes of their respective mistresses.

"Come," he urged Bassanio, "our ship awaits us, and I am told that Grimani has hired his craft for sailing in two hours. He who sups with the devil hath need of a long spoon. We'll not delay."

It was strange that a sudden loathness seized Bassanio as he wrung Antonio's hand.

"Would you were coming with us, amico," said he, "for I am reluctant to be parted even for a time from one in whose debt I lie so deeply."

"Nay," replied Antonio very earnestly, "there is no debt between us, Bassanio, save that of love. I shall be glad to hear of your happiness, which must be complete before you return to Venice."

"Or forever marred," sighed Bassanio, misgiving weighing on him for the first time. "But I do not dare to linger, though it takes all my courage to go, leaving one so dear. Still, Fate must decide for me before three weeks have passed, and there is that time wanting till the payment of the moneys."

With which self-encouragement he and Gratiano set forth for the quay, leaving Antonio to sit in the twilight of his solitary room, a smile on his lips, but a great weariness in his dark eyes, since for him life had but one beauty, one sunshine, amidst gray gloom—his friendship with Bassanio Ramberti.

Perhaps it was but in nature that the latter should look forward rather than back, forgetting for the time dear friendship in dear love.

Portia was in danger. For the second time she claimed him. But this time the claim was stronger, the danger more pressing, the reward—the reward—Bassanio must stop here, uncertain, diffident, leaving Gratiano to go forward alone along love's pathway.

Little Nerissa, having but herself to give, might be the lesser prize, but at any rate she was the more easily attained, so that Gratiano might dream on of reward, not bound down nor limited by difficult ordeal.

Still, it was not of the peril of the casket's fateful decree of which Bassanio thought as he and his companion lurked behind those trees through whose dark shade they could see the blue of a velvet doublet worn by some other watcher.

12

It had been a difficult task to get upon the track of Grimani and his accomplices, and more than once Bassanio had regretted not taking Antonio's advice and either warning the lady herself of her peril or telling Florio to set guards in the woods to protect his mistress.

But the mistake—if it were a mistake—had been made, and the young man was at pains to argue with himself that so wild a tale would scarcely have received credence either from the lady or her steward, since he accused a noble of Venice.

That Portia had already had proof of Grimani's importunities and lack of faith, Bassanio did not know. So he and Gratiano stood there, behind a thick screening of myrtles, ready to spring to a rescue at the first warning of danger. An hour dragged by, an hour when every breath was a peril and limbs grew racked by cramping pains as the two men stood rigid in their hiding.

From time to time they heard brief whispering amongst the men nearer the path, and once or twice one or other of them moved, stretching stiffened limbs and uttering imprecations on the tardiness of their prey in coming to a trapping.

Bassanio felt his pulses drum in fierce anger as he heard the words and marked the certainty of the villains in the accomplishing of an easy task.

Gratiano too gripped his dagger closely as he recalled the sweetness of a kiss.

Per Bacco! He would teach scoundrels a lesson which they might con over in purgatory, if they dare lay hands on his Nerissa!

The myrtles rustled in the wind. It was cold waiting here, and the woods were gray, sunless, ill-omened to-day. Mercurial spirits are easily damped by outward impressions and the young men were both growing more anxious than they cared to admit.

What risks had they chosen to expose their mistresses to in pursuance of their own self-glorification?

More than once was Bassanio tempted to leap out, challenge Niccolo Grimani to combat, and end the threatened encounter before the coming of Portia di Nerlini.

Yet he held back, since in such a case how would it be proven which of them had been waiting here as traitor or champion?

Clear and sweet-chimed, the tones of the convent bell drifted towards them down the hillside; each vibrant clang seeming a summons to prayer: prayer for the living, prayer for the dead, prayer for saints, prayer for sinners, importunate clamor of prayer stealing up towards the blue arch of the heavens.

Was it a summons to those already gone forth from sheltering walls to return to the deeper peace and safety of convent shade? Ah! Bassanio would not have a maid's sweet ears making such interpretation of the sound. Yet why was it she had been deaf to the call which might so easily have appealed to one girt about with threatening dangers and difficulties? What temptation was drawing Portia di Nerlini back to the world she had for so short a time forsaken?

Bassanio's pulses stirred. Did she know Love was waiting here—Love, strong-winged and ardent-souled, with golden lights in his eagle eyes and passion in his breath? Had some wandering nymph, stealing through the barred casement of a convent cell, whispered that sweet tale of Bassanio's devotion to one who knelt in pious prayer before the emblem of a far greater and divine love?

Clearly, sweetly, sounded the chimes, but to a lover's ears came another and nearer warning for his attention.

Footsteps on the pathway, voices talking together, a girl's laugh—Nerissa's glad rejoicing at her freedom, as she told her mistress it would be good to be home once more.

Then a rustling amongst the trees, a sharp exclamation in a man's tone, a shrill scream and a reassuring laugh. It was Niccolo Grimani who spoke—gayly, banteringly, with passion which was more mockery than devotion.

"Nay, nay," he cried, "command your servants to put up their weapons, lady, lest they suffer hurt. I do assure you that these blades are but the device of love to win its way. I love you, sweet Portia, and neither foolish oaths nor convent walls shall rob me of you. Come, smile, lady, since never yet have I heard of the woman who frowns on love?"

There was more anger than fear in the clear tones of Portia di Nerlini's reply.

"You sully a white name by your dishonoring speech, Signior," she replied. "How dare you speak of love, who have never learned the meaning of the word? I would not think worse but better of you if you stood there and said, 'Lady of Belmont, I do desire your wealth, and have no balking sense of shame or honor to keep me from oath-breaking or trickery on a defence-less woman.' But in that last you would be wrong too, for I am neither defenceless nor afraid. These two servants are not nobly born, yet by their noble defence of their mistress they'll show you how courage and loyalty are spelled, since I deem you backward in such learning. Stephano! Balthazar! I bid you clear my path; unless, Signior, you may choose to gather together such poor rags of honor as you still possess about you and leave one who despises you for your unworthy conduct."

So high was the lady's contempt that instead of shaming its listener, it goaded him to madness.

Swearing to himself that he would make the proud jade repent such scathing words, Grimani sprang forward with drawn sword upon Balthazar, with so unexpected a movement that he had run the poor fellow through his right wrist before he had time to strike one blow in his lady's defence.

Grimani's companions too were speedily engaged with Stephano, being at more pains to disarm than to kill him, since Grimani was aware that a bloodless encounter would benefit him in the future. Nerissa was screaming wildly by now, seeing Angelo Sutari before her, his dark face all a-grin with malice, whilst even Portia, with her back to a tall pine tree, was wondering what she must do to save herself in this dilemma, when two men, springing out from amongst the undergrowth changed the aspect of that brief fight.

Stephano had managed to wound the paid ruffian Giacope, though he himself was lying senseless beside his adversary, and Nerissa ceased to scream, but clasped small, trembling hands in prayer as she spied the champion who was thrusting with practised blade at the hulking figure of Sutari.

But Portia closed her eyes, swaying like some tall lily in the summer breeze as she saw on the path before her the man for whose coming to Belmont she had prayed —as she had prayed too for the rest of an honored father's soul.

Yes, he had come! the man who had stood with her in the moonlight and looked her heart away in the first glance from those keen yet merry eyes.   But he was not looking at her.   With back turned he stood there on the path, a slender figure in black hose and doublet, the silver girdle gleaming around his waist.

A champion come to save her a second time in this far greater peril, yet by odd trickery of fate almost in the same spot where she had first seen him.

Niccolo Grimani, within sight of swift success— cursed long and deeply, as sword to sword the two men stood—nobles of Venice both, splendid in their youth and strength, but with hate lurking on each face.

"So," cried Niccolo softly, "I must prove my right to this lady by the removal of so greedy and importunate a suitor.   I do not think, *Clarissimo*, that a di Nerlini's wealth will save you from the Jews."

But Bassanio did not answer; he only waited there on the path, his sword drawn in defence of the fair lady who stood with closed eyes and swelling heart under shadow of the trees.

.   .   .   .

To and fro leaped those two sable-clad figures.   To and fro under the pine trees, with stealing sunlight to show the glitter of a jewel on hand and collar or display the tense whiteness of the grim-set faces.

Portia di Nerlini was watching now—but she did not pray as Nerissa did—she had no mind for prayer, or hope, or love; only her eyes were fixed on the bending, swaying figures, which stooped and leaped, smote and defended, there on the narrow pathway.

Once she bit her lip till the blood dyed her chin, for she had seen Grimani's sword point buried for a moment in Ramberti's shoulder.   The blade was red when he drew it forth and yet her champion made no sign, but

fought with still fiercer energy as one who knew his time
was short. But Nerissa was crying now with laughter
and tears co-mingled, for it had dawned upon her why
Balthazar, at sight of those two new defenders, had gone
in hasty flight through the trees, too maimed for further
fighting, but swift of foot to play the courier. And now
he was returning—that wise Balthazar, though not alone.
From the direction of the palazzo, shouts and cries rang
long and loud through the woods.

The Lady of Belmont's retainers were not slow in coming to the aid of a beloved mistress, and Niccolo, hearing
the clamor of fast-approaching men, guessed what had
chanced, and cursed aloud since he had already begun
to number the moments before he could count victory
assured.

Bassanio still fought, parrying every subtle thrust,
but for all his efforts it was plain that loss of blood would
soon rob him of consciousness and place him in his
enemy's power.

Indeed, ere now, Grimani might have succeeded in
beating down his adversary's guard and slaying him by
fierce attack, but the wily Venetian was not so crazed by
anger as to lose sight altogether of the rashness of such
an act.

Reckless and improvident as Bassanio Ramberti had
shown himself in the squandering of his fortune, he had
won many friends in Venice—and amongst these was
Duke Niccolo da Ponte himself, who would requite the
slaying of a favored noble by the sentence of perpetual
exile from the city. This, Grimani would not risk,
having been confident that a few minutes would place
this tiresome meddler at his mercy.

So there was an added sting to this second failure

which might have been fashioned to success had he been more prompt.

As it was, however, caution warned the winner of that duel that his only safety from ignominious capture was in flight.

Angelo Sutari was already making his escape, with Gratiano at his heels, the lust of fighting in the pursuer's soul.

Bassanio staggered, swayed, his sword slipping from between nerveless fingers, then, as Grimani, also dropping his sword, sprang forward, Portia di Nerlini sank on one knee, her arms outstretched, thus breaking the fall of the man who had gotten grievous hurt in her defence and who now lay deep sunk in unconsciousness, his head pillowed on his lady's lap.

Nearer came the shouts of Florio and his men, the voice of Balthazar rising shrill in crescendo fear.

"This way, comrades—to the left of the cypress grove. Our Lady grant that we are in time!"

"In time!"

Portia looked up, and did not realize till later how Bassanio, unconscious, saved her yet again. For Niccolo's purpose had been to catch her in his arms and so make a reckless dash into the heart of the woods, trusting to the dense undergrowth of the shrubs to hide him from pursuit, and then essay to reach the spot not far distant where horses were tethered. But Portia, half kneeling, half seated on the ground, with the weight of her lover in her arms, could not be so easily raised and carried away. Nay! Even as Grimani stood glowering over her, irresolute as to how he should best accomplish his purpose, the foremost of the Nerlini retainers burst through the bushes and came running towards the spot.

Grimani swore aloud and, not daring to wait longer, followed Angelo Sutari in headlong flight to where their horses awaited them for a very differently planned journey.

The man—one Giacomo—did not attempt to follow the fleeing noble, but stood with mouth agape beside his mistress, staring in wide-eyed horror on the scene around.

Giacope still lay senseless, but Stephano, recovering had raised himself on one elbow, a sorry figure, with torn jerkin, and blood trickling in a slow ooze down his pale face.

Balthazar too, having spent his last strength on that well-conceived race, had slid prone onto a mossy bank, whilst a comrade, following hard after Giacomo, kneeled to bind his slit wrist and offer him cordial. For the rest, Gratiano, alone scathless after hard fighting, took advantage to comfort the nerve-racked Nerissa, whilst Portia bent weeping over Bassanio.

"He is dead," she made moan. "See how his life blood drains! And it was for me he suffered! For me he gave away that which I would have fain cherished forever. O Bassanio! Thus to die and never know Portia loved you!"

"Dead!" echoed Gratiano, startled from a more pleasant task, to read disaster in the picture near. "Bassanio dead? Nay, it cannot be. Life was too buoyant in him, lady, to be drained by so small a wound. If you had known how he dreamed of the moment when he should meet you—whose image has been so long shrined in his heart—you would not believe he could lie there unmoved, unconscious that his dream comes near to realization."

A long shiver shook the lady's form—to her it seemed

as though her own dreams of springtide and glowing summer were so far from realization that winter's cruel winds had blighted and killed them past recall.

So pale he looked, so lifeless, lying there, his shapely head pillowed on her lap—whilst with trembling fingers she essayed to open the doublet above his wound. As she bent to the difficult task Bassanio slowly opened his eyes, and looking up, saw a vision which he carried with him to his dying day; though at the first sight of it, he believed death past, and she who leaned above him some fair saint if not the Mother of Heaven herself.

The long black veil which had closely shrouded the lady's face had been flung back, dragging down by its weight the coils of fair hair which now hung over her slender shoulders like a mantle of burnished gold. Her face in such a framing was pale but very lovely, with great blue eyes wide in a tenderness far deeper than pity gazing down to meet the rapturous glance of the man who, coming slowly back to life and consciousness, thanked Heaven that he saw neither angel nor saint, but the woman he loved.

"Portia," he whispered, and her tears fell like healing balm upon his forehead.

But she did not answer—afraid to trust herself—with Florio and her people standing by bewildered by the enigma of this happening, so that Gratiano, having soothed Nerissa's terrors and seeing the plight of his friend, took matters in hand and, with the air of a prince, commanded that a litter might be brought and a leech sent for from Padua, since the sooner the illustrious Signior Bassanio Ramberti could be brought to shelter and away from these chill woods the better it would be for his health.

"But whither shall we take him, Signior?" inquired the doubtful Florio—who, having failed to plumb all this mystery, was uncertain whether or no his lady played the good Samaritan to a quondam foe. But Gratiano's hint had roused Portia from the maze of confused thoughts in which joy and grief strove for mastery.

"Whither?" she cried sharply, noting how wearily the sick man's lids had dropped after that one welcoming glance. "Why, whither but to the palazzo? Understand, Florio, that but for this illustrious gentleman and his friend I—I should have been the prey of a very evil plotter. But come, the Signior is right. There must be no delay; make you a litter with your swords and cloaks, and carry Signior Ramberti carefully, an' you love me. Nay, wait till the wound is bandaged, foolish one. Nerissa, a strip of linen quickly. So— that is better. Florio, you shall send instantly to Padua by a swift messenger for the best leech in the town. Sweet St. Ursula! he swoons again. Nerissa, be more careful in your touch; here, give me the bandage."

So impetuous was her speech, so quick her commands, that it was difficult to follow them as swiftly as she desired.

Nor had the Lady Portia patience with their slowness. Blaming herself for the first delay when she had feasted her heart's longings in that one long look of love, she grew angry and impatient now at the least delay on the part of others, railing in unusual irritation when some of the servants attempted to raise Bassanio on to the impromptu litter, and set the bandage about his shoulder awry, so that fresh blood stained the whiteness of the linen. Even Nerissa did not escape scoldings, but perhaps she better understood her mistress' mood, for, as the men proceeded at foot pace towards the palazzo, she came to Portia's side, slipping her hand into that of the lady.

"I think the Signior's hurt is not serious," she whispered. "And so, Signora, after all he comes to the Palazzo Nerlini."

Had she guessed, little witch, that that was the triumphant thought, rioting over present fears, in her lady's heart? At any rate a warm pressure of her fingers assured her that her words had not been unwelcome.

It was some hours later before the learned leech from Padua arrived to find that his nostrums and quackeries were not so very necessary.

The ladies of that time were all well skilled in the dressing and bandaging of wounds and the applying of salves and simples, whilst, after all, a sword thrust in the shoulder was nothing so very alarming beyond the first faintness attendant on loss of blood, which in this case had been considèrable; and, as it chanced, the faintness might have led to disastrous consequences had it not been for Balthazar's promptness in bringing assistance to his lady.

The Paduan wiseacre discoursed much, forbade wine, ordered the most meagre of diets and spoke at immense length on the wonders of the drugs and salves he prescribed.

Bassanio grew weary of so much widsom and openly yawned in the great man's face. His shoulder was stiff, he declared, and he was weary, but after a night's rest, would be as well as ever, and in spite of profound respect and gratitude for the illustrious physician's advice, felt he would be more perfectly restored by a full diet and generous liquor.

"The fever is on him," observed the leech, speaking afterwards to the fair chatelaine of the palazzo, "but the draught I have administered will cool his blood and produce sleep. I will visit him on the morrow and trust I shall find him on the road to recovery. Yet there must be care—the greatest care—since there ariseth much danger from indiscretion, and youth is ever impatient of sickness."

Which last words were the truest the learned doctor had ever uttered.

For the next few days Bassanio tossed to and fro in bed, fevered—not by his wound—but with impatience to be up and about, since the Lady Portia, in obedience to Dr. Cerello's injunctions, had not visited her sick guest. Bassanio, hearing of this mandate, through the indiscretion of Gratiano, raved in good earnest, so that Gratiano, playing the leech, boldly avowed to the lady that if she would see her visitor restored to health she must act the sick nurse herself in place of old Bettina.

So Portia came, and Bassanio forgot forthwith that his wound was stiff and sore or that a miserable weakness kept his mind drifting down into that shadowland which is only half-consciousness.

Surely there could be no shadow where this bright presence came—bending over his bed like some tender guardian-spirit—but thanking him as a woman thanks the man she loves.

Was that a fancy too—bred of desire? Or did blue eyes tell more of the truth than they might have done for pity's sake?

There were moments—when Portia was not by—spent by an anxious Bassanio in the asking of these questions, but in her presence all doubts were lulled, all fears forgotten, whilst it seemed that he and she were on a golden sea sailing towards paradise.

Thus the days drifted by, uncounted, unheeded, till Bassanio's wound was healed and his weakness more insisted on by Portia to keep her guest beneath the spell of those drifting days, than a reality.

And Bassanio—a true Venetian in his taste for pleasure seeking—was content to yield to her command and lie at ease upon the soft couch before the window, resting amongst soft cushions and silken coverings, watching his lady as she sat beside a dainty wheel, with gilded distaff in her hand, less because she loved industry than because she knew full well the pose was graceful, showing the whiteness of her little hands, the curving sweep of her lily neck, the elaborate dressing of golden curls and the daintiness of the velvet-slippered feet which rested on the stool.

Or at times she might read to him from one of the illumined scrolls by which her learned father had set such count, for she found something of a scholar in Bassanio, and it was pleasant to dip together into stores of written wisdom—though, be sure, they found the wisdom of each other's looks most pleasant of all—and the oldest tale in the world the one illumined in brightest colors of the soul.

Then again, the lady, at request, might take the lute, as she did that day when three short weeks had run their length unheeded, and sang in a voice as sweet and clear as the reed warblers amongst the hedges in nesting time— a tuneful voice and words atune to both their moods.

> Love me but well, I will be thine forever;
> As long as shall endure the winds of heaven;
> While pen and ink endure I'll leave thee never;
> Love me but well; I will be thine forever.

The refrain of the last line came twice in repetition, and the singer's voice had taken a deeper note, such as one hears on winter's nights amongst the pine trees.

"*Voleme ben, che saro sempre vostro.*"

And Bassanio, looking into her tender woman's face, knew that this was another Portia to the one who in a silver springtime had given him a pink carnation and smiled her girlish welcome into his eyes.

Yes, the child had become a woman during those short months; a wondrous change which thrilled him as that last line of her song had done.

Alas! Was it his love alone which should win her? If so he would have had no fear—she would be his forever. But were there not the caskets—those fateful caskets, which held kindly or adverse fate for him?

Portia laid aside her lute and came across to his couch.

"You are weary, Signior," she murmured. "Would you sleep?"

He looked up at her—his queen, his lady, between whom and himself rose the barrier of a dead father's decree.

"Aye," he answered passionately, "I would sleep, lady, if you could promise me all my dreams should be of you. Though then I should not wish to waken."

The rosy color tinged her cheeks, but she was not angry.

"Life is more than a dream, Bassanio," she whispered.

His eyes kindled and he rose, standing before her, his handsome head bent to a near level with her own.

"And because it *is* more—far more than a dream— I must not linger, Monna," he urged. "I cannot remain haunted by the threatening of uncertain destiny. Let me make my choice and know whether paradise or hell lies before me."

She looked at him, and her lips quivered.

"Nay," she pleaded, "you—are not fully restored from the hurt you suffered for my sake. Be in no haste to choose, for—for though I will not say what I hope from that choice—yet I should be sorry for the necessity for one who—who has served me so well to leave me forever."

But Bassanio's face grew stern.

"Talking of service rendered," he replied, "reminds me of duty neglected. I have a friend in Venice, lady, to whom I owe more than I can recount—such a friend as man seldom possesses. I swore to him I would return long since, and he though very patient, will ask himself why Bassanio tarries—though I think he will guess some part of the reason."

Portia di Nerlini smiled—then sighed.

She would have denied him, coquetted, teased him, resenting the knowledge that she had shown her heart too plainly in those days when she had judged him to be dying for her sake.

But it was too late now. How could she scorn him even in pretence when to-morrow he might be bidding her an eternal farewell?

To hide her distress she moved nearer to the window, watching how Gratiano paced the garden terrace with Nerissa by his side.

How happily they laughed, those two! And why should they not? Love had come to them untrammeled by hard condition and there was nothing between sweet confession and a lover's kiss.

She saw Nerissa's red lips raised in invitation, saw the sunlight play on brown, curling locks and a blushing face, and could not altogether suppress the jealous sob which strangled in her throat.

"Lady, you are sad?"

Bassanio spoke, and she turned to him impulsively, pride drooping under the ban of cruel necessity.

"It is hard, Bassanio," she whispered, "for—if I told the secret I should be forsworn, whilst if I tell it not— if I tell it not——"

"Why," he answered, stooping to raise one hand to his lips, "I will only listen to hope's song, lady. Why should we suffer twice what may not come? Has not Fate already shown herself our friend; since, but for Fate and your father's loving thought—for it was a thought of love, lady, and therefore cannot greatly err from its own purpose—you had been wooed and won by some insistent suitor who would have been hardly denied? And this would have happened whilst I lingered in Verona and Rome, little guessing the hidden secret of my own heart."

She took courage at these words, even smiling as she allowed herself one swift glance to what life would be if Fate, under command of Heaven in answer to her father's prayers, guided Bassanio's choice on the morrow—that morrow into whose mysteries she did not dare to gaze.

But she did not sing again that night—only prayed, kneeling by her bedside alone in the darkness long after Nerissa had left her. Prayed—with no words to offer, only a cry which went up in all the appeal of a loving woman's heart towards the starry heavens.

And Bassanio, sleepless too, stood watching a bright star climb slowly above the sharp outline of the cypresses and pour its single beam down, as it were, into his tumultuous heart.

"Love me but well—I will be thine forever."

13

His arms went out in a passionate gesture of longing. What guerdon could life hold comparable to this?

Fame, wealth, the gratifying of the highest ambitions, were but as nothing when weighed in the balance against love.

It was strange that as he went to bed he was thinking tenderly and very pityingly of his dear friend Antonio, who had never known the love of woman.

But then Bassanio, for all his superior wisdom and understanding, knew nothing of the light which had gone out of the life of Antonio his friend when the convent gates closed upon the fair form of Bianca Ramberti.

So true it is that our nearest and dearest know little of the inner secrets of our hearts.

CHAPTER XX

"**Y**OU have returned?"

Aaron Tubal inclined his head with slow dignity, folding his arms within his wide sleeves.

"I have returned," he answered, regarding Shylock with steady, inscrutable eyes.

It was twilight in that upper room of the Jew's house, where signs of wealth lay smothered under thick layers of dust, since the washing of vessels, hands and feet, did not extend to things in general, but were observed only by the strict letter in the narrow creed of the Jew. So tawdry geegaws lay side by side with priceless objects of art—a veritable medley—such as might be seen in some old curiosity shop of to-day—with its owner standing in the midst, a striking figure for all its shabbiness, the light full on the lean, shriveled face with its great nose, blear eyes and patriarchal beard. Shylock's claw-like hands worked ceaselessly.

"Did you find my daughter? Did you find Jessica?" he gasped. "Had she the jewels on her?"

His anxiety almost suffocated him; great beads of sweat broke over his forehead.

Tubal stared gloomily at him, his own fingers thrust into his short black beard.

"I often heard of her," he growled, "but never saw her. I did not spare myself in the search."

His somber eyes glowed.

But at the news Shylock broke out into bitter lamentation.

"May the curse of Abrahan light on the woman," he moaned, "and on the villain who tempted her to this sin! Think of it, Aaron! A diamond gone, cost me two tousand ducats in Frankfort! The curse never fell on our nation till now—at least, I never felt it till now. Two thousand ducats in gold! and other precious, precious jewels."

He wrung his hands, sobbing in impotent fury.

"I would my daughter were dead at my feet, and the jewels in her ears!" he groaned. "Would she were hearsed at my feet and the ducats in her coffin! No news of them! And, I know not what we shall have spent in the search. Why, it is loss upon loss! The thief gone with so much, and so much to find the thief! And no satisfaction! No revenge! No ill-luck stirring, but it lights on my burdened shoulders—no sighs but of my breathing—no tears but of my shedding."

Exhausted he sank into a chair, a pitiable object had it not been for the sordidness of his grief.

Tubal raised his heavy brows, shrugging his shoulders. "Why, as for that," he replied, "other men have ill-luck, too. Antonio Cainello, as I heard in Genoa——"

He could get no further.

Shylock was on his feet in an instant, his whole aspect changed to one of intense eagerness.

He caught at Tubal's sleeve, rending it in his excitement.

"What? What? What?" he gurgled incoherently. "Ill-luck, ill-luck?"

He was as some bald-headed vulture which spreads its

wings towards a distant fight in pleasant anticipation of dead men's flesh for feasting.

"Cainello hath an argosy cast away, coming from Tripolis," concluded Tubal, freeing himself from the other's grasp.

But Shylock had already loosed his hold, folding his' hands in blaspemous thanksgiving.

"I thank God! I thank God!" he cried, "Is it true, good Aaron? Dear Aaron, is it true?"

He stooped, his hands on his knees, to peer up wickedly into the other's face.

"There can be no doubt," Tubal assured him calmly. "I spoke with some of the sailors that escaped the wreck."

Shylock laughed—such laughter as might have made one think of devils rejoicing over the souls of the damned.

"I thank you, good Tubal," he cried. "Good news! Good news!"

For the moment he could think of nothing else, since during the past three months his hatred to Antonio— upon whom he placed all the score of his misfortunes— had grown like some leprous taint till it obsessed him. But Tubal quickly directed back his thoughts to less pleasant channels.

"Your daughter Jessica," said the younger man, not without some show of malice, "spent in Genoa, as I heard, four score ducats in a single night."

Shylock reeled, clasping his hand over his heart. "You stick a dagger in me," he moaned. "Alas! I shall never see my gold again! Four score ducats at a sitting! Four—score—ducats!"

He was dazed at such disaster.

Tubal looked at him in secret amusement.

"I journeyed back to Venice in company with some of Antonio's creditors," he said. "They declare he must be bankrupt—the wealthiest could not weather so much misfortune."

Shylock's restless eyes glittered with satisfaction.

"And to-morrow," he muttered, "the bond is due. Three months to-morrow—and if he cannot pay—his bond is forfeit." He clutched the air, gibbering like an evil ape. "I'll plague him," he whispered beneath his breath, "torture him too. At last, Antonio, the Jew's day will dawn. Look to to-morrow! I shall be waiting. And it is certain that thus three at least of his argosies have met with disaster. How well have I planned! How all falls out to my dearest wish! How——"

"One of these same fellows," quoth Tubal carelessly, "showed me a ring, that he had of your daughter for a monkey."

Shylock shrieked aloud, as though a torturer had wrung his limbs upon a rack.

"Out upon her!" he sobbed. "It was my turquoise, Aaron. I had it of Leah when I was a bachelor. I would not have given it for a wilderness of monkeys."

Tubal fingered his yellow badge meditatively.

"Antonio is certainly undone," he said. "I do not think we shall see him strutting it as of yore on the Rialto."

"That is true," retorted Shylock, showing wolfish fangs. "You may rest assured of that, good Tubal. Come, let us go out now and learn what further news of disaster there may be. I have hopes, Aaron, great hopes of to-morrow. You are sure Antonio's creditors spoke with certainty of his breaking? Good! Good!

We will go to the Rialto and hear more of the matter, which is sure to be buzzing from mouth to mouth amongst the merchants. Antonio broke! Why, it is the best news you could have brought me. You are coming?"

But Tubal shook his head.

"I returned from Genoa, as I promised," said he, "but I have not given up my search of Jessica and her Gentile lover. I almost had my hand upon them—but I think they had warning. Yet they have not wholly escaped. Have I not vowed to find them? I do not think I am a man lightly forsworn. So, by your leave, Shylock, I lose no time in starting for Rome, where I have good assurances I shall find them."

Shylock blinked in some astonishment.

"To what profit?" he demanded bitterly. "The jade will have spent the ducats and sold the jewels. I shall never see either again."

Tubal showed yellow teeth in a vicious grin.

"You spoke but lately of revenge," he retorted, "thinking of Antonio. I too speak of revenge—and think of the man who stole my bride. You understand?"

It was a creed which the elder Jew only too clearly understood, and he laughed a crackling, contemptuous laugh.

"So you will kill Lorenzo?" he said. "Well! I'm glad of it. But do not bring Jessica hither again, lest I should lay violent hands on my own flesh and blood, thinking of the jewels, my precious, lost jewels."

Tubal shook his head.

"Oh, no," he replied. "I will not bring Jessica to you again—though I shall hope to kill Lorenzo."

His eyes were inscrutable as he went out and away

down the staircase, crossing the bridge towards his own home.

But Shylock did not pause to consider the enigmatical words or ponder on what his daughter's ultimate fate would be should her lover be slain and she fall into the hands of her ferocious countryman.

Since his ducats and jewels were irretrievably gone, the old man had no tears to waste over a lost daughter.

So, as he stood waiting for a boat to take him in the direction of the Rialto, he yielded undivided thought to the more pleasant consideration of Antonio Cainello's misfortunes.

If 'all were true as Tubal had said, the morrow would have a crowning joy for Shylock the Jew, which almost compensated for past distresses.

There were many to turn and gaze at the shabby figure in its coarse gabardine and yellow turban as Shylock hurried past the drapers' shops set under the porticos of the Rialto.

Every now and then a group of bare-footed urchins would run after him, mocking.

"Hast found thy daughter, Jew?" one would cry, leering at him with lolling tongue, whilst another would add, "What of the ducats pretty Jessica stole, Shylock?"

And a third, seeing the victim wince, uttered another taunt, "Has she invited thee to her Christian home, Jew, so that thou canst eat pork? Good pork, paid for at price of thy ducats."

The little rascals were scattered at last by a pitying silk vendor, who noted how pale the old Jew had grown, and thought he suffered, little guessing that it was but rage at white heat.

Knots of merchants, richly clad in silks and velvets

of gay or sober coloring according to their wearer's fancy, stood together eagerly discussing the news of the day.

As Shylock had guessed, Antonio Cainello's name was on every lip. The young merchant's unprecedented successes, his wealth and bold trading had not—as is so usually the case—made him an object of envy and dislike. The man was too kindly, too generous, too fair in his dealing to rouse animosity or hate. In fact, there was no more popular man in all Venice than Antonio the merchant. Rich and poor admired, trusted, loved him for his noble uprightness. Shylock the Jew and his like were the sole exceptions.

So, when fortune, by the most cruel trickery, turned her face from her favorite, sending disaster upon disaster to wreck his hopes and bring ruin to torment him, the unfortunate victim of her caprices found many sympathizers on the Rialto, in the Ducal Palace, aye, and in those meaner streets where his kindly heart had taken him in charity for the poor and suffering.

And, in and out of the crowd, lingering here, listening there, like some black bird of prey, stole Shylock the Jew, whilst the more he heard the greater grew his satisfaction.

Not only was Tubal's story true, but there were other tales confirmed again and again, relating how not one or two, but every single venture launched by Cainello on the treacherous seas had been doomed either to wreckage or piracy.

Ruined indeed was he, beyond all hope and doubt. Already men wondered how it would go with him, and what his creditors might hope to receive when all his worldly gear was sold.

Idle speculations, pitying speculations—Shylock the Jew listened to them all, and laughed into his beard as he told himself that it was very certain he might wait in vain to-morrow for the coming of Antonio and his three thousand ducats.

Presently, in his wanderings up and down the Rialto, he came upon the merchants Salarino and Salanio, whom he knew as dear friends of Antonio and Bassanio both.

They looked glum enough, having no doubt been joining in that buzz of talk which raged around Antonio's name and misadventures.

Yet Salarino, disdainful in his twitting of the Jew, hailed him mockingly.

"How now, Shylock?" cried he, thrusting his thumbs under his armpits, and stretching his legs somewhat widely apart. "What news amongst the merchants?"

Shylock scowled evilly. He hated these men, who never disguised their contempt for him.

"You know," he muttered, "none so well—none so well as you—of my daughter's flight."

Salarino chuckled. "That's certain," he admitted slyly. "I, for my part, knew the tailor that made the wings she flew away with."

Shylock did not answer, but stood tugging at his beard, with vindictive glances towards the two young men who would have made sport of him. In their gay doublets and velvet cloaks they made fine show—whilst he, in his shabby gabardine, was the Crœsus who could have bought them and their fine prankings over and over again. Yet he hated them for this semblance of wealth which had so poor a reality.

But Salarino grew grave.

"Have you heard the news," he asked tentatively, "how our poor Antonio hath had losses at sea?"

Shylock showed his teeth in a vicious leer.

"There," he snarled, "I have another bad bargain. A bankrupt! A prodigal, who scarcely dare show his head on the Rialto! A beggar—who used to come so smug upon the mart. But let him look to his bond! He was wont to call me usurer; let him look to his bond! He was wont to led money for a Christian courtesy; let him look to his bond!"

As he proceeded the old man's whole being seemed to dilate with that venom which swells the head of some poisonous snake before it strikes its victim. His lips frothed as in a frenzy—he shook in the very voicing of his rage.

"Why," quoth young Salanio soothingly, "I am sure if *he* is forfeit you will not take his flesh. What's that good for?"

Both he and his companion stood, with arms akimbo now, eyeing the Jew as those who look on some new and hideous monstrosity; yet they neither of them could believe Shylock's significant threat was uttered in sober earnest.

"Good for?" echoed the latter shrilly. "Well— to bait fish withal! If it will feed nothing else, it will feed my revenge."

Salarino interposed. "Come," he urged, "what hurt hath Antonio Cainello ever done you, Jew? His is the kindest heart in Venice, aye, and in all Italy. If you were sick or sorry, instead of rich, his feet would be the readiest to come your way with succor and good cheer."

But Shylock was deaf to such reasoning.

Mayhap his brain, half crazed with sundry losses and adversities, had fastened in ill-proportioned hate upon this man whom he regarded as his bitterest enemy and cause of all his misfortunes.

"What hurt hath he not done me?" he squealed, spitting upon the ground. "He has disgraced me and baulked me of half a million ducats. He has laughed at my losses, mocked at my gains, scorned my nation, thwarted my bargains, cooled my friends, heated my enemies. And what's the reason for all his malice? *I am a Jew.*"

He paused, panting, giving vent for the first time to the full tale of his long-cherished grievances.

"Hath not a Jew eyes?" he demanded. "Hath not a Jew hands, organs, dimensions, senses, affections, passions? Is he not fed with the same food, hurt with the same weapons, subject to the same diseases, healed by the same means, warmed and cooled by the same winter and summer as a Christian is? If you prick us, do we not bleed? If you tickle us, do we not laugh? If you poison us, do we not die? And if you wrong us, shall we not revenge? If we are like you in the rest, we will resemble you in that! If a Jew wrong a Christian, what is his return? Revenge! If a Christian wrong a Jew, why should he not follow Christian example and take revenge too? The villainy you teach me I will execute, and it shall go hard if I cannot better the instruction."

He raised both lean arms aloft as though invoking Heaven itself to attest to his cruel vow. Thus his companions left him, shuddering as they moved back to the more crowded part of the Rialto, crossing themselves, too, as though at the sight of something evil.

"Would that Bassanio were back in Venice," said Salanio impulsively. "For I think yon Jew means mischief. Yet, after all, what can he do but throw our poor Antonio into prison for debt? Since assuredly neither the Duke nor Senate would listen to the demand for fulfilment of so wild a bond."

But Salarino was looking back to where a bent figure in shabby gabardine and yellow turban was hastening away from the Rialto.

He too pitied Antonio Cainello from the depths of his heart.

CHAPTER XXI

"MY lord Bassanio has not returned, illustrious Signior."

The servant's tones were respectful, yet his black eyes were inquisitive, since, like the rest of Venice, he had heard how disaster had engulfed the fortunes of the Signior Cainello, reputed one of the richest of the younger merchants of the city.

"Ah," said Antonio, concealing disappointment under a calm demeanor. "Not returned? And you have not heard from him?"

"No, illustrious."

Antonio Cainello sighed as he re-entered his gondola— he had hoped to have seen his friend, since already the day had dawned and passed for the redeeming of his bond to Shylock the Jew. And, though he might smile at the mere jest which fixed the forfeit of his bond, a sense of oppression weighed on him.

It was the hour of noon and the Piazza San Marco was crowded with pleasure seekers, sightseers, buyers and vendors, their bright-hued dresses, doublets, caps and veils making a blaze of color along the broad pavement of the Piazza.

Venice held carnival to-day for victories gained by her sons in foreign battlefields, and the spirit of gayety, triumph and pride was stamped on every smiling face amongst the jostling crowd, which sang and danced as

(206)

the jingle of lute and guitar drifted to them from the gayly-decked gondolas which plied to and fro across the lagoons.

It was a busy, stirring spectacle, which would have equally pleased patriot or artist. Vivid color was everywhere, and the winter sunshine blazed with summer warmth over the gay scene which was no uncommon one in these golden days of the great Venetian Republic.

Perhaps the most famous carnival of all in point of gorgeous display had been that which marked the receiving of the news of the victory of Lepanto, when the Turks had been defeated by the Christian allies. Then, whilst in the church of San Marco, the Government were offering up thanksgiving, the exchanges of the various nations were illuminated, and the porticos of the Rialto were hung with cloth of gold, turquoise and scarlet, trophies of Turkish arms and beautiful pictures. A great triumphal arch had been erected at the foot of the Rialto bridge, whilst every window had its flags or carpets, and for three days continuously the bells of all the churches rang joy peals. The masqueraders too, representing Stradiotti, Swiss, Turks, Moors and fishermen, had roused the wildest enthusiasm, forming as they did an escort to the procession of cars on which were represented Faith, Venice and the three quarters of the globe.

To-day the carnival was being carried out in less prodigal display, yet it was interesting enough; though, for his part, Antonio Cainello was in no mood for merry-making.

As quickly as he might he threaded his way amongst the laughing crowd and gained the more congenial asylum of the great church, where the Mass was nearing its conclusion.

The Duke, his train and most of the magnificoes of Venice were there kneeling in solemn prayer and thanksgiving for victory which had been the gift of Heaven.

But Antonio knelt alone, far in the background behind a marble pillar where the shadows fell thickly.

Why had he come hither? Had he thanksgiving to offer—he, the penniless bankrupt, down in the dust of humiliation and poverty?

A sigh broke from his lips as the organ pealed forth its triumphal pæan of victory and the voices of the choristers rose sweet and clear in praise.

The beauty of the Te Deum could not fail to find some echo in the heart of the soul-sick man. After all, was it necessary to despair because his ships were sunk and his fortunes broken?

One boy was singing a solo now—a fair-haired child in scarlet cassock and cap and lace surplice—his voice flooded the great church with the melody of angels and was answered by the thunder of the organ, the voices of his companions and the massed congregation. Then slowly the procession of tonsured priests filed out of their stalls and vanished from sight. The Duke arose and passed down the aisle, his head bowed in reverence, as he led the way out followed by his nobles and train of attendants. Out into the sunlight they went, and Antonio could hear the cries of "Il Duca—il Duca" —as the soldiers cleared a way for the ducal procession back to the Palace, where feasting and dancing would fill up the rest of the day and night. But he himself, kneeling in the shadows behind the pillar of white marble, was glad to be alone in the silence. The echo of that sweet boy's voice lingered in the aisles and dark corners of the great building, with its incense-laden atmosphere.

From where he stayed, Antonio could see how a shaft of sunshine, stealing through a high, stained window, fell athwart the white purity of clustering lilies on the altar. Fell too across the sculptured Figure of the crucified Christ, the Bowed Head drooping under the weight of its thorn-crown and infinite suffering.

It was then that Antonio could pray.

Few words and halting at first, barely articulate; though, as he raised his face towards the Figure of divine compassion and love, peace gradually stole to his heart—as the sunlight lay warm upon the flowers yonder.

After all, what mattered poverty if love remained? A sigh escaped him. From contemplation of the highest, his mind reverted to that other love which had shown him a golden path he might never tread.

"Bianca!" he breathed, and let his thoughts drift as they had so often drifted before in wonder as to whether in Heaven he might one day tell his lady what love of her had meant to him on earth.

A golden cord, pure and unsullied by carnal taint, drawing him upward to the infinite love of God. Bianca! He saw her now, as he had seen her, ah, so long ago— a slim, girlish figure, robed in white and gold, waiting on the steps of her brother's palazzo for the gondola which was to take her to some banquet at a friend's house. How lovely she had looked, the flush of expectancy on her sweet, childish face, her dark hair crowning the head which a long veil enshrouded—a veil only raised for a moment so that Antonio, breathless with longing, had seen the glory of those great gray eyes.

A child's eyes, clear of guile, looking out for an instant in amaze at the great world she was never to know.

That had been the last time Antonio saw her, but he

14

pictured her again, no less lovely though yet more angelic, in her gray nun's dress, kneeling alone in some narrow cell, her eyes grown mystical with looking not on earth but Heaven.

And yet again he saw her to-day, standing there near the altar, white robed, exultant, eternally beautiful, gazing neither towards the world—or Heaven—but at him.

Yes, he grew bold in his visioning. Here was the reward he prayed for—the reward, ah! how ill-deserved —for all his suffering and patience—that she should know him in eternity, come to him, laying her sweet hand in his, calling him "Antonio."

Again the echo of the little chorister's song of praise rang trumpet-like in his ears. Could he sing too— because Bianca, being dead, still lived, aye, and had looked towards him from amongst the lilies of the altar?

Tears filled the kneeler's eyes. He had forgotten that he had entered the church a broken, ruined man. He only knew that beyond death the angels sang the song of the Resurrection and Atonement, and that amongst them stood one whom he would call Bianca when he went to find her.

Then, since thoughts drift hither and thither, like feathers in a sportive breeze, even in most recollected moments, he fell to wondering how Bassanio fared, and of his own deep love for Bianca's brother.

Why, yes—who had called him ruined, bankrupt, when he held such a wealth of love all his own? He could smile at the bare suggestion.

Bassanio loved him—he loved Bassanio and would very gladly suffer all the pangs the future might hold for him in serving his friend. How noble and how true

a word that was! *His friend.* So closely locked in
each other's love that no reverse of fickle fortune could
sever them.   He prayed again—this time for Bassanio's
happiness, and saw the lilies sway in a little breeze as
a door opened somewhere behind the choristers' stalls
and an old priest came out to pass towards the altar rail
and there kneel.

He prayed for others, as was his office.   Antonio
prayed too, as was the obligation of his friendship.
Was Bassanio happy in his love? Would he win his
Portia after such long delay?

Antonio sighed very faintly.   A black shadow passed
across the golden sheen of prayer—the devil, come even
into the holy place to mar what he most feared.

And this time the devil took the form of Shylock the
Jew.

The day had passed when his bond should be redeemed,
and Antonio had not a thousand ducats in the world.
No, nor likelihood of gaining them.

Of course there was the hope that Bassanio, married
to a rich wife, would be returning anon to pay the debt
he more rightly owed.

But what of the bond?   An idle jest?   A folly to
cloak a generous deed?   Why, after all, that had been
out of nature in Shylock the Jew!

Moreover, last night, Salarino and Salanio in supping
with him had given no hint of his creditor's charitable
spirit.   Instead they had looked askance when Shylock
was mentioned, and Salanio had railed on the vile Jew
in no measured terms.

Chaotic thoughts were these, some of which had been
enough to weigh down Antonio's spirit before he entered
the church.   But now he grew more resigned, more

peaceful in his mind. Had he not watched the sunlight fade over a thorn-crowned Head? Had he not dreamed of Bianca's form, a lily amongst lilies, a messenger from eternal shores, sent by Love Incarnate to solace him in his pain? After all, if death *should* follow ruin he would not weep, but rather smile in offering sacrifice for a dear friend.

"Bianca—love," he whispered, "do you know, Bianca, you—amongst the lilies of Heaven?" Then he rose from his knees and went out from the cool church with its shadows and sunlight, its lilies and crosses, incense and praises, leaving a white-haired priest to pray for Venice in the hour of her triumphs.

The glare of the Piazza, the thronging garishness of the crowd in flaunting colors and merry hubbub, dazed Antonio, so that he put up his hand to shade his eyes.

Everything was still blurred and indistinct when a shrill note, dominant among other voices, pierced clear and startling to his clouded senses.

"It is he!" cried the voice of Shylock the Jew. "Take him, officers. Bind him, lead him away to prison. It is the Duke's command. I have his written order. Do not hesitate. Bind him, lead him away."

Antonio looked round, and saw his enemy beside him. Yes, his enemy. No cloak of disguise now. No fawning sycophant who held out a spurious olive branch, crying, "Take me for your friend. By this bond, this merry bond which holds no breath of usury, take me to your heart of friendship."

It was hate undisguised which blazed from blear eyes into the face of Antonio Cainello, so that the latter knew the truth even before it was uttered.

And for a moment the young merchant stood silent,

"The Duke shall grant me justice."

dumfounded by such hate as he saw directed towards him. Shylock without a mask! No pleasant sight forsooth—so that mothers hurried by, clasping their babes to their breasts lest the little ones should be overlooked by some fateful glance, whilst young girls drew their veils of golden tissue closer over their faces after one scared peep towards the group gathered near the church.

A small guard stood by the Jew, yet it was obvious that the men were as reluctant as they could be to obey his behest, for it went against the grain, in those days of fierce racial feeling, for a Jew to have the better of a Christian. And in this case the natural feeling was strengthened by the knowledge of the two men and their characters.

But Shylock grew impatient, seeing the gathering throng and hearing the murmurs which called shame on him and urged the guard to refusal of his will.

"Will you gainsay the Duke's command?" he snarled. "If so you shall suffer for it. Bind the man, bring him on his way to jail."

Antonio understood now, and the color dyed his cheeks, whilst he could not forbear protest, useless though he might have known it.

"Hear me, Shylock——" he began.

But his enemy cut him short.

"I'll have my bond," he gibbered. "Speak not against my bond! I've sworn an oath that I will have my bond. You called me dog before you had a cause. But since I am a dog, beware my fangs. The Duke shall grant me justice."

The guard, impressed by the last words, reluctantly approached their prisoner.

Still Antonio urged, seeing how his good friend Salarino hastened through the crowd towards them.

"I pray you, hear me speak," he entreated.

Shylock only shook his head. "I'll have my bond," he reiterated. "I will not hear you speak. I'll have my bond. Speak no more. What! Shall I, a son of Abraham, yield to Christian intercessors? I'll not be made a soft and dull-eyed fool to sigh, relent and pardon. I'll have no speaking. I'll have my bond."

The guard had gathered about Antonio now, and though there were passers-by who stopped to gape, calling curses on the Jew and pity on his victim, yet, seeing the ducal liveries, they dared not interfere.

Salarino, however, had forced his way almost to his friend's side. He had been utterly dismayed to hear the news, which had already reached the Rialto, of how Shylock had been since early dawn at the Ducal Palace importuning the Duke for Antonio's arrest, even threatening if his request were not complied with. In vain the Duke had tried to withhold consent. The Jew had him on the hip with his reiteration of the Duke's own motto, "Justice in the Palace." So justice had her way, though Salarino could have wept aloud as he saw Antonio, the kindly, revered merchant of lofty standing and unimpeachable character, standing like any common criminal under arrest.

"Cur!" he gasped, "will nothing change your humor? Come, we will bargain with you on the Rialto. Your favorite game, Shylock. You'll not miss the opportunity, vile Jew?"

Shylock made no reply. He was urging the guard, who moved slowly forward towards the prison, to hasten their steps.

"Let him alone," said Antonio quietly, turning to his friend with gentle dignity, as Salarino strode by his side, cursing and weeping. "I'll follow him with no more bootless prayers. He seeks my life—nothing less will satisfy him. Nor is his reason far to seek. He hates me, amico, because I have often saved those who had come under his extortioner's lash."

"I am sure," responded the other hotly, "the Duke will never grant this forfeiture to hold."

Antonio shook his head—he would not accept the hope of such hollow comfort.

"The Duke cannot deny the course of law," he replied. "Justice is justice and must be administered without favor or travesty. See you, Salarino. It is impossible it should be otherwise, since so many strangers live and trade amongst us from other lands. These must see that the law holds no devious cause. The Jew is right there—and so I suffer. Nay, do not weep at that. I am so worn with grief and losses that I cannot hope to spare a pound of flesh to this bloody creditor and live. Yet, if it might be, I would see Bassanio again. He is not in the city now—but at Belmont."

"He would not linger in returning did he dream of what may happen in Venice," replied Salarino in a voice choked by grief.

A slight shadow crossed Antonio's face.

"I know it well," he replied. "And if I could would send a messenger with my letter—if pen and ink are allowed me, as I think they will be. Salarino, in this perchance you'll stand my friend? There is a man who feels himself in my debt—one Tito Scappini, who has repaid my trifling service many times in love. Yet he'll not grudge to pay again, and I can trust to finding him

willing to go to Belmont for me, deliver my letter to
Bassanio and show him my case. There is no need for
more, since Bassanio will not tarry in coming if but to
clasp my hand in fond farewell."

"Nay," retorted Salarino stoutly, "this Scappini
whom I have often seen at the quays and whom I know
well enough for an honest lubber, is no messenger to
send on such an errand. But fret not, Antonio; there
are feet as willing, hearts as fond and brains more nimble
than this poor fisherman's, who I warrant would be too
mazed by despair at hearing of your plight to have one
grain of understanding left in his simple pate. So you
shall send me in Scappini's place; or, if not, I'll take
myself, since I vow this day shall see me at Belmont
and that before the sun is near its setting."

Antonio smiled gratefully into the other's twisted
face, where grief, anger, and determination struggled
together for predominance.

"Why, this is kind," he said, "and I thank you,
Angelo. Yet I hesitate to accept this service, knowing
how your own affairs engage you on the Rialto, needing
your constant care and attendance. I would not have
you light on disaster for my sake."

Salarino shrugged his shoulders with the careless
gesture of one who hides deeper emotion.

"For that," said he, "I am better out of Venice,
both wit and body, than that my body should be on the
Rialto whilst my wit wavers between your prison and
Belmont. Say no more, Antonio, and I will visit you
in less than an hour's time, when you shall have the
letter written. I will have my gondola ready, and
hey, presto! before you have time to wonder what
Bassanio thinks of your news he will be here himself

cudgeling his brains how to save a friend from a churlish devil who shall find Venice at the same heat as his native pit if I have my way."

And the speaker scowled across to where Shylock shuffled along by the side of the captain of the guard, whose glum face showed that he found him no pleasant comrade.

"The letter shall be writ," declared Antonio, with more confidence, "and commended to your care and love, my Salarino. Why, trouble but proves to a poor man his better wealth. I thank you, friend, for this proof of friendship."

"If I could wring yon Jew's scraggy neck, I would count the service of more esteem," growled Salarino, winking away his tears, as the grim gates of the prison loomed in view. "However, Bassanio shall have your letter, and you shall have Bassanio before another dawn, if friendship doth not miscarry as justice hath at times a trick of doing."

So saying the merchant strode hastily off towards the Rialto to spread dismay there by a vivid recountal of the day's tragedy and convene a deputation of twenty of the most notable merchants to wait on the Duke—and if necessary on Shylock himself.

CHAPTER XXII

NERISSA MAKES CONDITIONS

"**B**UT, Nerissa——"

Poor Gratiano's ready eloquence was checked. Mumchance he stood before the dainty little figure in its green gown, which poised on a step above him, where a shallow flight of wooden stairs led to a rustic bower.

Nerissa knew her powers—who better?—and that she was altogether charming and delectable as she stood, with dainty arms akimbo, swaying to and fro very slightly, so that the long ends of her sleeves, falling from the elbows of her gown almost to the ground, gave a soft swishing sound against the shrubs as they brushed them.

"*But*, Signior Gratiano," she mocked teasingly, allowing him to see the dimples which rioted over the plump smoothness of her cheeks.

He stretched out his right arm, trying to imprison her hand, but she was too quick for him, and retreated up another step, looking for all the world like a kitten who wants a game of play with the puppy dog who insists in misinterpreting arched back and ruffled fur.

It was the first time in his life that Gratiano had been at a loss for words. Had you asked his reputation of a score of friends in Venice, all would have been in one tale about him as a boon companion, a merry jester, an incessant chatterer—and an arch flirt.

But this time he was serious—and in the art of serious persuasion he was a novice.

Yet, after all, simplicity was, as it always is, most eloquent of any.

"I love you," he said, and the distant splashing of a fountain echoed the words.

Nerissa ceased to mock—she even deigned to descend one step.

"Why, you've told me that before," she whispered. "Take care, Messer Gratiano, for if you repeat yourself too often you will end by believing your own words. And then, hey! for gay bachelorhood and all the delights of the town."

The words inspired him with hope, so that he rashly repeated his offence and tried to take her hands.

"Nerissa," he pleaded, seeing her retreat once more— three steps this time, and a frown between white brows into the bargain. "If you love me, torment me not. What shall I say to teach you reason? I love you, I would marry you, and——"

She stretched her fingers wide before her face in mock dismay. "And make me one of your fine Venetian dames," cried she, "prancing in clogs so high that I vow I should break my legs if I tried to walk in them, and wearing my hair crisp and dyed about my shoulders, like any flaunting courtesan. Fie, Messer Gratiano! I prefer Belmont, if it please you."

"It is not so!" he cried passionately. "If you will wed me, Nerissa, I vow by the sword of San Marco and every other saint. in the calendar that you shall dress as you please, walk as you please, be served as you please. Have no fear, carissima. Do you not believe I love you?"

Of course she believed it, but would not admit it just yet. So she stripped a leaf from the shrub near and began idly to twist it.

"For that matter," she replied, "you are no doubt a past-master in loving, but here at Belmont we have so little practice." And she sighed in forlorn fashion.

"I swear to you," urged Gratiano, mounting one of the steps, "that till I met you I never loved."

She raised drooping lids just high enough to let him see the smouldering depths of black eyes beneath. "Nor ever told a woman you did so?" she demanded.

He did not answer, unable to lie in so wholesale a manner.

Nerissa frowned. "After all," she summed up, "the holy nuns are probably right. Men are born but to deceive silly women, and it is better to forswear their company altogether."

So incongruous a sentiment, coming from lips plainly created for kisses, set Gratiano laughing.

"Monna Nerissa," he retorted, "I shall certainly become a monk the day that sees you take the veil."

She was offended by his levity and tilted her chin with lofty disdain.

"After all," said she, "it is no such very unlikely happening, since I have vowed never to wed the man of my choice till my mistress marries hers."

Gratiano's face grew glum.

"What difference can that make to your lady?" he urged. "If she be sick or sad, will it restore her to see you sick and sad, too?"

Nerissa shrugged her dainty shoulders.

"I am no lawyer to stand arguing," she declared, "but I'll not wed, leaving my dear lady to plait Saint

Catherine's tresses alone. You will not argue against a vow, Signior."

"At least I deplore it," groaned Gratiano, "for till now I congratulated myself that no barrier lay between me and my love such as makes that of Bassanio and the Lady Portia a thing of hopes and fears, with fear outstripping hope."

"Fie! You speak confidently of my love, Messer Self-Assurance."

He came up another step, and not attempting to take her hand, boldly encircled a slim waist with his arm.

"Carissima," he whispered very earnestly, "I love you, and I have dared to read an answering passion in those sweet eyes. Look at me, Nerissa, and tell me I have read aright."

She hesitated between fleeing up to the shelter of the arbor and obeying; and perhaps the dread that she might, after all, lose a lover in her devotion to a mistress made her kind, for she looked down into the smiling, handsome face a little below the level of her own, and gave him a silent answer.

"Nerissa!" he cried, and then and there would have folded her in his arms.

But this the little coquette would not allow. She must be sparing of her favors if she intended to keep her vow; so she slipped from and past him, reaching the lawn before he had fully realized his arms were empty.

"Why are you cruel?" he complained. "Why will you not listen, Nerissa? Is not the tale of a man's love sweet to you? Why should we not enjoy a sunlit hour? What in life shall ever be found so sweet again?

You must not deny me, by your own love. Come back."

He held out his arms, but she only shook her head.

"No, no," she reiterated—the more stubbornly because her heart cried "Yes, yes."—"I have told you my vow, and lay command upon you not to speak to me of love till after this momentous choice to which your friend the Lord Bassanio will be going at once in company with my lady."

Gratiano came slowly down the steps.

"The choice?" he echoed. "Is it indeed to be made to-day?"

He had not realized what a grave occasion this was till he heard Nerissa's vow.

"Already," declared Nerissa, "we have lingered too long in selfish dalliance. Without loss of a moment I must go in to my mistress, who will need me sorely, even if the Lord Bassanio be so cool-blooded that he desires not the support of a friend in such an hour of crisis."

"I blame myself," replied Gratiano, "that I was not with him before. But, Nerissa——"

"Yes, illustrious?"

"You are not—in earnest about—a vow?"

"Indeed, Signior, I am not accustomed to use lightness in such grave matters. If the Lady Portia does not wed the Lord Bassanio she vows none shall have her but Holy Church, whom she will wed straightway. And as I have vowed to follow my lady's example in all things, it remains that if she weds not, I must remain maid and attend her to the nearest convent."

Gratiano groaned aloud.

"Oh, rash vow!" he complained. "What issues are at stake here? If the choice—if the choice——"

Then natural optimism overcame bitter dread.

"If," he whispered, "the choice is happy, and Bassanio weds the Lady Portia?"

. .The dimples flashed over his companion's face, though she answered demurely.

"Why, Signior, I have vowed to make a double bridal of it, if so be I do not have to sing 'hey nonny' for a groom."

And thus far Gratiano was forced to be content.

CHAPTER XXIII

"SO I go to find fortune or disaster. You'll wish me well, Gratiano?"

"With all my heart, Bassanio."

The two young men gripped hands, then in silence turned towards the marble staircase which led down to the great hall, where Portia already awaited them, with Nerissa by her side, and the usual throng of attendants in the background.

It seemed fitting that the destiny of so fair and wealthy a lady should be chosen with due pomp and state, though in this case the aspiring bridegroom came very slenderly attended.

Yet he made a gallant figure as he stepped forward, the white cloth cloak worn only on great occasions flung back over one shoulder, jewels sparkling at his collar and upon his sword hilt. Portia herself was a veritable queen in crimson velvet gown broidered most gorgeously with delicate needlework, long sleeves of gold tissue hanging loose from her shoulders, the under sleeves of soft embroidered satin. Her long veil floated to the hem of her dress and she carried a fan of ostrich feathers.

A prize indeed—to be won or lost this day.

No wonder Bassanio's heart beat till its throbs threatened to suffocate him.

Low he bowed over the lady's hand after one swift glance into her flushed and lovely face.

(224)

"You are prepared," she whispered, "to take an oath which binds you to perpetual bachelorhood if you lose me?"

"I am well prepared," he answered, in the same low tones. "Since if I lose you I shall never desire another woman for my wife."

She sighed, tears filling her blue eyes. At the moment she could only read tragedy into her father's decree.

Gratiano had moved to Nerissa's side. He was a far gayer figure than his friend, since, not belonging to the *nobili*, he was not restricted as to dress, and wore doublet and cloak of turquoise color with hose of white and yellow.

Nerissa had no words for him—but her eyes were as tender as they were anxious, showing how much she too staked on this venture.

"Let me come to my fortune and the caskets," urged Bassanio, seeing a certain reluctance on his lady's part.

She took his offered hand, signing to her servants to precede them, and thus allowed Bassanio to lead her to the dais-like seat where she had so often sat of late with very different hopes and fears animating her breast.

"While he makes his choice let music sound," she commanded old Florio. "Silence is terrible whilst we sit or stand around, holding our breaths in fear, too numb for prayer. In music, if he fails—Bassanio must not fail—but if he does he makes a swan-like end, fading in music. Whilst if he wins, what so befitting as sweet strains heralding the king new-crowned, who turns to meet the homage of his servants?"

Tears and laughter were on the speaker's face, her little hands clasped passionately upon her knee, where lay her fan. She could not look towards Bassanio at

15

first as he approached the table from before which the curtains had been drawn back.

At her desire soft strains of music, played by unseen musicians, filled the room and a child's sweet treble sounded clear and lute-like from the adjoining balcony.

Portia turned her head, gazing dim-eyed towards the window, through the open casement of which the music drifted in.

> Tell me where is fancy bred,
> Or in the heart, or in the head?
> How begot, how nourished?
>
> It is engendered in the eyes,
> With gazing fed; and fancy dies
> In the cradle where it lies;
> Let us all ring fancy's knell;
> I'll begin it—Ding, dong, bell,
> Ding ... dong ... bell.

The last echoes sounded faintly. The music was hushed. Portia di Nerlini was leaning forward now, her fan unheeded at her feet; one hand gripped the gilt side of her chair, the other supported her chin as she rested her elbow on her knee. She was unconscious that the music had ceased, unconscious that her servants stood around watching with curious gaze, unconscious that little Nerissa had turned aside and instinctively clasped her lover's hands as though seeking encouragement in their close pressure; all Portia saw or understood was that the man who held her heart and had yielded her the treasure of his own, stood there faced by a dead man's irrevocable decree. From casket to casket Bassanio moved, neither irresolute nor halting, though it was plain he communed inwardly with himself.

"Here choose I. Joy be the consequence."

He had passed by the golden casket, though long had he halted there, seeing the glittering ornament of the precious metal for which since the world's foundation men had risked their lives in vain service.

He would not, however, be deceived by outward seeming. The food of Midas, hard, inexorable gold, was little to him in such a search. Nor would he look long on the paler luster of the silver casket, but laid a firm hand upon the unattractive casket of lead.

"Here choose I," said he simply. "Joy be the consequence."

But Portia had sunk back into her chair, her face covered by her hands as though a sudden flare of sunshine had dazzled her, whilst Nerissa was weeping with her pretty face hidden against Gratiano's shoulder.

So joy at times counterfeits pain in her expression. Hardly had Bassanio raised the lid of the leaden casket than Portia at least had recovered from that first overmastering ecstasy of joy.

With clasped hands she leaned forward, light and laughter transforming the anxious woman to the very embodiment of girlish happiness. He had won! He had won! And the crowning joy of happiness was theirs.

Her pulses throbbed in tumultuous glee, the color ebbed and flowed in her cheeks, her eyes were as the heavens on a spring morning.

As for Bassanio, he had scarcely realized his good fortune yet, though in his hand he held a portrait which should instantly have told him the truth.

"Portia," he whispered, as pictured eyes looked up in shy innocence to his. "Fair Portia's counterfeit. Her very self. Why, the eyes have her trick of smiling

to the life, and here in her hairs the painter plays the
spider; weaving a golden mesh to entrap the hearts
of men, faster than gnats in cobwebs.   But her eyes!
How could he see to do them? ̦ Having made one,
methinks, it should have power to steal both his and
leave itself unfurnished.` Yet how poor my praise for
such an object, and how poor an object in comparison
with its living substance!   And here's the scroll to
acquaint me with my fortune."

Drawing a deep breath, the impatient lover unrolled
the parchment, and turning for the first time towards
Portia, read aloud its brief contents:

> You that choose not by the view,
> Chance as fair, and choose as true!
> Since this fortune falls to you,
> Be content, and seek no more.
> If you be well pleas'd by this,
> And hold your fortune for your bliss,
> Turn you where your lady is,
> And claim her with a loving kiss.

The scroll was laid aside, and Bassanio, flushed and
eager, wholly oblivious of the many gazers, came straight
to his lady's side.

She had risen to meet him, an answering flame in her
beautiful eyes; and so they stood, like children too
bewildered by their happiness to know at first how to
take it for their own.

Then Bassanio's hands went out, clasping those so
ready to find shelter in his grasp.

"Is it true?" he asked, in an oddly choked voice,
never having realized the full horror of his fears till he
saw them vanish into oblivion.   "Am I so blessed?

Thrice fair lady, I cannot believe this great good fortune until you confirm it with your own sweet lips."

He saw those same red lips, parted in dewy fragrance, mutely echoing the invitation of the written scroll, and without more ado stooped, thus sealing that strange betrothal.

One by one the attendants moved away, filing through the door, whilst the heavy velvet curtain fell in place behind Florio, the last to go saving only Gratiano and Nerissa, who, intent on their own affairs, had moved towards the balcony.

"My lady," whispered Bassanio, and looked so deep into the blue depths of her eyes that surely he must have learned all their owner's secrets, so there was no need for the question a lover never tires of asking.

"You love me?"

She leaned towards him. "Do I not, my lord?" she murmured. "Cannot you answer me?"

He laughed very softly, with the reverence of one who laughs for joy in the sacred precincts of a church.

"I am giddy with happiness. Dazed by sudden fortune," he confessed. "So that till you tell me all the tale of your love I cannot believe it. Words are empty things. Thus I say, 'Portia di Nerlini is my promised wife. To-day I have won her by a fortunate choice.' Yet that tells me little of my happiness. So teach me, gentle lady, so that I may believe and enter into the kingdom of your heart."

She laughed, a little tremulous laugh, no longer the stately lady of Belmont, who had awed so many a greedy suitor for her wealth, but the young girl, all innocent of the great world, ignorant too of many things save the secret of her heart.

"You see me, Lord Bassanio," she said, standing so close that his arm stole naturally about her slender waist, "here where I stand, such as I am. For myself I would not be ambitious. Yet for your sake, whom I love so well, I would be a thousand times more fair, ten thousand times more rich, exceeding in virtues, beauties, friends, all that I am or have—for you, because I am yours. And yet you take me as I am, an un-lessoned girl, unschooled, unpractised; happy in this, that I am not too old to learn. Happier too in not being too dull of wit to learn, and happiest of all in committing myself to your care, my governor and king, to whom I and all I have belong. Till now, see, Bassanio, I was lord of this mansion, master of my ser-vants, queen over myself. But now this house, these servants and this same myself are yours, my lord. I give them with this ring, which, when you part from, lose or give away, I shall know that Bassanio has no more love to bestow upon his Portia."

So she spoke, pride, which so many had been wont to condemn in her, abased, self-humbled before the shrine of love.

Being of a generous nature she showed it now by such sweet humility that would not let this dear lover feel the shame of being her pensioner, looking to the bounty of her wealth on which to live.

Knowing his poverty and straitened circumstances, she gave royally, kneeling as a subject to bestow her crown. And never herself more truly regal than in her self-abnegation.

Womanhood crowned! So stood she in her sweet perfection before the man whose great love grew to something akin to worship as she showed him more clearly the value of his prize.

Could he answer her? Could he tell her that if he were king she must be empress-queen, reigning forever in his heart?

Words were so poor and weak in such an ecstasy. Life's cup brimming with a surfeit of happiness so that he became dumb for lack of adequate language.

So together they stood, locked in a close embrace, apart, aloof from all the world, their eyes telling each other of joy transcendent.

Then Bassanio spoke.

"Lady," he whispered, as he set the ring with its single splendid sapphire upon his finger, "I cannot show you all my heart, nay, not in a lifetime of devotion. But this you shall know, if this ring parts from this finger you shall be certain that Bassanio is dead. No enemy but death shall rob me of so fair a gift."

Slowly their arms unclasped—since one cannot stay forever in that seventh heaven where none may dare intrude; and in turning, they found Nerissa close beside them, with Gratiano holding her hand as though he feared to lose her.

Nerissa's piquant face was bright with smiles, and be sure she was spokeswoman!

"My lord and lady," she cried, "it is now our turn that have stood by and seen our wishes prosper, to cry good joy. Good joy, my lord and lady!"

Portia laughed, and pulling the girl to her side, kissed her very kindly.

"My lord and my gentle lady," repeated Gratiano, slyly gay, yet withal a trifle sheepish too, as men are on such occasion of speech-making, "I wish you all the joy that you can wish; for I am sure you can wish none from me. And may I ask when you mean to solemnize

this marriage, which is in the making? For, by your
leave, I should like to wed at the same time."

Bassanio struck him a merry blow on the back.

"With all my heart, friend," cried he, "if you can
get a wife."

And he looked with some amusement towards Nerissa
who was whispering secrets in her lady's ear.

"I thank you," retorted Gratiano, with whimsical
humor. "You yourself have got me one. My eyes,
Bassanio, can look as swift as yours. You saw the mistress—I beheld the maid. You loved—I loved. In
more still we were alike. Your fortune stood upon the
caskets there. And so did mine. For in wooing and
swearing devotion—till my very roof was dry with oaths
of love—at last I got a promise of this fair one here to
have her love if you won that of her mistress and her
mistress's self."

Bassanio held his sides with laughter.

Per Bacco! It was good to laugh now, be free to
laugh, knowing the world was good, love better and
Portia best and dearest of all.

So he could find jest in hearing how past anxieties
had been shared by this anxious friend, since now love
and happiness rang joy bells all around.

"Is this true, Nerissa?" asked Portia, her own fair
face mirroring her lord's merriment.

Nerissa hung her head, though no whit abashed.

"Madam, it is," she confessed; "so you stand pleased
withal."

"And do you, Gratiano," demanded Basssanio, with
much gravity, "mean good faith?"

He had heard of certain merry escapades on his
friend's part in Venice.

, "Why, yes, indeed," quoth the latter, with much fervor, taking his sweetheart's hand.

"Well then," cried Bassanio heartily, "our feast shall be much honored by your marriage; and of this same marriage and its fixing we must talk, sweet, presently, when you walk with me in the garden."

He took his lady's hand, for though vastly pleased by the tale of these other loves, his own had first place in his mind, whilst yet the wonder of it was on him.

So, leaving the others to follow at their pleasure, he led Portia towards the balcony and thence to the garden, where shaded paths tempted lovers' confidences and promised coveted seclusion from unwelcome interrupttion.

Yet, alas for selfish desire! since scarcely had they reached the spot where a mighty ilex stood sentinel to a wilderness walk than Portia called her companion's attention to two distant figures which approached the mansion up the long avenue.

Bassanio, none too pleased, shaded his eyes against the slanting rays of sunlight, than gave a low exclamation of surprise.

"If I be not deceived," quoth he, "it is one Lorenzo Fortunato, a friend of mine, sweet Portia, and his wife, a Jewess named Jessica—and a very gentle lady."

CHAPTER XXIV

AN ILL-OMENED MESSENGER

BASSANIO'S guess had been correct; it was Lorenzo Fortunato himself who came towards them across the lawns, whilst his companion, so closely veiled that her features could not be seen, halted under an acacia tree as though her courage had failed—or mayhap fearing that her presence might not be welcome.

Lorenzo seemed to possess far less of his customary swagger, and whilst he bowed very low before the lady of Belmont, he regarded Bassanio with an interrogatory glance which sought to read the riddle of the other's mind and know whether he had been presumptuous in taking advantage of a casual invitation.

But Bassanio's greeting quickly dispelled all doubts.

"Why, good Lorenzo," he cried, taking the other's hand in his own. "We meet at Belmont in a happy hour. Welcome hither. Sweet Portia, you see I take your office in bidding a guest welcome to your home with no other introduction than that he is my friend."

Portia di Nerlini came forward, a very gracious lady, Lorenzo thought, as he bowed again.

"You are indeed welcome, Signior," she said gently, one hand slipped within the curve of Bassanio's arm, "as all my lord's friends shall be in this his home. He says truly that you come in a happy hour since already we think of preparations for a speedy marriage. We shall hope to keep you with us to witness your friend's——"

(234)

"Most unmerited happiness," added Bassanio, kissing her with lover-like ardor. "As this gentleman will understand, being, as I guess, newly wed himself. You shall beg your lady, Lorenzo, to allow us the honor of her acquaintance. Ah, but here she comes, brought by a kindly friend."

Gratiano and Nerissa had approached the shy stranger, who had been seized by a fit of sudden nervousness, feeling herself alien amongst these fine friends of her husband.

But shyness could not be long retained under Nerissa's sunny influence, and Jessica had already been persuaded to draw aside her suffocating veil and allow her dark, beautiful face to be seen.

Portia advanced at once to meet her, her simple friendliness chasing away all the stranger's fears of the lady who had appeared so magnificent and imposing at a distance.

"You are weary, poor child," said Portia kindly. "Nerissa, you shall take her within doors presently, for I wager sleep has been stranger this long time from her eyes."

But Jessica shook her head, shrinking back to her husband's side.

"Indeed, madam, I am not weary," she confessed, "only—only afraid, lest you might have refused us asylum."

Her dark eyes were haunted by swift fear as she glanced up at Lorenzo, who, with one arm protectingly about her, asked leave to tell his tale.

"Why, most certainly," cried Portia. "We are most eager to hear, and if you will neither eat nor sleep at present, let us rest and listen to what I do not doubt will prove to have been strange adventures."

"In sooth I'll wager that," added Bassanio, as he followed with the others to where, under a wide-branched tree, seats were invitingly spread with cushions and brightly-striped rugs.

Very briefly Lorenzo related, for the benefit of the Lady of Belmont, the story of how he and Jessica had stolen away from Venice, and without more adventures than their fears engendered at the thought of pursuit, they reached Genoa, where the priest, whose services Lorenzo had before engaged, was awaiting them.

This Father Lawrence had first baptized Jessica into the Christian faith before wedding her to the eager lover. Then, because Genoa seemed a fair city to them, and their happiness complete, they had lingered there week after week, merry as children newly escaped from the discipline of school. Never in all her secluded life in the old corner house of Venice had Jessica dreamed of all the glittering splendor of life beyond, and Lorenzo had never tired of waking new wonder in the dark eyes of his little bride.

But alas! The dream was rudely dispelled on the day when Lorenzo returned home to the vine-clad inn, where Monna Bianca, the plump, kindly landlady, had mothered his child-wife since her first coming to Genoa, and brought the news that Aaron Tubal was in the city.

Jessica had remained indoors all next day, trembling and anxious because Lorenzo so long delayed his return. She knew something of Tubal's fierce humor, and also that her father had promised her to this friend of his in marriage.

Somehow Genoa no longer appeared a place of sunshine and laughter, but full of mournful dirges and ill omen. At last Lorenzo came, tried to kiss away the many terrors on a small, pale face, but finally confessed that from what he had gleaned of one and another, Tubal was ransacking the city in search of them, nor did there seem any doubt as to his temper.

"Let us go," Jessica had entreated, clinging to her young husband. "He is a very terrible man. He will perhaps kill you and then there is nothing but death before me."

It was then that Lorenzo had remembered Bassanio's laughing invitation to Belmont; and, desperate though it was, had determined to come and beg asylum here till the search for his wife had abated. Perhaps later he would be able to settle in Padua or Verona, in both of which towns he possessed friends. He did not suggest Venice, yet Bassanio, seeing the shadow on his merry face, guessed that this light-hearted friend felt his exile keenly, whilst Portia, looking from one to the other, was convinced that the groom counted all well lost for the sake of such a bride.

It was a romance such as could not fail to appeal to any woman's heart, and when Lorenzo had finished with many expressions of gratitude for the generous welcome they had not dared to hope for, Portia took Jessica's hand, kissing her dark cheek again, telling her that neither she nor her husband need have any more fears.

"You shall both remain here so long as you choose," she promised, "and we shall be glad of your company, my lord and I."

Whereupon she looked across to Bassanio, who was regarding her with tenderest affection, noting her kindness to this stranger.

It was Lorenzo who put the diffident question regarding his friend's fortune, and was told the tale of how that very day had been witness to Bassanio's happiness.

The story of the caskets was retold by those who sat beneath the trees there on the peaceful lawns, whilst twilight crept in gray beauty over a fair scene, and Portia would have risen, declaring it to be time to return to the palazzo and prepare for supper, had not the appearance of Florio on the terrace changed the current of their thoughts.

The old steward bowed low before his mistress—since these were early days to grow accustomed to the presence of a new lord.

"A messenger from Venice, Signora," he averred, "on very urgent business to my Lord Bassanio."

The name brought recollection in the utterance, and Florio made up for neglect by many bows in Bassanio's direction.

Jessica drew closer to Portia's side.

"It may be Tubal," she breathed fearfully. "Before now he will have returned to Venice and may have guessed of our coming here."

"What name gave the messenger?" asked Bassanio, fingering the dagger in his girdle.

Again Florio bowed.

"Messer Salarino, an' it please you, illustrious," he replied.

Bassanio started. "*Salarino!*" he echoed in surprise. "Santa Maria! What brings the merchant from Venice? I hope it bodes no ill for Antonio. I beseech you bring him hither without loss of time."

"You see," whispered Portia to Jessica, "there is no reason for your fears. This messenger is known to my Lord Bassanio."

"Known well indeed," replied the latter. "But what can he want here? Has he come—too late—to discover the secret of the caskets?"

He smiled whimsically at Portia as he spoke, but the smile could not hide the deeper anxiety of his eyes, nor did he really suppose the sedate Salarino to have come on any such errand.

The group on the lawn sat or stood together watching the pompous Florio escort the visitor towards them with due ceremony.

Bassanio went forward to meet one who was merely his friend since he was that of Antonio.

"Your hand, amico," said he genially, contriving to cry down the growing fear which sight of Salarino's grave face quickened within him.

"What's the news from Venice? How doth that royal merchant, good Antonio? I know he will be glad to hear of our success. We are the Jasons—we have won the fleece."

Salarino bowed to the seated ladies, grasped hands with Gratiano, and after a few brief words of congratulations, turned, gloomy-eyed, to Bassanio.

"Would you had won the fleece that Antonio hath lost," he replied, handing the other a sealed parchment.

Bassanio hastily broke the seal, moving apart from the rest, as, with trembling fingers, he unrolled the scroll of paper.

Gratiano, paying small heed to Salarino's grave manner, took the latter by the elbow, chatting gayly of how he had lighted on a bridal group. To Gratiano the world was a golden arcadia just now, all piping, dancing, kissing and vowing of devotion.

But Portia had risen and was moving towards her lover.

"See," she urged, looking back towards her companions. "There is ill news indeed in that paper. How pale Bassanio grows! All color drained from his cheeks! Alack! This must be tidings of some dear friend's death. Poor Bassanio, a black death on a golden eve. This is sad, indeed."

She reached Bassanio's side, taking his arm.

"With leave, dear lord," she whispered, in tenderest sympathy. "Will you not tell me your trouble, since I am half yourself to share sorrow and joy together?"

He looked at her, too dazed at first for her comfort to reach him, whilst slowly he raised his hand to his forehead, pushing back his cap and wiping aside the beads of sweat which had gathered on his brow.

"Sweet Portia," he stammered. "Ah, dear, this is ill news indeed. The cruelest words that ever blotted paper though penned by a hand of love. Gentle lady, do you recall how, when I first confessed my love to you, I told you frankly that I was very poor? All that I could claim was nobility of birth. I am a noble of Venice—but that is sum and total of all my possessions."

"What matter?" replied Portia gently. "Since I am rich and all I have is yours."

He took her hand, raising it to his lips.

"Alas!" he sighed, "there is more to tell. I should have told you I was worse than nothing. I am in debt, lady. Worse still. My friend, to furnish me with the ducats to come hither, bound himself to—to a Jew. That Jew is Jessica's father. Another time you shall learn what he is besides; how lost to all semblance of humanity in his lust for as foul a vengeance as ever was conceived by a man. Oh, the agony of this! It stuns me with its swift horror. Antonio in danger.

Antonio ruined. Antonio in prison for my sake. Antonio in danger of a bloody death."

The speaker wrung his hands, tears filled his eyes, he was so totally unstrung that he scarcely knew what he said or did.

Even Portia was powerless to soothe such grief, and as she listened to the explanation which Bassanio gave, her own cheeks paled and her blue eyes dilated with horror.

Bassanio turned feverishly to Salarino.

"Is it true, Salarino?" he cried. "Is it true? Have all our poor Antonio's ventures failed? What!—not *one* hit? From Tripolis, from Mexico and England? From Lisbon, Barbary and India—and not one vessel escaped shipwreck or the pirates?"

Salarino shook his head.

"Alas! not one," he replied. "Besides, I fear if he now had the money to discharge the Jew, the latter would not take it. He seems to have a rancorous hate against Antonio, which sees the light now that he counts to have him in his power. Never has a man been known to be so keen and greedy in seizing on his victim. Night and day he haunts the Ducal Palace, crying for justice, railing that if he does not get it, he impeaches the freedom of the state. None in Venice can talk or think of anything but this business which seems unique in its character."

"But something must be done," cried Bassanio, striking his hands fiercely together. "The Duke could not permit the iniquity of this bond's fulfilment—to hack the life from an honored and reputed citizen in payment of a bond which Shylock himself mocked at as a pleasant jest."

16

"He does not term it so now," retorted Salarino grimly. "The fellow is like nothing but a lean gray wolf, which howls about a lonesome house during winter nights. He'll have his bond, he cries, defying all Venice to rob him of his due."

"Have any tried to persuade him?" asked Portia. "Have they shown him the uselessness of such revenge?"

Salarino bowed. "Why," quoth he, "for that matter all Venice has been at the task of 'suasion. A deputation of twenty merchants waited on him. His only answer was, 'I claim my bond.' The magnificoes of greatest port urged mercy and a more human spirit—he would have none of either. The Duke himself tried to argue with him. 'My bond—and justice,' was all the answer. It is that bond—or rather Antonio's life—for which he alone appears to thirst."

All shuddered as they listened to the hideous tale. Whilst Jessica raised her veil to speak.

"When—I was with him," she faltered, "I have heard him swear to Tubal and Chus, his countrymen, that he would rather have Antonio's flesh than twenty times the value of the sum he owed him."

Silence followed this speech.

It was to all those who stood on that shadowed lawn as though they gazed upon some fearful picture where the hand of genius portrayed hate personified, a deep and treasured hate which has waited long and patiently for fulfilment.

At last Portia spoke.

"What sum owes he the Jew?"

Bassanio raised a haggard face to hers.

"Three thousand ducats," he muttered, "borrowed for me. Three thousand ducats." His chin sank for-

ward on his breast.   This grief was greater than he
could bear.

Love and despair for this closest, dearest friend even
obscured the bright dream of love which had come so
near to fulfilment to-day.

Portia leaned forward, touching his arm.

"You love him?" she asked softly.

"Love him!"   Bassanio's laugh was bitter.   "He is
the dearest friend to me," he goaned, "the kindest man,
the noblest spirit that ever breathed.   When yet did
Antonio think of himself?   Never, I fancy.   Always of
others, always for others he spends himself, his life, his
substance.   The only reason he possesses this enemy is
because he took too much pity on the victims of greedy
avarice.   Three thousand ducats!   How should they
weigh against the life of an Antonio?"

"Pay the Jew six thousand," cried Portia, her face
flushing, her eyes kindling.   "Double six thousand and
then treble that, before a friend of this description shall
lose a hair through Bassanio's fault.   You shall have
gold, dear lord, to pay the petty debt twenty times
over.   When it is paid bring your true friend along—
that he may be your wife's friend too."

Bassanio caught her outstretched hands, pressing
them to his heart.

"Sweetest of ladies," he murmured, "how can I thank
you for this generous love?   It is true I must go to
Venice.   See, shall I read you this letter which claims
that necessity?   So will you find unselfish sacrifice an
easier thing."

"There is no sacrifice in speeding you to such a
duty," replied Portia.   "Yet, read me his letter, for I
would know all I may of such a man as this Antonio."

Bassanio unrolled the parchment, reading the contents in a voice which halted and grew husky with emotion.

"Sweet Bassanio, my ships have all miscarried, my creditors grow cruel, my estate is very low, my bond to the Jew is forfeit; and since, in paying it, it is impossible I should live, all debts are cleared between you and me. Yet—if I might but see you at my death: notwithstanding, use your pleasure; if your love do not persuade you to come, let not my letter."

Tears stood in Portia di Nerlini's eyes as she listened. Nerissa was sobbing in helpless, tender-hearted fashion, whilst Jessica sat, shamed beyond expression, as though she were some leper amongst these others, since she must call Shylock the Jew her father.

"Listen, Bassanio," quoth Portia very gravely. "First let us go to church, where you shall wed with me—Gratiano with his Nerissa; and from the church's door we'll speed you on your way to Venice. Save your friend, if that be possible, then return, both of you, to claim those who shall be praying for your good success."

Bassanio bowed his head.

"If you will do this, and let me so play my part," he whispered, "be sure there'll be no tarrying by the way, sweet Portia. Let me but call you wife and save Antonio, I do not think the world will know a happier man than your Bassanio."

"Saving one Gratiano," whispered the latter in Nerissa's ear. "Tell me, sweet, are you as ever obedient to your mistress' will?"

And Nerissa, smiling through her tears, gave mute assent.

CHAPTER XXV

"**H**E has gone," murmured Portia, and sighed as she looked out upon the velvet darkness of the night, "but he will return."

Looking up into the mysterious vault of the curtained skies she saw a star, and smiled the rapt smile of one whose heart sings an unworded psalm. For the time she had forgotten Antonio and threatened tragedy. Only she remembered that her prayers had been answered, and Love, bright-winged and eagle-eyed, stood on the threshold of her life.

After all, her father had been wise—or had it been some clearer inspiration conceived in the chill atmosphere of death which gazed beyond to where all things lie plainly discerned in futurity?

Had he known that he should give her love, shielding her from all spurious imitations such as fifty suitors had offered at her feet?

Love! She thought of the men who had come and gone, men of various nationalities, aspirations, ambitions, who had vowed their vows, pleaded their faith and gone, unregretted by the woman whose fortune they came to win.

She shuddered as she thought of the importunate wooing of Niccolo Grimani, and how nearly he had captured her by unknightly fraud and scheming. It was then that she saw her Bassanio—the gallant hero of every

(245)

maid's dreams—come to her in the flesh, to be loved as
soon as seen, to woo and win her as no maid had hereto-
fore been won; and to leave her at her own command
on the day which had seen her betrothal and wedding,
to perform a duty claimed by friendship's bond.   Aye!
and a double bond it seemed, since but for Antonio her
Bassanio—brought low by extravagance confessed—
would have lacked the means to come to her, and in
coming, save her from an ignoble thief, to be—his own
dear wife.

No wonder Portia smiled as she watched that star,
which shone down so clearly with its golden beam to
touch and stir her heart.

Love!   Yes, it was hers—and she at last was rich, who
before in the midst of wealth had deemed herself poor.

Then she sighed, growing sad as she drooped her
head over folded hands.

Could she laugh whilst her lord wept?   Smile when he
grieved?

And supposing this friend should die—killed by the
cruelest vengeance ever conceived by human brain?
Antonio was Bassanio's dearest friend, worthy of all
loving regard.   She felt him to be so, judging him by his
friendship, and a sudden wrath rose in her heart against
this Shylock who had so marred the perfection of her
wedding day.

If she could but save Antonio!   If she could but
bring gladness in place of despair to her Bassanio!

All her woman's wit, her courage and that daring
which had strengthened in her during the past months
of a difficult independence and loneliness rose to help
Portia di Nerlini in her dreaming.

And what a dream it was!   Fantastic—shadowy at

first, bringing reluctance to combat impetuosity, hesitancy to cling to the skirts of rash urging, but gradually a definite purpose growing out of the chaos, whilst tightening lips, lurking laughter and the erect poise of a proud little head told that what Portia di Nerlini had resolved on finally would not easily be relinquished. And she told herself the dream should become reality. Was there then any question of drawing back?

"There is no time," whispered the girl very softly to herself, "no time for deliberation, no time to look this way and that, questioning of expediency, maidenly modesty, all those warring tales which would hold a maid back from the swift prompting of a purpose. Blessed St. Ursula guide me in this!—since it is for the salvation of one man and love of another. For Bassanio, known and loved. For Antonio, unknown, but deeply reverenced. Come, I'll think no more—but act—as I think Bassanio my husband would wish me."

She laughed softly, not rebuking herself this time for undue levity, whilst, striking a bell which stood on a table near, she summoned a servant.

"Bid Stephano speak with me," she commanded peremptorily, and the woman hurried away wondering as to her mistress' pleasure.

Meantime, Portia awaited the coming of a trusted messenger with impatience. Like most women she was inclined to rush at all enterprises without due reflection, fretting till her purpose was accomplished.

But in this case there was excuse for her restlessness, since haste was necessary to her design.

Not that Stephano kept her long waiting, and his mistress, beckoning him forward, bade him come near, since she would entrust him with a service which was very private.

Stephano, a straight-limbed young Italian, clad in the dark blue livery of the Nerlinis, bowed low. Like the rest of the servants he was devoted to his beautiful mistress for whom he would gladly have laid down his life.

"Attend very carefully to my instructions, good Stephano," commanded the Lady Portia kindly. "I have ever found thee honest, true and faithful; let me find thee so still. Here is a letter. Guard it carefully, and with all possible despatch hasten to Padua. Thou wilt be ready to start within the hour?"

The Italian's black eyes flashed. "I shall be on my way when I leave your presence, noble Signora," he replied quietly.

"Good. I can trust thee, Stephano, to use all possible despatch, since not only the life of a man but much of thy mistress' happiness depends upon it; and when thou hast reached Padua seek out the house of my cousin, Dr. Bellario. Give this packet into his hand. He will give thee his answer together with notes and garments. Attend carefully to his instructions and bring all he gives thee to the inn which stands close to the common ferry trading with Venice. Thou knowest the place?"

Stephano colored. "Yes, lady," he replied. "It is known as the sign of the 'Golden Fig.'"

Portia smiled, for she guessed that the fellow's confusion could have been explained by the fact that Monna Francesca—though a widow of three years' standing— was as pretty as many a sly-eyed contadina who took her fruits and vegetables across the ferry to the market places of Venice.

"Do not forget all that I bid you," she repeated, "for indeed it is very urgent, and I would have you thinking more of the illustrious Signior Bellario's messages than the chances of Monna Francesca being kind."

Whereat Stephano blushed still more furiously, vowing that a dozen Francescas, nay, a hundred! could not possess the power of misdirecting a thought which should be given to duty.

"Why, then, you're a very Stoic," smiled his mistress, "or do not know what a will-o'-the-wisp of torment true love may be. Heigho! How wise one can grow in a day!"

She laughed gayly, bidding Stephano begone.

"Swiftness, discretion and a speedy meeting with me at the 'Golden Fig,' with full weight of directions from the Signor Bellario, will win thee a golden guerdon of thanks, good knave," said she, with so much winning grace that Stephano thought of nothing but pleasing so sweet a lady, as he hurried forth on that midnight errand, which in those days of insecure and bandit-fested roads was by no means an easy one.

Portia, left alone once more, drew a heavy breath, as one who having taken a daring plunge or leap, looks back wondering at her own temerity.

The messenger was sent. Would she have called him back? Not she! Too much hung on the issue of this adventure which she would undertake for love's sake.

"You called me, lady?"

The door closed softly upon Nerissa, who stole forward to her mistress' side.

Portia stretched out her hand and pulled the girl down to the stool by her side.

"If so," she replied, "it was my heart, for indeed I crave the company of a friend."

Nerissa laid her hands on the other's lap, bending

forward so that the eyes of the two girls sought and found an answering gaze.

"The Signior Lorenzo and his wife have retired already?" asked the maid.

Portia nodded.

"Else, I had not left my guests?" said she. "They were very weary, so weary that little Jessica could scarcely keep her lids apart for all her efforts. I think they were glad to go to their rest undisturbed by the ghosts of any avenging pursuers. Indeed, I am sorry for the Jewess; she is sweet and gentle, loving too. Nor do I blame her for finding happiness by such daring means."

"She has found a loving husband in the venture, lady."

"I do not doubt it. As for this Tubal whom the girl fears so much, he will not think of Belmont, nor dare come hither even if he thinks of it as a possible asylum. So we will keep our pretty love-birds here, Nerissa— for kindness' sake as well as because Lorenzo is Bassanio's friend."

A smile rippled over Nerissa's piquant face.

"Ah, lady," murmured the maid, "little did we dream that the choice of caskets would bring such happiness."

"True. It was as you first said, child, an inspiration whispered in my father's ear by some guardian-angel. Yet, because I'm foolish, I shudder even now, torturing myself by such thoughts as these. 'Supposing one of those other grasping suitors had seized the leaden casket in choice'—or—'Supposing my lord Bassanio had picked the one of gold.'"

"Have no such fears, dear lady. Are you not wed already? It is not a dream that the Signior Bassanio placed that ring upon your finger whilst Gratiano set this upon mine. It is no dream that they wear our rings in change. It is no dream that we lately stood within the chapel near whilst Fra Angelo laid our hands in those of our dear lords and loves—giving us each to each."

Portia sighed.

"Was ever such betrothal or such wedding planned?" she reiterated. "And scarcely had their clasp unfolded about those hands than they had gone—these lords of ours—riding forth as though they had but one thought in their minds—and that assuredly not of the wives they left behind them."

"Gratiano told me, lady, that never was there such a bond of friendship between man and man as between Bassanio and this Antonio. He said Antonio lives but for Bassanio's sake, so close their souls are knit. I do not wonder that my Lord Bassanio was so much affected at this direful news, which hinted of swift and bloody death, compassed by scheming vengeance."

"We must scheme deeper then, Nerissa," retorted Portia eagerly. "We must plot yet more craftily than this greedy Jew. Oh, my heart! If this might be. Hold my hands closer, Nerissa, and tell me if you would be willing to win your husband's yet warmer regard?"

Nerissa blushed.

"If that might be, lady," she confessed.

"It shall be," promised Portia confidently. "Ah, Nerissa, shall I ever forget the joy of that moment when I stood but lately in the chapel near, seeing the last glow of daylight fading to darkness over the high altar, before which stood the dear old priest whom I have known and loved all my life long, and listened to his solemn blessing on the new life which lies before us now? And, whilst my heart beat, half fearful in its joy, I turned to see the lovelight in Bassanio's eyes and forthwith yielded all myself to him in loving trust.   What happiness for one who dreaded lest wealth should stand a coldly, cruel barrier to all a woman longs for!   *Love*, Nerissa— he loves me!   Is that the echo in your heart to-night?"

"Why, yes, dear lady.   I am very happy.   It is all joy to which we look.   I see no past—only a future, rose-crowned and lovely."

"Ah!" sighed Portia.   "So I told myself but now as I looked out into the velvet darkness of the night, saying, 'Bassanio loves me, my cup of happiness is full, to-morrow he returns—my loving lord.'   But then, Nerissa, alas! a black shadow fell athwart the sunshine. What if our grooms, returning to their brides, bring gloomy countenances, weeping for friendship lost, a tragedy enacted too ghastly to frame into words, though its ghost will haunt a lifetime?"

Nerissa shivered.

"It is very true," she replied; "the messenger from Venice was positive that none would turn this cruel Jew from his bloody purpose.   And if Antonio dies for sake of the money borrowed to speed Signior Bassanio to your arms, I fear the grief will rack your lord with bitter pangs and remorse."

"So much so," moaned Portia, "that at last he will say, 'but for you, lady, Antonio would have lived!'   Do I not know the canker of such thoughts?   I vow I would give my fortune to win the right to hear him say, 'But for you, Portia, Antonio would have died!'   Does not the repetition of such words thrill you to the desire for great deeds, Nerissa?"

The younger girl looked puzzled.

"I would we could help," she confessed, "and by our prayers we may.   Yet alas! what other way could there be?"

Portia laughed merrily, her dreamy, wistful mood slipping from her like a cloak.   She was the gayest and most eager of girls as she sprang to her feet, bidding her companion light candles, since she wished to unrobe to get to bed.

"What if I have work on hand that you know not of?" she demanded as she watched the taper-flare above the tall wax candles.   "Listen, Nerissa, would you see your husband before he thinks of you?"

Nerissa flushed.

"I think you would be talking in riddles, lady," she averred.

"Such a riddle," declared Portia, clasping her hands, "as you shall never unravel without the key.   Oh, Nerissa, Nerissa, what folly is in a woman's heart!   One moment I am beset with fears, weakness, regret, a hundred palpitating reproaches; the next I laugh at risk, mock at the very hint of failure, and hear the loud acclaims for victory won.   Tell me, Nerissa, do love's devices ever fail?   I do not know!   But this I'll whisper in your ear.   A woman's wit is quicker than a man's when she is put to it for clever invention.   A woman's thoughts travel post when a man's go ambling behind at a jog trot.   And a woman will find a way where a man sits down and writes an epitaph on failure."

"Which means," retorted Nerissa, coming to her lady's side, her black eyes dancing in excitement, "that you have found a way, madam, to save this worthy merchant of Venice?"

Portia danced a few steps of a stately minuet, curt-sying with wreathed arms about a well-poised head.

"An' it please you," she mimicked merrily, "I have seen a way; but what of its fashion?   You shall tell me, for instance, what sort of a man I shall seem when I don the clothes of one?   I vow that of us two I'll make the prettier fellow, turn mincing steps into a manly stride"—she set her hands on her hips and went swaggering up the room—"wear my dagger with the braver grace, and brag!   Ah, la, la, Nerissa, you shall hear me brag of frays—in which I ever have been winner—tell quaint lies of the honorable ladies who have sought my love, which, failing to attain, they have fallen sick and died, making moan of broken hearts.   You'll stand agape to hear me, Nerissa, but you'll try to copy too, so bravely shall we don our cloaks, swords, doublets and robes."

Nerissa frowned, perplexed, for this riddle was past her unmasking.

"Why, what would you be doing, lady?" she asked. "Join in some masque whilst our lords weep for a friend?"

She spoke reproachfully.

But Portia drew her down side by side with her upon her couch, and with arm entwined around the girl's waist told all the tale of how Stephano had gone in haste to Padua and would be returning by early morn to the sign of the "Golden Fig," just opposite the common ferry.

Here would Portia and her faithful maid meet him, and there at the inn—with no other confederate than Monna Francesca—would the transformation take place which would send two adventurous damsels to Venice, without loss of time, to carry out Portia's daring scheme for the saving of Antonio Cainello, and thus winning to herself a bridegroom without the shadow of grief and remorse to cloud the joy of their happiness.

"And so at dawn we leave the palazzo," cried Portia

in triumph, when all the story was related. "You shall call me very early, Nerissa, since I must make excuse to Lorenzo and Jessica for seeming rudeness in quitting guests with such claim on our hospitality."

And Nerissa was very punctual in her obedience, so that greatly to their surprise Lorenzo and Jessica found their young hostess awaiting them on the terrace when they came out next morning whilst the rosy cloudlets of dawn still lingered in the skies.

It was a fair day and Jessica had been eager to rise early and wander out into the pleasant gardens, which she had been too weary to notice on the preceding evening.

But she hung back, bashful and shy, at the unexpected sight of the Lady Portia and her maid pacing to and fro in the sunlight, wrapped in cloaks and hoods as if for traveling.

Portia came forward, however, with the kindliest of morning greetings.

"I am very glad to meet you so early," said she, "for I have pardon to crave, nor could I leave the plazzo before asking it."

"You are leaving the palazzo, Signora?" replied Lorenzo anxiously. "Then we must——"

But Portia interrupted with a sunny smile of apology.

"Pardon have I to crave," she said, "and boon to ask. I will explain. You know under what circumstances my Lord Bassanio and his friend left last night; and, alas! I fear this day will be a hard one for him, since a dear friendship is threatened with bloody dissolution. Could I be gay, then, thinking of this suffering? I am sure you, lady, and your husband here will understand that his sorrow is mine even though I do not know

the worthy gentleman whose peril is so imminent. Therefore, Nerissa and I would wish to withdraw to a convent
near till our lords return. But, though we would go
without loss of time, courtesy withholds me. So you
shall hear my boon. Will you, Signior Lorenzo, and you,
fair Jessica, look on this house and all it contains as
yours till our return? Command what you will, do as
you will, act in all things as though you were lord and lady
here. I have given my steward Florio instructions,
and you will find all obedient to your pleasure, which is
also mine."

Jessica might have hesitated, too abashed to accept so
much honor, but Lorenzo, with readier understanding,
saw the lady's need for a brief acceptance so that she
might more easily bid farewell—being in evident haste
to depart.

"Your hospitality, gracious Signora," he said, bowing
low over Portia's little hand, "is only equaled by the
generous kindness of its bestowal. Accept our humble
gratitude as we accept this very welcome offer. We will
await your return, praying it may be in a happy manner,
Heaven interposing to save our noble Antonio from a
cruel fate."

Portia inclined her head gracefully. She liked this
blue-eyed rogue, whose merry face wore tragic expression
most unnaturally. Certainly the dark-eyed little Jewess
had won a lively husband, and though a casual observer
might not have supposed their dispositions to have been
the least in tune, yet they were plainly devoted to each
other.

Slowly they moved forward together to where Portia's
coach awaited her at the head of the avenue—presum-
ably to take the lady to her convent shade.

"This Antonio," the latter observed, tentatively, "must be a very noble man; for though he is no more than a one-time wealthy merchant, yet all seem to hold him in very close esteem."

Lorenzo bowed.

"There is no nobler in all Venice," he declared, "no, not excepting the Duke himself.   He is a man of the loftiest honor combined with the kindest heart.   And though it is said that only knaves manage to win the good word of all, yet Antonio Cainello has won and deserved the love of every decent-living man or woman. His charity is of the widest, his patience untiring.   Yet, of his many friends, I am sure the Lord Bassanio is the one to hold all his heart.   If you knew the man as I do, lady, you would be prouder of your bounty, which I pray may successfully win his life from a hard creditor."

Portia glanced with quick sympathy towards Jessica. It must be hard, she thought, for the girl to hear such words against her father, though they seemed well deserved.

But Jessica had drawn the folds of her veil closer so that her face could not be seen.

The coach was reached now, and both Portia and Nerissa stepped into it.

"To meet again," cried the Lady of Belmont, leaning from the window, the veil flung back so that she could see the two who stood in the avenue watching her departure.   "And, as you say, Signior Lorenzo, may that meeting be in a happier hour—if prayers and love can win life for sweet Messer Antonio."

The last word seemed to echo in the speaker's ears, as, leaning back amongst the cushions of her coach beside the eagerly expectant Nerissa, they were rapidly

17

driven, not—as was supposed—to the Convent of St. Ursula upon the hill top, but twenty miles away to where the picturesque little inn of the "Golden Fig" stood, facing the ferry where boatmen plied a busy trade between the mainland and Venice.

CHAPTER XXVI

THE hour of triumph!

Shylock the Jew laughed as he stretched wide his arms as though embracing that elusive form of a success for which he had schemed and plotted these long months past.

He had won revenge! At least the winning was assured. Already he had tasted the sweets of his desire, and he was tasting them again as he sat alone in the deserted house awaiting the hour when he should go hence to the Court of Justice.

A lonely, deserted house, but Shylock did not think of that. He did not recall how death had knocked at his door, carrying hence—long years ago—the wife whom he had wooed in the heyday of her youth and beauty. He did not think of Leah's daughter either—*their* daughter, their little Jessica. Had he ever loved the child? Perhaps many years ago, before the gold-lust had become his one absorbing passion. To-day, however, he had neither affection for Leah's child nor curses for the daughter who had stolen his wealth and brought disgrace on his name by the renouncing of her faith and marriage with a Christian.

And yet the strongest and most powerful force in the old man's breast was his pride.

Pride of race—the implacable, tenacious pride of the Jew who saw himself apart and immeasurably superior to the rest of mankind.

(259)

Pride of wealth, in subservient degree, but real too, glorying in the power which gold gave of crushing and humbling the despised Christians.

And here was the hidden crux of his hatred to Antonio. It was as if the merchant had laid his finger on that vulnerable spot in the old man's armor and sought to wound him there.

Antonio Cainello, single-minded, charitable, upright, could not be expected to understand the tortuous windings of Shylock's pride-hardened mind. The merchant of Venice only saw the sordid usurer, who in his lust of gain trampled ruthlessly the souls and bodies of fellow-men in the mire of despair.

Cainello did not read the more complex reasons of ingrained pride which saw in every Gentile a natural enemy and persecutor. The young Venetian, in common with most Christians of those days, despised the Jewish nation, and he had plainly shown his contempt for Shylock. And there was not a scornful phrase, a mocking word, a contemptuous look, which the old Jew had not noted, treasuring it in his rancorous breast against the day of vengeance. It was as if in Antonio Cainello he saw the whole antagonistic force of Gentile hate consummated. And his hatred, nourished and cherished by months and years of brooding, blazed now in a passion which almost overwhelmed him in its intensity.

So now at last he triumphed! Pride, crushed and bruised by slight and insult, leaped in his veins, singing its pæan of exultant joy. He was on the threshold of seeing his vengeance gratified. Seated there in that lonely room of an empty house, the old man rocked to and fro, hugging himself in his ecstasy.

It was Antonio Cainello who would suffer now—the man who had cheated his malice, rescued his victims, paid the debts of those he had hoped to tread under his heel. Had he not too played the usurer; claiming no interest but that of love, so that Shylock grew sick in listening to tales of the good Antonio, the generous Antonio, the noble Antonio, who bearded Shylock on the Rialto, making a scorn and mock of him in his fiery condemnations?

But there would be neither mocks nor gibes now. Men would fear Shylock the despised Jew, who had taken slow but sure revenge on his enemy.

He would walk with head erect upon the Rialto and see others shrink back in terror, whispering, "There goes the man who had the life of Antonio Cainello because the merchant mocked him."

Shylock threw up his arms, crying a thanksgiving which to a Christian listener would have smacked of blasphemy.

His hour of triumph! Had it not already begun? He had known it to be his, when twenty of the wealthiest merchants from the Rialto had waited on him—on *him*, Shylock the Jew, offering to pay Antonio's debt, if he would forego the bond. It had seemed to those dignified Signiors that they had come to seek a gray wolf in its den, which drew back thin lips above yellow fangs screaming at them, "My bond! I'll have my bond! It is the Duke's justice."

He had had the same answer for the Duke himself when Niccolo da Ponte had summoned him to the Palace to argue with him in suave and stately manner, treating him with a courtesy which should have made Shylock forget the shame of the yellow badge he wore upon his breast.

But he did not forget it or the times Antonio the merchant had pointed to it, spitting upon it in his reviling as though to be a Jew were to be the very scum of the earth. So Shylock's lips set firm in sinister fashion as he answered the Duke that he asked for nothing but justice, and desired nothing but his bond.

It had been the same with the pleading of the mangificoes of Venice themselves, great nobles who had recognized the nobility in Antonio Cainello and called him friend. They spoke at length to Shylock, bringing forward argument after argument as to why he should show mercy; how it would be to his advantage, what profit it might bring him.

But to each and all came but one answer: "My bond. I'll have justice—and my bond. The law gives it me. I abide by the law."

So they had gone at last, merchants, magnificoes, the Duke himself, worn out by futile reasonings, seeing only a hatred so malignant, so unquenchable, that they shrank back appalled. And none could have traced that hatred by its devious courses back to the source saving Shylock himself.

But Shylock knew—and now he made his offering to that outraged pride which, after all, was his birthright.

From across the waters of the lagoon, floating on the breeze down the narrower precincts of the canal, came the sound of the bronze hammers of San Marco's great clock, striking the hour. Shylock rose, set his yellow turban more closely on his head, and shuffled towards a walnut-wood chest which stood in one corner of the room. Raising the lid he drew forth a long knife. It had been lately sharpened and polished, so that it lay there in an open leather case like a streak of silver in a dark place.

There was a wicked glitter on the blade as Shylock held it aloft, staring at it fondly, as a young mother might look on the crowing babe she holds at arm's length, before catching it back to her heart. Many a long hour had the old man spent in whetting this instrument of his vengeance. And he was satisfied with his work. The knife was sharp—very sharp. It would cut deeply, even if it were only an old man's hand behind it.

Shylock drew a trembling finger along the edge and smiled as he watched the thin trickle of blood which oozed from the self-inflicted cut.

He would be cutting more deeply presently—but not into his own flesh.

Carefully he wiped the slight stain from the glittering edge and hid the weapon in the folds of his gabardine. He was ready now—quite ready. He would go forth to take vengeance after long delay. He would go forth to lay the pride of these hated Gentiles in the dust, and exalt the pride and strength of the Hebrew nation; a strength which many a cringing, beggared suppliant had felt before now.

Coin for coin in payment of old mockeries, present contempt. Coin for coin—but the interest to be claimed by the Jew over and above all!

A long, exultant thrill shook the old man as he fingered his yellow badge once more. That token would stand for a sign of power and fear to-day, when the Jew had his will in spite of Duke Niccolo and all his magnificoes.

The shutters of the opposite houses were open as Shylock passed in his boat down the canal, but no head craned forth to see the old Jew pass. A crimson curtain blew out across the whiteness of a wall. It looked like some blood-stained banner waving to victory in Shylock's eyes.

There were flowers on the balconies, swaying graceful stems in a breeze. Would flowers deck Antonio's bier?

The distant droning of water against the sea wall might have been a requiem for some passing soul.

Whose soul? Why, that of the Jew's enemy, since Antonio would die to-day.

Drawing his gabardine more closely around him Shylock stepped from the boat which had brought him to the Piazza near to the Court of Justice. A crowd of people stood around the building. Fishermen in their bright-hued caps and sashes, pert flower girls, market-folk and merchants jostled with sightseers from all parts of the city, who, hearing of the strange case which would be heard in court to-day, had come all agog with curiosity to know what went forward.

At sight of Shylock's sinister figure all shrank back, whispering and nudging. They seemed afraid that a glance from those blear and crafty eyes should fall on them, lest they might be "overlooked" by some wizard's spell.

Here he came—the well-known haunter of the Rialto —shuffling along, carrying a set of scales in one hand, whilst the other caressed his side, making sure the knife was safely set in his girdle.

Once a man leaped out before him, a sunburned fisherman, his red cap set back over black curls, his black eyes sparkling in fury as he cursed the vile Jew, who stood like some expectant bird of prey before him.

Then, before Shylock could answer, a young girl caught at the man's sash and drew him back into the crowd. They were Tito Scappini and his daughter,

Gemma, who had wept and prayed incessantly since news of their benefactor's arrest had reached them.

"He has death in his eye," groaned Scappini, drawing a sun-scorched arm across his face. "Santa Maria!—if it were not for Lucia and the children I would stab him now, before he entered the court."

But alas! even now he would have been too late for such an act, since Shylock had already mounted the marble steps and passed between the imposing doors.

The Jew's hour had indeed come.

The court was thronged, except for that part reserved for thé Duke, the councilors and such magnificoes of Venice as were likely to attend so unprecedented a trial.

Many merchants were gathered together, pale and anxious-eyed, self-reproachful too, since all would have subscribed to pay Antonio's original debt had any dreamed the Jew meant to claim his bond.

Here and there an unveiled courtesan laughed shrilly at the jest one of her cavalieri had whispered in her ear, but beyond such as these there were no women in court, since Venetian ladies were strictly guarded, never venturing out of doors without being closely shrouded by a veil and accompanied by male relatives or servants.

Bassanio was here, standing near the door, Gratiano and Salarino by his side. The young noble was awaiting the entrance of his friend, and appeared pale, agitated and very anxious.

He drew back at sight of Shylock shuffling in with his scales and groaned out a curse which merely brought a smile to the Jew's lips. For once Shylock found a Gentile curse as music to his ears—for there was pain in it —suffering in it, inflicted, as he knew, by himself.

Bassanio hid his face for a moment in his cloak, but

whether to pray or weep his companions could not determine, though they noted how he shuddered, when a brazen-voiced courtesan laughed shrilly, crying some jest at the expense of Shylock and his scales.

Then Gratiano plucked Bassanio by the sleeve.

"I think Messer Antonio comes," he whispered, and his eyes were full of a great pity.

With obvious effort Bassanio turned to see that dearest friend enter the court surrounded by his guard.

What havoc the last three weeks had wrought in Antonio's mien and appearance!

A broken man, both in outward seeming and reality. Though he still bore himself with quiet, almost stately dignity, the young merchant's shoulders were bent as if under too heavy a burden, and he had grown thin to emaciation—yet at sight of Bassanio weeping near, his face lighted up with a joy bordering on triumph.

So Salarino had sped well—his friend had come to be near him in death, to clasp his hand in love—to whisper tender words which should ring in the ears of the dying man who went to find Bianca in that Great Beyond, where men and women understand so many of the secrets never explained on earth.

"Antonio!"

Though the other spoke hardly above a whisper the guard must have heard; and being altogether in sympathy with their prisoner, contrived to halt so that the two might clasp hands in one all-comprehensive touch. Then, as Antonio passed to his place, Bassanio turned away, weeping unrestrainedly.

Gratiano touched his shoulder.

"Courage, amico," he urged, "do not despair. Think of the Lady Portia's generosity. Would any Jew, however greedy for revenge, be able to refuse so rich an offer? Shylock will take the gold. Have no fear on that score. Else he would be a traitor to his own nature. He'll take the gold—with our curses to flavor it; and Antonio will be free."

It was so easy for Gratiano to see everything rose-tinted to-day, though he chafed to think of the long hours which must intervene before he saw his Nerissa again.

But between Bassanio and his happiness stood the shadow of a friend's approaching sacrifice. For the moment, in his present agony, Bassanio would have been willing to renounce his claim on Portia herself, if by so doing he might win his friend's salvation.

Yet he could not believe Gratiano's cheerful convictions.

"Look at Shylock," he muttered, "and read me the purpose in his eyes. But do not speak of hope or mercy after noting the twisted hate of yonder features."

And Gratiano looking, beheld, as it were, the face of a devil.

CHAPTER XXVII

A MURMUR of welcome sounded without. Muffled cheers greeted the popular ruler, Niccolo da Ponte, as he and his train approached the Court of Justice.

The Duke had come. All eyes turned to the door to watch him enter, a very stately figure in his crimson velvet tunic and robes. He was a handsome, kindly-looking man, bearing himself with regal grace as he passed slowly to his seat, followed by a long train of the highest nobles—or magnificoes—of Venice, a somber group in their black doublets and hose, though the gloom of their attire was relieved on this occasion by the short scarlet cloaks which they wore flung back over one shoulder.

They looked grave enough, though, as they took their seats, for this was no ordinary trial, but as it were the judgment on some racial feud.

Jew versus Gentile! But the law of the land was on the side of the Jew, and try as they might, those scarlet-robed councilors yonder, seated in semicircle, could not deny it.

It was an imposing scene upon which winter sunshine blazed down—the scarlet robes of the councilors, the black and red of the magnificoes, which did not lack a suggestion of the satanic, combined with dark faces and black, pointed beards, the brilliant-hued dress of

(268)

the rich merchants and the glitter of gold tissue which adorned the flaunting figures of the courtesans.

And outside, the expectant crowd, the blue waters of the lagoons and the pigeons circling about the gilt and marble domes, of churches and palaces.

There was a breathless pause after the Duke had seated himself, then all eyes turned to the central figures in that strange drama as Niccolo da Ponte spoke.

"Is Antonio Cainello here?" he asked.

Antonio raised his head, answering very calmly, "I am ready—so it please Your Grace."

The Duke was silent, staring gloomily around the crowded court.

He fully realized what would be required of him to-day—and never had he found it so difficult to maintain his proud motto, "Justice in the Palace."

Yet what could he do? Shylock had shown himself implacable, and his threats were significant.

If the Duke once made the precedent of setting mercy before justice, law and order would be imperiled in Venice, and he would be found guilty of betraying his trust for the sake of mere personal feeling.

Yet Antonio's quiet bearing and brave fortitude wrung a groan from his judge.

"I am sorry for you, merchant," said the Duke, glancing from plaintiff to defendant. "You are come to answer a stony adversary, an inhuman wretch incapable of pity, void and empty of any spark of mercy."

It was an unusual denunciation on a judge's part, yet to none did it seem out of place at this unprecedented trial.

But Shylock merely smiled as he set down his scales upon a table and stood with lean arms folded within the wide sleeves of his gabardine.

He was quite aware that he had no friend or advocate in that crowded court, and the knowledge increased the pride of his triumph. He, the despised Jew, was here to bend the necks of these mocking Gentiles. He was here to confound them by their own cherished laws. He was here to take revenge upon his enemy—and in doing so exalted his whole down-trodden race to the level of their tyrants.

Antonio was replying courteously to the Duke's impetuous outburst.

"I have heard of the kindness you have shown towards me in this matter, Your Grace," he said, "and thank you with all my heart for this great condescension and love towards me that you should so interest yourself on my behalf. Yet at the same time I know the law— and that this man, whose debtor I am, hath that law on his side. So, for the sake of justice, for Venice and for the people, my dear countrymen, I am content to oppose my patience to the fury of my enemy. There is no other way—but to pay my debt in the fashion which this bond dictates."

But the Duke, still impetuous, turned in one last appeal to Shylock, who waited, no less mocking than patient, for the moment of fulfilment when vengeance should be complete.

"Shylock," cried Duke Niccolo, "is it not time to finish with this play-acting which grows cruel when carried too far? We will not wrong you, Jew, by believing you to be in earnest. This is but an ill-timed jest, by which you would prove to Antonio here the folly of setting his name to so wild a bond, which it were death to fulfil. Come, I will prophesy, good Shylock, and tell you how 'tis thought you'll act to-day, for in sooth we believe that presently you will lay aside this cloak of strange apparent cruelty and instead of exacting the penalty of a pound of this poor merchant's flesh, will not only free him of his bond and refuse to take any forfeiture, but, touched with human gentleness and love, forgive at least a part of the principal of his debt."

Shylock stood with bent head, not raising his eyes from the ground, so silent that the Duke, fancying that his appeal had touched a seemingly obdurate heart, continued his persuasive speech.

"You will have pity, Shylock," he urged with more confidence, "considering the losses of this poor merchant, which, coming one after another in such cruel fashion, have been enough to wreck the most royal fortunes and crush their victim to a dark despair, enough to rouse commiseration in the stoniest breast and bring compassion to hearts which have never before felt such kindly feelings stir them. I do not believe I plead in vain, but, having shown you plainly this debtor's sad estate, shall have a gentle answer from you."

A gentle answer!

Did he indeed expect it? Was it expected by those gravely-watching councilors who sat listening to the judge's brief petition on the prisoner's behalf? Did those who crowded that sunny court expect to hear the welcome words of forgiveness issue from the lips of the man who stood defying all present in his indomitable lust of hate and pride?

Shylock had raised his face and stood scanning those who watched him, with a deliberate stare before he turned to his noble interrogator.

"Have I not already told Your Grace my purpose?"

he demanded scornfully, raising a lean right arm aloft.
"And by our holy sabbath I have sworn to have the
due and forfeit of my bond. If you deny it, you threaten
your own charter and your city's freedom with the
danger of injustice committed. I am here to claim my
due. *Justice*—no more nor less. You'll ask me why
I rather choose to have a weight of carrion flesh than
to receive three thousand ducats? ' I'll not answer that,
but say it is my humor."

A murmur ran through the court. Men looked in
horror at the man who stood before them making such
a statement in callous tones of hate.

A murderer, claiming justice to stand beside him
whilst he performed his deed of blood.

Shylock flung them a snarl in answer to that low-
voiced abhorrence, turning to right and left to confront
that crowded audience, like some gray wolf at bay.

"What, are you answered yet?" he cried, his voice
rising shrill in his scarcely pent rage. "If my house be
troubled with a rat, who shall say me nay if it be my
pleasure to give ten thousand ducats to be rid of it?
Is there any more reason in hatred than in love? Some
men there are who are mad if they see a cat, another
faints at sight of a crawling reptile. Can you tell me
what is the reason for each passion which sways a man's
mood? Bring your wise men, your learned philosophers,
to argue the point with me. Give your reasons, sirs—
and I'll give mine. Till then you shall be content to
know that without given reason but by natural instinct
I so hate this smug merchant, this Antonio Cainello
here, that I am content to follow a losing suit against
him. Aye, content with what is due to me—that
which justice and your Duke, your Senate and your

councilors, cannot deny me—the payment of my bond."

The last words rose to a shriek such as fiends might utter in some nethermost hell as they guide their victim's feet towards the pit. He defied them all, this old, frail man, whose shriveled form seemed to swell and dilate with the flame of his hate so that he towered amongst them—a conqueror—using their own tools to confound them. The Duke leaned back in his gilded chair. Here was such a quandary as it seemed his wisest councilors could not deliver him from. His cherished goddess—that justice whose sword he was so proud to wield—was in danger if this old Jew's demand was refused. He dared not risk the State by this. Yet, equally impossible did it seem that one of Venice's most reputable citizens should be hacked to death before his eyes and those of all present to gratify the hate and blood-lust of this alien usurer.

Bassanio Ramberti had stepped forward and was confronting Shylock with clenched hands and a face grown ashen in the effort of mastering fierce emotions.

He was here to plead—yet never had he felt less like such a task. His fingers itched to be at this old murderer's throat and squeeze the vile life from such a heartless rogue.

Yet he conquered the instinct and tried to speak calmly.

"Unfeeling wretch," he said, "this answer is no excuse for such cruelty as you conceive."

Shylock shrugged his lean shoulders in contempt.

"I am not bound to please you with my answer," he retorted.

18

Bassanio bit his lip. "Do all men kill the things they do not love?" he argued in more level tones.

Shylock sneered. "Does any man hate the thing he would not kill?" he replied subtly.

"Every offence is not a hate at first," quoth Bassanio.

The old man laughed. "What?" he queried. "Would you have a serpent sting you twice?"

And he shuffled back nearer to the table where the scales stood.

Antonio stretched out his hand, touching his friend's arm gently.

"Bassanio," he said, "I pray you not to question with the Jew. You do but waste your time, for indeed you might as well stand on the beach and try to lull the storm; or question with the wolf upon his cruelty in making the ewe bleat vainly for the lamb. You might as well bid the mountain pines forbear to sway under the fury of the winter storm. Or any harder task you might essay more easily than hope to soften this man's Jewish heart. So, amico, I do beseech you, make no more offers, use no more arguments, since both and all are vain, and but waste the time and patience of these kindly friends. Let me therefore have judgment—and the Jew his will."

As he spoke the doomed man began to loosen the fastening of the long furred robe he wore in place of hose and doublet, but Bassanio, passionate in his despair, checked him. Even fury against Shylock was forgotten in the agony of his desire to save his friend.

"Come, Jew," he cried, "listen to my offer. An honest, sober offer which you'll not despise since I have the gold here. For three thousand ducats here are six."

Shylock scarcely deigned to turn his head.

"If every ducat in six thousand ducats were in six parts," he replied, "and every part a ducat, I would not draw them. I would have my bond."

Bassanio groaned, catching at Gratiano's shoulder and hiding his face—he had made so sure that Portia's generous offer would win life for his friend.

That last speech of Shylock's had damned all such bright expectations.

"How shall you hope for mercy, rendering none?" asked Duke Niccolo sternly.

Shylock looked up quickly towards the judge, and there was that defiance bred of long persecution in his reply.

"What judgment shall I dread, doing no wrong?" he replied. "You have among you many a purchased slave, which, like your asses, your dogs and mules, you use in slavish parts—because you bought them. Shall I say to you, 'Let them be free. Marry them to your heirs! Why sweat they under burdens? Let their beds be made as soft as yours. Let them dine at your table in honorable place, eating the same food, drinking the same drink.' You will answer, 'The *slaves are ours.*'

"So do I answer you. The pound of flesh, which I demand of Antonio here, is dearly bought, is mine and I will have it. If you deny me, fie upon your law. There is no force in the decrees of Venice. I stand for judgment. Answer, Your Grace, and you, learned councilors of the Senate? Shall I have it?"

He stretched forth claw-like hands, swaying to and fro—a mummy in the wind. Yet the hurricane which swept him was that of hate, a quivering, sensient hate which filled with horror those who gazed at it.

No less appalled than the rest was the Duke himself. In this meanly clad and despicable Jew he met a pride equal to his own or that of the proud nobles who stood around; and this pride, clamoring in the name of justice, demanded the only panacea which hate could contrive to soothe its wounds.

"Upon my power," groaned da Ponte, glancing helplessly around, "I can do nothing but dismiss this court unless Bellario, a learned doctor of Padua, for whom I have sent to unravel so nice a point between justice and humanity, come here to-day."

There was a slight stir at the back of the court, and Salarino, who had gone towards the door, after speaking with Bassanio, now hastily approached the Duke.

"Your Grace," said he, bowing very reverently, yet speaking with scarcely concealed eagerness, "a messenger stands without even now, newly arrived from Padua, with letters from the doctor you mention."

The Duke's gloomy face cleared.

"Bring us the letter," he commanded briefly. "Call the messenger."

Bassanio turned to where the prisoner stood resting his elbow on the rail before him, his face covered by his hand, whilst his lips moved in silent prayer.

"Good cheer, Antonio," he cried huskily. "What, man? Courage yet! The Jew shall have my flesh, blood, bones and all, before you shall lose one drop of blood for me."

Antonio raised his head. He was very pale, but there was neither fear nor dismay upon his countenance, which wore the lofty courage of one who, having made his peace with God, looks forward to speedy dissolution with calm tranquility, regarding less the horror of pain or dark charnel house of the tomb than the hope of a life to come, widening out into the sure expectation of an eternity of bliss where love reigns triumphant and hate cannot abide.

"Hush!" he replied. "I am prepared to die, as you to live, Bassanio; if you will write my epitaph hereafter you shall say, 'Here lies a man who knew what love might mean.'"

He smiled with something akin to triumph in his look, knowing that Bassanio might not wholly read the riddle of this speech, though he himself would soon be telling it to fair Bianca in the fields of paradise.

Yet at sight of his friend's tears, his own came near to brimming, for with Bassanio's hand warm in his own, and his heart knit fast in tender bonds to this Bianca's brother, his own youth and strength cried, "Live! Aye, life can be good and sweet and true here on earth. Live —and love."

Yet, whilst the voice echoed loudly in his heart, he heard a sound which thrilled him with a new-born horror.

Shylock had drawn his knife from beneath the folds of his gabardine and was sharpening its already keen point against the sole of his shoe as if in pleasant anticipation.

CHAPTER XXVIII

A SLIM, dingily-attired figure passed up the court towards the Duke's seat.

A lawyer's clerk he appeared to be, who held himself straightly, though he kept his eyes on the ground, whilst he clasped a roll of parchment fast against his breast.

The Duke glanced curiously at him. The clerk was but a boy, possessing the swagger born of excessive shyness. But, after all, what of a lawyer's clerk? It was his master who concerned those present.

"Come you from Padua, from Bellario?" demanded Duke Niccolo.

The boy bowed jerkily.

"From both, Your Grace," he answered in low tones. "Signior Bellario greets Your Grace."

And he held out the folded parchment, with its binding of ribbon and seals, to the Duke, who hastily unfastened and began to read the contents.

Silence prevailed in the court, saving where here and there one whispered to another in undertones concerning the likely issue of this sinister business.

A woman—painted and bedecked in gaudy fashion, was being borne, half swooning, by two cavalieri, from the place where death, grim and terrible, seemed hideously personified by the shrunken figure in its coarse gabardine which stood near the Duke's seat.

(278)

Men, looking at Shylock the Jew, crossed themselves as though in that gray-bearded old man they saw the father of evil himself. But he, for his part, neither looked up nor around him, but stood, resting his left hand upon the table where his scales were placed, whilst in the right he clutched the knife whose blade he drew to and fro across the sole of his shoe with a monotonous swishing sound which grated so hatefully upon Gratiano's ear that he stepped to the Jew's side, hoping to arrest this hideous occupation.

"Why do you whet your knife so earnestly?" he asked.

Shylock chuckled, nodding towards Antonio.

"To cut the forfeiture from that bankrupt there," he retorted.

Gratiano shuddered.

"Not on your sole, but on your soul, harsh Jew," he reproached, "do you make your knife keen. But no metal, not even the hangman's axe, can be half so keen as your sharp envy. Can no prayers pierce thee?"

He thought as he spoke of little Nerissa in distant Belmont, and grieved for the sorrow in which he and Bassanio must return to those who so lovingly awaited them.

"Prayers?" mocked Shylock contemptuously. "None that thou hast wit enough to make."

The taunt stung Venetian pride to the quick. "May you be damned for this, inexorable dog!" cried Gratiano softly, but very sincerely. "Can justice spare the life of so vile a thing? If so she wrongs her name. Are you a man, gifted with a human soul? I cannot think so ill of my kind. A wolf's heart beats in your bosom, Jew. Aye! and a wolf, which in some past and better age hanged for human slaughter. Would it be possible for one like thou art to conceive any desires but such as are wolfish, bloody, starved and ravenous?"

He paused for want of breath and perhaps because the venom of this rage choked him.

But Shylock stood unmoved, continuing the sharpening of his knife against the leather of his shoe. Had Gratiano spoken in most sugared compliment he could not have gratified better the Jew's delight in thus witnessing the impotent wrath of those whom he saw metaphorically so fast beneath his heel.

"Till you can rail the seal off my bond," he retorted suavely, "you but injure your lungs in speaking so loudly. Repair your wit, good youth, or it will go limping past cure for the rest of your life. I stand here for law."

He justified Gratiano's likening to a wolf by the snap of his jaw. He was hard as flint, this old man, and surely no soulless beast of the forest had so fierce a lust against its victim's life.

Duke Niccolo was refolding the parchment scroll with due deliberation and bent to hand it to the clerk, who sat beneath his seat.

Then, turning to the young messenger who had brought the writing, he addressed him kindly and with lightened brow: "This letter from the illustrious Bellario commends a young and learned doctor to our court," he said. "Where is he—your master as I take it?"

The youth bowed, this time with more assurance.

"He attends hard by, Your Grace," he replied eagerly, "till I shall bring him the answer as to your pleasure in admitting him."

Duke Niccolo smiled, nodding towards a little group of attendants standing near.

"With all my heart," he said. "Some three of four of you go give him courteous conduct hither. Meantime, the court shall hear Bellario's letter."

The young men hurried away, bearing the dingy little clerk in their midst so that he might bring them to his master.

As soon as they had gone the Duke signed to the man who held the parchment to proceed in his reading, and a great hush fell forthwith on all the court.

Men craned forward, anxious not to lose a word of what was said, though as they listened many shook their heads, deciding that if the wit and affection of all Venice had failed to save its beloved citizen, this youthful stranger was little likely to achieve success.

Yet to Bassanio, ever optimistic in his thoughts, there showed some ray of hope in a very dark and gloomy despair.

"'Your Grace shall understand,'" read the clerk in high-pitched tones, "'that at the receipt of your letter I am very sick; but in the instant that your messenger came, in loving visitation was with me a young doctor of Rome; his name is Balthazar. I acquainted him with the cause in controversy between the Jew and Antonio the merchant. We turned over many books together; he is furnished with my opinion, which, bettered with his own learning (the greatness of which I cannot enough commend), comes with him, at my importunity to fill up your Grace's request in my stead. I beseech you let his lack of years be no impediment to let him lack a reverend estimation, for I never knew so young a body with so old a head. I leave him to your gracious acceptance, whose trial shall better publish his commendation.'"

This with many courteous salutations ended the letter of the illustrious doctor Giralomo Bellario, and its reading was received by a low murmur of comments from the listeners.

Not many hopes were, however, entertained by those present that the young substitute in whose praises a great man did not stint himself, would triumph where a Bellario might probably have failed.

What argument could outstand Shylock's claim? The bond was made and signed; forfeit was due. Justice claimed its payment.

Even Shylock expressed no shadow of fear that his triumph stood in jeopardy. This was but a prolongation of his victim's torture, and as such he was ready to welcome it in this day of exultation and revenge.

"You hear what the learned Bellario writes?" said the Duke, glancing eagerly towards the door. "And here, I take it, comes the doctor he has sent us."

Bassanio, turning with the rest, though with his hand still clasped within that of Antonio, saw a flutter of red robes and the glimpse of a young dark face which, for a moment, had something familiar in it, though as he racked his brain to place a name to the likeness, it escaped him and he saw only a good-looking youth, who wore his dark locks somewhat ragged and untidy about the nape of his slender neck, yet bore himself with easy grace and confidence as, bowing, he kissed the Duke's extended hand.

"You are welcome," quoth Duke Niccolo very graciously, "seeing you come from our friend the illustrious Bellario with such credentials as shall presently, I pray, make you more welcome still for your own sake, wise young sir. Take your place. Are you acquainted with the case which presents such difficulties to the common cause of justice with mercy?"

His keen glance searched the newcomer's face and person anxiously. It seemed but that of a youth, after all, comely and well set up in slender fashion, though his flowing robe hid his figure to a great extent.

Was this one, thought the Duke, to crack so hard a nut, unravel so tangled a skein and preserve this court of justice from what, under cloak of law and justice, was little short of a bloody and unnatural crime?

And at the question his hopes sank as low as those of Bassanio, who eyed the stripling doctor with much disfavor for all the latter's confident carriage. Certainly Balthazar of Padua did not share in his clerk's shyness, for having quickly arranged his papers, he answered the Duke in clear, ringing tones, which, resounding through the court, again awakened elusive memories in Bassanio's breast; memories which were soon forgotten, since in listening to the doctor's speech, he quicker ceased to ponder on the doctor's tones.

"I am informed of the case, Your Grace," said the young lawyer very deliberately. "Which is the merchant here and which the Jew?"

He glanced as he spoke towards the spot where Bassanio stood beside his friend, but the glance was too brief `for Bassanio to have told what color were the speaker's eyes.

"Antonio Cainello, and you Shylock, stand forth," commanded the Duke.

Balthazar leaned forward over his desk, regarding the two intently. But he addressed himself to the Jew first.

"Is your name Shylock?" he asked.

"Shylock is my name," was the grudging response.

"This is a strange suit you follow," mused the lawyer aloud. "Yet you claim the Venetian law, and so this man stands your debtor, do you not?"

He turned to Antonio, who, truth to tell, found this respite from speedy consummation of his sacrifice most trying of all, so sure was he that the delay only meant the longer torture of suspense.

"Aye, so he says," he replied quietly.

"Do you confess the bond?"

"I do."

Balthazar looked to the rearrangement of his papers— his hands were very small and shapely, though as dark-skinned as his complexion.

"Then must the Jew be merciful," said he.

Shylock's claw-like fingers sought his beard, tugging it restlessly.

"Why? Why?" he demanded. "On what compulsion must I? Tell me that?"

The young lawyer spread out both arms, raising his face so that the light from an upper window fell on it.

"The quality of mercy is not strained," he cried; "it droppeth as the gentle rain from Heaven, upon the place beneath. It is twice blessed; it blesseth him that gives and him that takes. 'Tis mightiest in the mightiest. It becomes the throned monarch better than his crown: his scepter shows the force of temporal power, the attribute to awe and majesty, wherein doth sit the dread and fear of kings. But mercy is above this sceptered sway. It is enthroned in the hearts of kings. It is an attribute to God himself. And earthly power doth then show likest God's when mercy seasons justice. There-fore, Jew, though justice be thy plea, consider this— that in the course of justice, none of us should see salvation. We do pray for mercy, and that same prayer doth teach us all to render the deeds of mercy. I have spoken thus much to mitigate the justice of your plea; which, if you follow, this strict Court of Venice must needs give sentence 'gainst the merchant here."

He paused—awaiting Shylock's answer as though he and the Jew were here alone, man to man, pleading a brother's cause. He seemed oblivious to the fact of how his eloquence had stirred the court, moving the Duke himself nearly to tears, whilst a deep breath rose like a mighty sigh from every listener in silent admiration of so noble a speech.

So all listened—for the answer which must come from one who alone had remained unmoved, unstirred by that passionate appeal which carried its case far beyond the limits of earthly justice to a greater Court, pointing the proud, vengeful old man who clamored for such a cruel right to the mightiest of reasons for his mercy.·

The Duke, the law of Venice, the pleas of friends, the bribery of gold, might all fail to rescue Antonio Cainello from his enemy. But this young doctor of law placed this question on another basis, crying to the creditor to remember how one day he, a debtor would stand before the Judge of judges.

Could he look for mercy then—rendering none here? It was a terrible thought, suggested by the subtle reason of one who knew the strong belief of the Jew in a hereafter, near and tangible to the holder of a narrow but powerful creed.

It was no matter of love or hate, forgiveness or vengeance, for Antonio the merchant, but, based on this other standpoint, a personal question to the soul of Shylock the Jew.

Here was what others had failed to find. A reason for an avenger's mercy. And as all listened in that pregnant silence, some there were who thought to pray that the appeal had not been vain.

Alas! Hope was barely born before the raucous voice of Shylock rose in fierce outcry as though defying some deep, inner whisper of his heart.

"My deeds upon my head! I crave the law. The penalty and forfeit of my bond."

With a groan Bassanio turned his head away. Only a fool or madman could still hope for mercy after that appeal had been vain.

The young Paduan glanced for the second time towards where Bassanio stood beside Antonio's side.

"Is he not able to discharge the money?" he asked, indicating the latter.

Bassanio stepped eagerly forward. He had ceased to puzzle over elusive memories awakened by Signior Balthazar's voice and face. His whole soul was absorbed by the desire to save his friend.

"Yes," he cried, holding out a leathern bag which bulged in weighty fulness. "Here I tender it for him in the court. Yea! Twice the sum! If that will not suffice, I will be bound to pay it ten times over, on forfeit of my hands, my head, my heart. If this will not suffice then malice must be proved stronger than love and truth. Oh, I beseech you, ye who judge this case even as you would plead for it, will you not once bend the law to your authority? To do a great right do a little wrong, and cheat this cruel devil of his prey?"

With hand outflung the young noble stood, imploring the Duke and his councilors with such vehement distress that the tears which ran down his cheeks seemed to draw similar signs of emotion to the eyes of others.

Never surely was justice in such danger of outrage.

The Duke covered his face with his mantle, more than one grave Signior wept aloud—but before Niccolo da Ponte could make reply, the voice of the advocate sent by Bellario broke in, calm and decisive.

"It must not be," he ruled. "There is no power in Venice can alter an established decree. 'Twill be recorded for a precedent; and by so ill an example, many a wrong and error will creep into the law of the Republic. It cannot be as you demand."

Bassanio drew back, disappointed, baffled. For a brief moment he had thought to read relenting on the faces of Antonio's judges. Alas! that the very man sent to save his friend should be the one to confound him.

But whilst the rest of those present were silent for very grief, Shylock was loud in his applause.

Shuffling a little nearer to the lawyer's desk, he raised his hands in admiration, saluting Balthazar respectfully.

"A Daniel come to judgment!" he exclaimed, showing yellow teeth in a wolfish grin. "Yea, a Daniel. O wise young judge, how I do honor you!"

The Paduan leaned towards him. "I pray you, let me look upon the bond?" he begged.

Thrusting his hand within the breast of his gabardine the old man drew forth the parchment with its ponderous seals.

"Here it is, most reverend doctor," he cried, offering it to the young lawyer; "here it is."

Balthazar took the scroll and began reading it very carefully, his fine brows knit in a slight frown. Another wearisome pause, during which Antonio resumed his attitude of silent prayer, whilst Bassanio stared moodily before him, hearing nothing, seeing nothing but the haunting picture which, despair cried in his ear, must soon be witnessed by his waking sight.

"Shylock," quoth Balthazar sharply, "there's thrice your money offered to you here."

The old Jew shook his head.

"An oath, an oath," he clamored fiercely. "I have an oath in Heaven. Shall I lay perjury upon my soul? No! Not for Venice!"

The lawyer sighed as, refolding the parchment, he looked around that crowded court.

"Why," said he, "this bond is forfeit, and lawfully by this the Jew may claim a pound of flesh, to be by him cut off nearest the merchant's heart. Shylock, be merciful. Take thrice your money; bid me tear the bond."

He held the paper high between his hands in full view of all, as though in the act of tearing it. But Shylock's tone rose shrill.

"When it is paid according to the tenor. But not till then! It doth appear you are a worthy judge. You know the law, young sir, your exposition hath been most sound. I charge you by the law, whereof you are a well-deserving pillar, proceed to judgment. By my soul! I swear there is no power in the tongue of man to alter me. I stay here on my bond."

Alas! Was not all in vain? Threats, bribes, entreaties, all that tongue could urge had been urged in that court that day.

Yet it counted for nothing against an old man's jaundiced will and pride.

It was Antonio himself who set a period on his friends' distress.

"Most heartily I do beseech the court to give the

judgment," he said, and his voice rang clear and calm, with never a tremor of fear to add to the horror of the scene.

Balthazar laid his papers aside.

"Why, then, thus it is," he replied, "you must prepare your bosom for his knife."

A cry of anguish broke from Bassanio's lips, echoed by many in the court.

But Shylock was inexorable. Catching up the knife he had laid aside, he approached his victim, who, in spite of his friend's detaining hands, was essaying to unrobe himself.

"O noble judge!" cried Shylock, waving his terrible weapon as though in salutation to one who so favored his cause. "O excellent young man!"

The Duke would have spoken, interposing his authority. But what could he do? Was he not Niccolo da Ponte—the Duke of Venice, who, above all things, prided himself on administering a fair and equal justice?

And Balthazar for the moment seemed to have usurped his place.

"For," continued the young Paduan, "the intent and purpose of the law hath full relation to the penalty."

" 'Tis very true," gibed Shylock. "O wise and upright judge! How much older art thou than thy looks?"

"Therefore," concluded the lawyer, "lay bare your bosom, Antonio."

"Aye," interrupted Shylock, gloatingly. "His breast; so says the bond. Doth it not, noble judge? Nearest his heart, those are the very words."

"It is so," agreed the Paduan. "Are there balances here to weigh the flesh?"

"I have them ready," cried Shylock, pointing in an

19

ecstasy to the table where the balances had been set, swaying with sinister motion up and down, as though drawing attention to the hideous meaning of their presence here.

Bassanio was past speech. These details were too terrible, too ghastly for contemplation. As in a trance he saw the figure of Shylock the Jew hovering near, between the table on which the balances stood and his victim, who—alone calm amidst that nerve-racked audience—waited with bared breast for the first thrust of the knife.

The Jew's face was diabolical in its vengeful lust. Nought, as it seemed, but an angel from Heaven could have held his hand now.

Dignity, pride, everything was forgotten in that glutting of insensate hate which flamed in his blear eyes making them bright and keen; whilst, though every other limb shook in the transport of his triumph, his raised right arm was steady for its purpose. The flash of the polished steel shone aloft as a streak of light, stationary only for a moment.

The Duke and his councilors sat with averted eyes, appalled, dismayed, yet silent before a swift judgment, which could not be gainsaid.

Gratiano was vainly trying to draw the stunned Bassanio away, but the latter refused to move from Antonio's side.

At the back of his mind the young noble had some subconscious plan of interposing his own body between that cruel knife and its victim's breast. Surely, if *one* died in expiation of a bond, justice would be satisfied and Antonio's life spared.

Yes, justice would be satisfied. Yet Bassanio, resolved on such a sacrifice, did not pray—he only thought of Portia, and wondered vaguely whether she would say the sacrifice was well made.

Being a noble lady could she do otherwise? He stared past the Jew to where the Paduan lawyer stood, erect, alert, in his place, the sun aflame upon his doctor's robes, his handsome face calm as that of some Radamanthus, who gave judgment without thought for aught but barest justice.

And looking at him thus, Bassanio knew his own dear lady, doubtless praying for him and his friend in distant Belmont, would say it was right her lord should pay his own debt.

"Stay," quoth Balthazar peremptorily. "You must not fail to have by some surgeon, Shylock, on your charge, to stop Antonio's wounds, lest he bleed to death." Shylock glanced back over his shoulder.

"Is it so nominated in the bond?" he muttered.

The lawyer made pretext to unroll the scroll once more.

"It is not so expressed," he replied. "But what of that? 'Twere good you do so much for charity."

Shylock had returned, and was peering over the other's shoulder, tracing every word of the script with a claw-like forefinger.

"I cannot find it," he growled; "it is not in the bond."

No! It was not in the bond, and Balthazar the Paduan, relinquishing the parchment, left Shylock to study it further at his leisure whilst he turned to Antonio, who stood patiently awaiting sentence.

"Come, merchant," quoth he softly. "Have you anything to say?"

Antonio smiled the faint, sad smile of one who already

accustoms his eyes to look beyond this sphere towards eternity.

"But little," he replied. "I am armed and well-prepared. Give me your hand, Bassanio—fare you well. After all, fortune is more kind in meting me this fate than is her custom. At least I escape the doom of watching poverty slowly overwhelm me. It is difficult, after knowing the joys of wealth, to learn the hard lessons of the poor, in middle life. Commend me to your wife, and tell her the tale of your friend; say how I loved you, and when she hears how I died bid her judge whether Bassanio had not once a love. Nay! Weep not for me, do not so much as repent the loss of your friend since he repents not that he pays your debt. I vow, if the Jew cuts deep enough, I'll pay it instantly—with all my heart."

Bassanio raised his head, showing a face so grief-stricken that those who saw it turned away to weep for very sympathy of a fellow creature's agony.

Yet he found voice to answer that last farewell.

"Antonio," he cried, despair battling fiercely in his words, "I am married to a wife as dear to me as life itself. But life itself, my wife and all the world, would I lose, aye! sacrifice them all if in so doing I could deliver you, my friend, from this devil."

The lawyer from Padua stroked a smooth and rounded chin.

"Your wife would give you little thanks for that," he murmured, "if she were by to hear you make the offer.

Nor was Gratiano behind his friend in protestations of love.

"Antonio," he cried huskily, wringing the young

"A pound of that same merchant's flesh is yours."

merchant's hand, "I have a wife whom I protest I love. I would she were in Heaven, so that she might entreat for some change to be made in this currish Jew."

The lawyer's clerk was close beside his master—no longer shy and diffident, but pert in the tilting of his head, whilst his lips were thrust forward in a pout as he listened to this last speech which appeared mightily to displease him.

But to Shylock these farewells were over-long, and he pushed Gratiano aside.

"We trifle time," he snarled. "I pray you pursue sentence."

Balthazar still stroked his chin.

"A pound of that same merchant's flesh is yours," he declared. "The court awards it and the law doth give it."

It was as if the last stroke of a death-knell sounded.

But Shylock laughed aloud.

"Most rightful judge!" he cried.

"And," went on the lawyer solemnly, "you must cut this flesh from off his breast. The law allows it, and the court awards it."

"Most learned judge!" cried the Jew once more. "A sentence! Come, prepare!"

He was close to Antonio now. Many of the merchants in the court had risen and stood with the other folk who crowded the place, huddled together, shuddering, whispering, gesticulating as though contemplating interference.

The group of nobles too were talking in animated fashion, more indignant than pitying, with angry glances for the red-robed young lawyer, who stood in his place, a flaming figure of doom, with arm upraised, usurping as it seemed, the power and majesty of Duke Niccolo himself; whilst the Duke, as though only half realizing this, had risen from his seat as if about to forbid the execution of a hideous butchery.

It was a moment of crisis, the blood of all spectators chilled by horror as they looked upon that small central knot of figures.

Antonio, his breast already bared, in the midst, Bassanio and Gratiano beside him as though guarding him from the avenger who crept forward, his knife upraised, his face devilish in its malice, whilst behind him the sinister balances swayed softly up and down, awaiting their bloody burden—and beyond the table, the erect figure of Balthazar the Paduan, watching intently, his hand resting on the shoulder of his slim, dingily-clad clerk.

Then, before any could interfere, the clear tones of the young lawyer rang out:

"Tarry, Shylock," he cried. "There is something else first."

CHAPTER XXIX

JUSTICE!

THE Jew turned, glowering over his shoulder.

"What mean you?" he snarled.

The lawyer held up the bond.

"This bond," said he, "doth give you here no jot of blood. The words expressly are—*a pound of flesh.* Take then your bond—take your pound of flesh; but, in cutting it, if you shed one drop of Christian blood, your lands and goods are, by the laws of Venice, confiscate unto the State of Venice."

Shylock slowly faced round, the light fading from his eyes, his complexion changing from dusky swarthiness to ashen gray.

A knell indeed! But rung for him this time.

A crack of doom in the hour of triumph which seemed to stun him down to some lowest hell at a moment when all the longings and desire of years had been gathered to fruition.

But Gratiano had flung his arm about Bassanio's neck, whilst the latter, too dazed at first to read the full meaning of these words of hope, stood gaping like the rest of the spectators, whose nerves had been previously strung to breaking point.

"O upright judge!" cried Gratiano, joy overwhelming him in merry laughter and mockery, which, whilst half tears in gladness for Antonio, was for the rest a spice of devilment flavored to chastise the stricken Shylock.

"Mark, Jew," he rallied, wagging his head towards the old man, who still clutched his knife to his own breast. "O learned judge!"

Balthazar the Paduan raised his hand.

"Will you see to this?" he asked the silent Hebrew. "For, as you urge justice, be assured you shall have justice—more than you desire."

Again Gratiano's merry laugh rang high through the court, as he pointed a mocking finger at his enemy, then slapped his thigh in exquisite enjoyment.

"O learned judge!" he cried. "Mark, Jew—a *learned* judge."

Shylock shuffled forward. He was as a man in a dream. A man, too, grown suddenly very, very old— almost palsied in his movements, whilst the knife—that beautiful knife so zealously sharpened—fell clattering to the ground at the feet of the man who should have been its owner's victim.

"I take his offer then," he muttered dully, stretching out his lean, claw-like hand. "Pay the bond thrice. Let the Christian go."

Bassanio was eager in his compliance.

"Here is the money," he cried, extending the leathern bag.

But the lawyer from Padua interposed.

"Softly," quoth he. "The Jew shall have justice. Softly—no haste. He shall have nothing but the penalty."

"O Jew!" groaned Gratiano, writhing in delight. "An *upright* judge—a learned judge."

"Therefore," continued Balthazar, "prepare to cut off the flesh. Shed no blood, and cut precisely a pound of flesh—if you take more or less than a just pound—

be it but so much as makes it light or heavy in the substance, or the division of the twentieth part of one poor
scruple—nay! if the scale do turn but in the estimation
of a hair—you die and all your goods are confiscate."

Shylock shrank back, glancing around him as a rat
which, begirt by terrier dogs, watches to find the best
way of escape.

Hatred was chastened now by failure, the lust of pride
was brought low, yet not so low but that the Jew strove
with bitter courage to drag its tattered cloak about
him.

Sullen he stood, fierce and dogged in his discomfiture,
whilst Gratiano continued to point the finger of scorn.

"A second Daniel," mimicked the merry Venetian.
"A Daniel, Jew. Now, infidel, I have you on the hip!"

No sign gave Shylock, save to draw his gabardine more
closely around him as though the atmosphere of the
court were cold.

"Why doth the Jew pause?" asked the Paduan.
"Take you your forfeiture, Shylock."

But the old man only scowled.

"Give me my principal and let me go," he demanded.

Again Bassanio, transported by joy, left Antonio's
side to proffer the gold.

"I have it ready," cried he joyfully. "Here it is."

But the young lawyer motioned him aside.

"He has refused it in the open court," said he sternly.
"He shall have merely justice—and his bond."

"A Daniel, say I," gurgled Gratiano in supreme
enjoyment. "A second Daniel! I thank you, Jew, for
teaching me that word."

Shylock raised his bent head for a moment.

"Shall I not even have my principal?" he asked in
hollow tones.

The lawyer shook his head. "You shall have nothing but the forfeiture," he declared, "to be so taken at your peril, Jew."

Inexorable decree.

The old Jew clenched his fists, shaking them vehemently, as though calling down curses upon those whom he had sworn to bring beneath his heel, those whom he had hoped to make afraid, despairing, brought low by their agony of loss, but who now gathered around sneering and baiting him in his failure.

"Why, then," he snarled, "the devil give him good of it! I'll stay no longer question."

He shuffled towards the door, a huddled, broken old man, so evil in his misery that the most tender-hearted had no pity for him.

But his misery had not yet culminated. Balthazar the Paduan had not finished his case yet. This Daniel, whom Shylock had deemed his friend, read deeper into the law, and called back Antonio's remorseless creditor once more.

"Tarry, Jew," he cried. "The law hath yet another hold on you."

Slowly Shylock returned. He had no strength left for argument. The passion of his hate, the despair of failure had broken him, leaving him weak and exhausted physically.

He seemed a very, very old man as he stood there—yet it was an age which none respected.

The Paduan lawyer, half turned towards the Duke, half towards Shylock, was rearranging his papers. Antonio and Bassanio had withdrawn to the background, too happy in this unlooked-for deliverance to trouble about the further issues of the case.

"It is enacted by the law of Venice," quoth the lawyer sternly, "that if it be proved against an alien that by direct or indirect attempts he seeks the life of any citizen, he whose life he thus unlawfully seeks shall seize one-half of his goods; the other half comes to the privy coffer of the State; and the offender's life lies at the mercy of the Duke only, against all other voice. This, Shylock, is your present predicament, since it appears you have contrived against the very life of the defendant. So, since you have incurred the danger of this judgment, down on your knees and ask mercy of the Duke."

Shylock did not stir. His chin was sunk forward on his breast, and so motionless did he stand that it seemed as though he swooned.

"Beg leave to hang yourself," mocked Gratiano, remorseless in his gibing, "though, since your wealth is forfeit to the State, you have not the value of a cord left, and so must be hanged at the State's expense."

The Duke silenced the speaker with a frown, then turned to Shylock, speaking with the grave dignity of one who at last finds the giving of sentence easy.

"Shylock," said he, "you shall see the difference of the Christian spirit. I pardon you your life before you ask it. For half your wealth it is Antonio's. The other half comes to the State, though your humility may help to change this to a fine."

Shylock looked to where the Duke sat upon his judgment seat. His lean hands gripped at the folds of his robe above his breast, he panted as a man exhausted by running, despair was on his haggard, ashen face, and pride too, the indomitable pride of the Jew which neither humiliation, despair nor failure could utterly crush.

"Nay," he cried fiercely, "take my life and all. Pardon not that! You take my house, when you take away the prop that sustains it. You take my life when you take the means by which I live."

The Paduan lawyer looked towards the two who stood apart, rejoicing in the gladness of reunion.

"Antonio," quoth he very clearly, "what mercy can you render your enemy?"

Gratiano shrugged his shoulders.

"A halter gratis," he muttered. "Nothing else, for Heaven's sake."

But Antonio stepped forward, the same quiet dignity marking his bearing as aforetime.

He bowed before Duke Niccolo.

"So please my lord the Duke," he replied, "and all the court, to quit the fine for one half of his goods, I am content; so he will let me have the other half in use— to render it at his death to the gentleman who lately stole his daughter. Moreover, in gratitude for mercy shown him, he must presently become a Christian and also record here in this court a gift of all he dies possessed to his son Lorenzo and his daughter."

Shylock's face was hidden—he would not look upon the man who, if his malice had been rewarded, should now have been dead.

But fate had been too strong for the Jew, and a slim stripling from Padua, learned beyond his years, had robbed him of his prey.

Yet pride forbade the old Jew to show outward sign of his inward agony.

"He shall do this," declared Duke Niccolo, unable to conceal his relief at this ruling of the case, "or else I recant the pardon I have lately pronounced."

"Are you content, Jew?" asked Balthazar. "What do you say?"

"I am content."

The words were spoken monotonously but quite audibly. The lawyer motioned to one of the clerks of the court, bidding him briefly draw a deed of gift.

Shylock raised a trembling hand to his head.

"I pray you give me leave to go from hence," he requested the Duke, swaying as he spoke. "I—I am not well. Send the deed after me and I will sign it."

He clutched at a railing to steady himself; it was very evident his weakness was no feint.

"Get you gone," replied Duke Niccolo, "but fail not in signing."

Without another word the old man shuffled off, reeling in his gait, pitiable in his pride and misery had he shown one spark of pity for his foe.

As it was men did not forbear to laugh at Gratiano's farewell taunt.

"In christening," cried the latter, "you shall have two godfathers. Had *I* been judge you should have had ten more—to bring you to the gallows—not the font."

But Shylock made no sign of having heard the speech; he was deaf just now to any sound but the knell which seemed to ring the warning of his own death in his ears.

He had failed of revenge. Not only so. Vengeance, like some mongrel cur, had turned on his cherisher—and devoured him.

CHAPTER XXX

THE Court emptied slowly. As men of all classes poured out into the street they were busy discussing the strange events of the day. So certain had seemed Antonio's fate; so swift the turning of the tables by the clever arguments of the youthful lawyer from Padua.

All were agreed with the great Bellario's commendation of this wise young doctor, who had surely saved Antonio's life that day, and saved Venice, too, the shame of a bloody stain upon her records of justice.

On the Rialto, the Piazza, in palace and wine shop, nothing was talked of that evening but the case of Shylock and Antonio, and how the former had been confounded and the latter saved by a lawyer from Padua whose chin was smooth as a girl's and his shape as slim as a boy's.

Duke Niccolo, however, had not immediately left the court, but had withdrawn to an inner room accompanied by some of his nobles and followed at his request by the young Paduan doctor, Bassanio and Antonio.

The Duke was vastly relieved that the case had been settled in so highly satisfactory a manner. His motto, "Justice in the Palace," remained unchallenged; yet Antonio Cainello had been rescued from an unmerited fate, and a cruel usurer had received a drastic lesson which would be a future warning to all his tribe.

(302)

So da Ponte's manner was very gracious in addressing Bellario's young substitute.

"Sir," quoth he courteously, "you will accompany us to the Palace? I would fain have you dine with us presently."

The young man bowed respectfully.

"I humbly desire pardon of Your Grace," he replied, "but urgent business recalls me to Padua this evening, and I may not delay my return."

The Duke seemed disappointed. This paragon of wisdom interested him, and he would have enjoyed bettering his acquaintance.

But he saw it was useless to press the invitation, and after a few very courteous expressions of regret, together with warm praise and gratitude for the service which he declared was no less to the State than to Antonio himself, Duke Niccolo took his departure back to the Palace, followed by his train of nobles and attendants.

Bassanio and Antonio were left alone with the lawyer, who seemed anxious to escape their thanks—but could not contrive it.

Bassanio—ever the more impetuous—barred the way, his handsome features flushed by a joy which set his whole face aglow.

"Most worthy and illustrious Signior," said he, extending the leathern bag which he had twice proffered to Shylock, "I and my friend have, by your wisdom, this day been acquitted of grievous penalties. We do earnestly crave your acceptance of this bag of three thousand ducats as some slight acknowledgment of our debt."

"And," added Antonio softly, "stand indebted over and above, in love and service to you evermore."

But, to the surprise of both, the lawyer shook his head, obviously intent in escaping both thanks and reward.

"He is well paid, Signiors," he replied, "who is well satisfied. My best reward—the only one I desired— was in saving you, Messer Antonio. And having won success in this, I count myself well paid. So, as I am in haste, I take my leave, praying you know me when we meet again."

Still Bassanio barred the way.

"Dear sir," he urged, "I implore you take some remembrance of us as a tribute, not a fee? Grant me two things, I pray you. Not to deny me, and to pardon me."

It was strange how the lawyer avoided his petitioner's glance, keeping his eyelids lowered and his face in shadow under his flat cap.

"You press me far," he replied diffidently, "and therefore I will yield. Give me your gloves—I"ll wear them for your sake. And for your love, I'll take this ring from you. Do not draw back your hand. I'll take no more—and you in love shall not deny me this."

But Bassanio had indeed withdrawn the hand on which Portia's ring glittered so sparklingly. The young man's cheeks were suffused with shamed blushes and he displayed the greatest embarrassment.

"This ring, Signior," he stammered. "Alas, it— it is but a trifle. I'll not shame myself to give you this!"

"I'll have nothing else, but only this," retorted the young Paduan, with some animation. "And now, methinks, I have a mind to it."

Still Bassanio hesitated.

"There's more depends on this than on the value,"

he explained. "But in its place I will give you the most valuable ring in Venice, and find it out by proclamation. Only for this, I pray you, pardon me."

But the other merely shrugged his shoulders, after the fashion of a man sorely offended, and moved towards the door, beckoning his clerk.

"I see, Signior," he replied coldly. "You are liberal in offers. You taught me first to beg, and now teach me how a beggar should be answered."

He reached the door, raised the curtain and would have gone without further farewell, but Bassanio followed him.

"Signior," he pleaded, "this ring was given me · by my wife, who, when she put it on, made me vow I should neither sell, nor give, nor lose it."

The lawyer did not turn. "That excuse," he retorted scathingly, "serves many men to save their gifts. If your wife be not a mad woman, and learns how well I have deserved this ring, she would not be angry at your bestowing it. However—peace be with you."

Bassanio watched the slender figure in its red robes pass down the passage followed by the young clerk, and heavily he sighed as he saw both disappear round the corner.

Antonio's hand was on his arm, the merchant's tones were urgent in their beseeching.

"Bassanio," he begged, "let him have the ring? Let his deserts and my love weigh in this against your wife's command."

The young noble could not withstand the plea, though, strangely enough, Portia's image was most vividly before him, the echo of her voice seemed to ring in his ears. Portia! Of whom was it that that Paduan doctor had

20

reminded him? Illusive fancy—it could not be Portia herself? His fair and lovely lady could have no resemblance with yon dark-skinned youth.

Antonio still urged his request, and, with his friend new-won to him from the grave itself, Bassanio could do nothing else than yield. Yet even for Antonio, and the claim of gratitude which urged him too, he was reluctant to draw his lady's ring from his finger and hand it to Gratiano.

"Gratiano," he begged of the young man who had been lingering in the passage without, "I pray you hasten after the doctor from Padua, to whom we owe so much to-day; give him this ring, and bring him if you can to Antonio's house."

Gratiano took the ring, turning it curiously in his hand, whilst he wondered greatly, knowing from whom Bassanio had accepted it—and on what conditions. Yet a shrewd glance at his friend's face warned him to hold that readily-wagging tongue of his. So without a question he hurried away in pursuit of the lawyer and his clerk, who had by this time reached the street and were turning down one of the narrow lanes which ran parallel with a canal.

Signior Balthazar, the learned friend of Dr. Bellario, had caught his clerk's hand in very eager fashion, as they turned out of sight of the court.

"Nerissa," he whispered, "quick! We must reach the house of old Lisabetta in the Via Cheriati and rid ourselves of these disguises. Santa Maria! To be a woman again!"

The dingy clerk echoed the low laugh.

"You will essay to return to Belmont to-night, lady?" she asked breathlessly.

"No, no," replied Portia di Nerlini, glancing nervously behind her. "It is already late, and we shall sleep safelier under my old nurse's roof. Our husbands are not returning till the morrow's noon, so we shall be home in time to welcome them. If only I could have won Bassanio's ring I should be very content! What a jest we should have played, making accusation that other fair ones had claimed our guerdons. Nay, more slowly, Nerissa, we must consider carefully, for, before you don petticoats again, I want my nimble clerk to search out the house of Shylock the Jew, give him this deed and make him sign it. I think the Signior Lorenzo would be grateful for the sight of it, and I would have all glad hearts at Belmont on our return, though it shall be our humor, if may be, to play the teasing scolds first. If I had but that ring! I do not give up hope that Bassanio will repent his churlishness and seek me out."

"If I mistake not, lady, someone already does so. There are footsteps behind us, and I would wager my hopes of happiness that I heard Gratiano's voice."

"Gratiano? Softly, softly then. Without doubt he comes with my ring from my lord. If this be sooth I will ask his favor in taking you on your way to Shylock's house, whilst I seek Lisabetta—and my proper self."

Nerissa laughed beneath her breath.

"If Gratiano takes the clerk to the Jew," she murmured naughtily, "I'll wager the clerk finds some way to jew him of his wife's gift and then chide him on the morrow for a false swearer. We live in merry times, lady."

The voice of Gratiano calling them to stay checked Portia's reply, and the next moment the young Venetian came panting after them.

"Signior," he gasped, holding out a ring to the disguised Portia, "you are well overtaken. My Lord
Bassanio Ramberti on consideration prays your acceptance of this ring, and further entreats your company at
dinner."

Portia took the extended trinket between slim fingers.

"I pray you tell your friend," she replied suavely,
"that I most gratefully accept this ring, though at the
same time I beg you to make my excuses, since it is
impossible I should dine with him, having already explained to the Duke that necessity recalls me home.
Yet, fair sir, I shall be greatly in your debt if before taking
my message you would show my youth here old Shylock's
house?"

Gratiano bowed.

"Most willingly," he answered. "Come, boy, this
way. Illustrious Signior, I am forever your devoted
servant."

Portia returned his courteous salutations with easy
grace, and having slipped Bassanio's ring upon her finger
and bidding Nerissa seek her out speedily at the house
she knew of, turned away in the direction in which old
Lisabetta Strozzi, her childhood's nurse and faithful
friend, lived.

Nerissa was smiling slyly to herself as she followed
Gratiano along the ill-lighted street to where Shylock the
Jew lived. She wondered what this very patronizing
gentleman would say if he guessed that the shabby youth
he treated so cavalierly were his own wife.

CHAPTER XXXI

"**L**ORENZO!"

"Why did you call, carissima?"

"Only because the moon shines yonder amongst the trees, and whilst we wait the coming of the Lady Portia why should we not go out? Is it too late to dream our dreams, dear love, because we have told each other so often the riddle of them?"

The young Venetian laughed as he flung his arm about his wife, drawing her down the shallow flight of steps towards the terrace and the more distant groves of trees.

Here at Belmont they had found the joy of an unclouded happiness, since here they seemed in safety from the haunting fear which had dogged their steps at Genoa.

Jessica especially had known what reason there was not only to fear the anger of her father but the remorseless vendetta of Aaron Tubal. And as she recounted her fears to her husband, Lorenzo had bitterly reproached himself with selfishness, for he was too poor to be able to seek safer asylum far from his native Venice, since he had no means to procure a livelihood such as his business in the city won him; and so recklessly had they squandered the Jew's ducats during the first weeks of their marriage, that only a mere handful of coins stood between them and abject penury. There was nothing, as far as Lorenzo could see, but to return to Venice and his business there; yet this would also mean a return to the vengeance of Shylock and Tubal.

But to-night Lorenzo the light-hearted put such sordid cares to one side as completely as though they had never existed, whilst he gave himself up to the enjoyment of a romantic hour. His love to his pretty Jessica was as passionate as ever. He could have dreamed thus with her throughout an eternity, not troubling in the least even if he might never see Venice again.

It was the fear of what that return might cost them both which had weighed on his mind.

Yet now the moonlight fell on wide lawns and caught the sparkling waters of a softly plashing fountain. Jessica was beside him, tragedy and poverty far away.

So, with happy carelessness, Lorenzo laughed, kissing his wife's upturned face with all the ardor of a lover.

"The moon shines brightly," whispered he. "In such a night, when the sweet wind did gently kiss the trees, Troilus, methinks, mounted the Trojan walls and sighed his soul towards the Grecian tents where Cressida lay that night."

Jessica nestled closer to his embrace.

"In such a night," she breathed, yielding to the rapture of the dream, "did Thisbe fearfully o'ertrip the dew; and saw the lion's shadow ere himself, so ran dismayed away."

"In such a night," laughed Lorenzo, as they crossed the moonlit lawns, "stood Dido with a willow in her hand upon the wild sea banks, and waved her love to come again to Carthage."

"In such a night," mused Jessica, half-cradled in lover-arms, "Medea gathered the enchanted herbs that should renew old Æson."

"In such a night," teased Lorenzo, "did Jessica steal from the wealthy Jew and with a thriftless lover, ran away from Venice."

Jessica pouted her red lips, looking up through half-closed eyes, which sparkled where the moonbeams kissed them.

"In such a night," she mocked, "did young Lorenzo swear he loved her well; stealing her soul with many vows of faith—and ne'er a true one!"

"And in such a night," he retorted glibly, "did pretty Jessica, like a little shrew, slander her love and he forgave her."

Whereat they fell to laughter and kisses like the light-hearted children they were, tender and teasing by turns, as they stood beside the silver-shining fountain, under cypress shade, knowing no fear or pain till the moonlight fading showed them the blacker shrouding of the night.

It was then that Jessica, her head upon her husband's breast, whispered a fear which ever returned goblin-fashion in the dark.

"If we could always stay here—always dreaming—always loving!" she sighed. "But I grow afraid, Lorenzo, thinking less of my father's anger—though that must be great—than of Tubal's jealous vengeance. You will not return to Venice, dear love of mine?"

But Lorenzo, recalling his state of poverty and the grim necessity for that return, could not reply, only holding the slim little figure to his heart and whispering passionate vows of love and protection again and again, till Jessica allowed herself to be persuaded that there would be moonlight nights in which they two should dream even in Venice; and so, presently, they went back to the palazzo, where long since the servants had retired to rest. But little did Lorenzo and his wife guess, as they looked out upon the sleeping darkness which surrounded this safe asylum of theirs, that away in Venice an old man bent cursing and groaning over a parchment scroll, most unwillingly setting his name to the paper which should be the seal to his daughter's happiness and freedom.

So the night passed, and at length the slow dawn broke in eastern skies.

It was not without surprise that Lorenzo and Jessica received a hard-riding messenger, who bade them prepare for the speedy return of the mistress of the mansion.

Sweat and dust covered the man's face, so that Jessica wondered whether it were possible he had only ridden from the Convent of St. Ursula scarcely two miles away.

But the fellow seemed in no mood to be questioned, and having delivered his message, went stumbling away in search of refreshment.

"They keep empty cellars it seems up yonder," quoth Lorenzo whimsically, as he pointed in the direction of the hill on which the convent stood, "and poor Pietro must have the knack of collecting the dust of the highway down his throat. But come, Jessica, this shall—if it please the saints to answer our poor prayers—be a happy dawn. So let us seek Florio, and bid the good old man set the musicians piping to hail their lady's return and give her welcome home."

But Florio had already heard Pietro's news and did not need the Signior Lorenzo's hint concerning the welcome of a beloved mistress.

Being an old and favored servant, he was perhaps a little resentful of the stranger's interference, though brief ill-humor passed under the tactful gentleness of Jessica's suggestions.

So all was gay bustle at the Palazzo di Nerlini, and everything was in readiness long ere Lorenzo and his wife paced side by side down the wide avenue, to be first in their greeting of this noble chatelaine, to whom they already felt they owed much.

The sound of returning coach wheels was heard as they paused near the great gates, and as they drew aside for the Lady Portia's carriage to pass, Portia herself cried to her coachman to stop.

Then, quickly alighting, with Nerissa, demure and modest as though she would have died sooner than dream of strutting in manly hose and doublet, following her, the lady dismissed the coach, embraced Jessica very kindly, and gave her hand for Lorenzo's kiss.

"Dear lady," cried the Venetian gallantly, "welcome home to Belmont."

Portia laughed joyously. She was radiant as any Aurora this morning, in her beauty and happiness, nor was there any stain on her fair skin to show how she had once played the part of dusky Balthazar, whose wig and robes were already on their way back to Padua, with her grateful thanks to her illustrious cousin Bellario.

"We have been praying for our husbands' welfare," she lied naughtily, "who speed, we hope, the better for our words. Are they returned?"

How her blue eyes sparkled in the sunlight, whilst laughter rippled like dancing beams over her lovely face!

"They are not here yet, Signora," replied Lorenzo respectfully, "but just now we received the messenger who warns us of their coming."

The lady nodded, beckoning to her maid.

"Go in, Nerissa," she commanded. "Give order to my servants that they take no note at all of our having been absent. Nor you—Lorenzo; Jessica, nor you."

She turned impulsively from one to other of her perplexed guests, whilst Nerissa ran blithely off across dew-sprent grass, light as a lapwing on her mistress' errand.

As for Portia, she was like a girl just home from school, laughing, radiant, bewitching in this new mood.

Yet presently, after they had drunk their chocolate together on the wide-arched veranda, she grew a thought more pensive, the bright color· flushing her cheeks at sound of distant horsehoofs beating the dusty highway. Was she shy, filled with new-born maiden bashfulness at this meeting with her lord?

Yet, even as those who watched her asked the question to themselves, she was laughing more merrily than they all, whilst in her freshly-donned gown of blue velvet, whose high ruff framed the lovely, girlish face as a rosebud is garnished by its leaves, she led the way down the veranda steps.

"Surely they are come," cried she, "and we must go to welcome and rejoice with these our lords."

And her sweet lips parted in dewy expectancy as she held out her hand to Nerissa, whilst with the other she clasped Jessica's waist.

But Lorenzo, left forlorn behind such a galaxy of youth and beauty, piped on a doleful note.

"It may be, lady," said he, "that they return in sorrow. For, though I would not be banned as a croaker, I cannot forget the sad case Antonio Cainello found himself in."

But Jessica, being Shylock's daughter, was the only one of that trio to shudder at her husband's words. Portia only caroled the more gayly, refusing to be sad on such a morn, though she gave no good reason to Lorenzo for her mirth, save the fairness of the day.

"Fie!" she scolded. "The sun shines too brightly and my heart beats too lightly for ill to be near. It is a day for mirth, not tears; life, not death; and love in place of hate."

Nor had she finished on an upward lilting note before three men came into sight at the farther end of the long terrace, and Lorenzo's gloomy prophecies gave place to his glad cry of relief, as in the central figure he recognized Antonio Cainello himself.

Be sure that was a merry greeting on a merry morn, though at first Antonio stepped aside to speak with Lorenzo and his wife, leaving those other four, twain and twain, to welcome each other as love should teach them.

No shadow was there in earth and sky for Portia di Nerlini that day; no, nor for Nerissa her friend and maid; yet both girls, looking deeply into their husbands' eyes, fancied to see a lurking trouble, carefully hidden indeed and only observable by those who sought it.

Yet, because, after all, a woman, like a tiger or a cat, has the element of teasing cruelty in her nature—be it of the gentlest fashion—both Portia and Nerissa laughed more gayly in spying that trouble by which they meant to profit.

But for the moment the time had not arrived, so Bassanio, leading forward his dearest friend, brought him before the lady who found him less stranger to her than she to him.

Yet so demure was her stiff curtsy that none could

have suspected they had clasped hands the day before as comrades and equals.

"You will give welcome to my friend, carissima," said Bassanio in his eager, impetuous tones. "This is the man, this is Antonio, to whom I am so infinitely bound."

And his gray eyes kindled as he looked from that dear friend to his yet dearer love, thinking how fair she must seem to Antonio's eyes since she never had been fairer in his own.

Portia was smiling rarely as the young merchant raised her hand to his lips, but she looked at Bassanio.

"You should in all sense be much bound to him, since, as I hear, he was much bound for you," she replied quaintly.

Antonio raised himself, looking with affection to his friend. "No more than I am well acquitted of," he answered.

"Signior," said Portia gently, "you are very welcome to our house. I hope that we may show it in better proof than words."

And she glanced across the terrace to where, at the head of a flight of stone steps, Nerissa stood beside Gratiano.

Lovers they should have been, since so lately had they plighted their troth to love and cherish each other till life should end. Yet, unless appearances were vastly deceiving, something very like a quarrel was in progress.

Nerissa had her back to her lord and master and was moving towards the group on the terrace, her rounded chin tilted high, lips scornful, cheeks flushed, whilst Gratiano followed her, protesting volubly.

"By my love I swear you do me wrong," they heard

him crying, his voice high-pitched in distress. "In faith, Nerissa, I gave it to the judge's clerk. Would he had reproached me as the vilest ingrate sooner, since you, dear love, take it so much to heart."

Nerissa did not even deign to reply to this protestation. She seemed intent on tearing a tiny lace handkerchief to pieces between trembling fingers. Temper, not tears, sparkled in her black eyes—in truth, she was very defiant.

Portia, one hand set on her hip, fell to laughing.

"A quarrel, ho, already!" she teased. "What's the matter?"

It was Gratiano who, in sore trouble, made haste to explain away his guilt.

"About a hoop of gold, Signora," he said. "A paltry ring that she gave me, whose poesy was, for all the world, like cutler's poetry upon a knife, '*Love me and leave me not.*'"

The explanation lashed Nerissa into words, which came pouring forth in sobbing accusation, denunciation and condemnation.

"What talk you of the poesy or the value?" she cried, dabbing her eyes with the torn fragments of her handkerchief. "You—you swore to me, when I did give it you, that you w—would wear it till the hour of your death; and —and that it should lie with you in your g—grave. For your oath's sake, even if not for mine, you should have kept it. Gave it a judge's clerk! Oh! Oh!—the tale! But well I know the clerk who had it will ne'er wear hair on his chin."

Gratiano groaned in helplessness of spirit against such a tornado. "He will if he lives to be a man," he replied.

Nerissa was round on him in a trice, as an angry kitten upon a sportive terrier.

"Aye," she sniffed, "if a *woman* live to be a man."

"Now, by this hand!" vowed Gratiano, very earnestly, "I gave it to a youth—a kind of boy; a little, scrubbed boy, no higher than yourself—the judge's clerk; a prating boy, who begged it for a fee till I could not for my heart deny it him."

Nerissa hid her face in both her hands, whilst her shoulders shook—as though with sobbing.

Portia regarded Gratiano the culprit severely.

"You were to blame," she said. "I must be plain with you, Signior. You were wrong to part so lightly with your wife's first gift—a gift placed upon your finger with many oaths, so that it should have been riveted by faith into your flesh."

She looked confidently towards Bassanio, over whose smiling face a cloud of guilty uneasiness had gathered.

"Now," she continued, "I gave my love a ring and made him swear never to part with it, and here he stands; I dare be sworn for him, he would not leave it, nor pluck it from his finger for all the wealth of the world. In faith, Gratiano, you give your wife cause for grief by this unkindness, which would have maddened me had it been practised at my expense."

Bassanio had edged away from the group, making pretence to pluck a flower from a shrub near. He was in mortal fear lest his lady-love should call for proof of that highly prized faith; and even meditated whether he had not better cut off his finger, vowing he had been so maimed in defending his treasure.

Could he not, however, change this argument to a more profitable subject, and one less likely to cause heart burnings?

Alas! In excusing himself Gratiano did not hesitate to accuse another on the old supposition that blackening a friend or foe helps to whiten one's own character.

"My Lord Bassanio gave his ring away," he retorted sullenly, "to the judge that begged it—and indeed deserved it too And then the boy, his clerk, who took some pains in writing, begged mine. And neither master nor man would take aught but the two rings."

Bassanio did not dare to meet his lady's gaze; he was pretending to be absorbed in fastening a flower in his doublet—yet every word of Gratiano's speech had rung a knell in his heart.

And Portia was regarding him—did he not know it only too well? Did he not feel the burning accusation of those blue eyes before he met their fire?

"What ring gave you, my lord?" he heard her question in coldly measured tones. "Not that, I hope, which you received of me?"

Bassanio pulled himself together with a mighty effort. Never had he in all his life felt so conscience-stricken, so mean and guilty.

Yet he tried to smile in would-be whimsical fashion as he stretched out his hand.

"If I could add a lie to my fault," he confessed, "I would deny it—but you see, my finger hath not the ring upon it; it is gone."

He dropped his head a little as he made the simple statement which sounded so bald when voiced. Yet how should he broider the fact with argument, since he could not deny it?

And denial only would satisfy the woman who stood before him.

Antonio had moved away with Lorenzo and Jessica,

not having waited to hear the full controversy, since in staying to listen they might seem to intrude. So there was no intercessor to cry "Mea culpa"—nor would either Bassanio or Gratiano have shirked the blame their ladies put upon them by blaming in turn their friend.

Each was answerable to his mistress—and it seemed that neither Portia nor Nerissa was minded to be lenient.

Recalling their many oaths, perhaps the forsworn lovers read their guilt in clearer light than the deed had shown itself in Venice, when the rings had been bestowed by generous impulse born of impetuous natures.

Yet, guilty as they now seemed, surely the doom pronounced was hard enough.

Empty fingers told their own tale.

So void, summed Portia, were their wearers' hearts of truth.

And false lord she would have none of, nay, nor Nerissa either.

"Till I see my ring," the lady cried—and kept her blue eyes hidden from Bassanio's despairing gaze, "I will not again look upon your face, false lover that you show yourself."

"And I—as always wait upon my lady," added Nerissa. "Her will is also mine, as you must understand, false Gratiano."

So they turned away, crossing the terrace and re-entering the mansion, without a backward glance, leaving their new-wedded lords to stare upon each other's moody countenance and wonder what perverse devil had marred the beauty of that sunny morn by whispering so vile a misinterpretation of their impulsive action into the ears of wayward womanhood.

And where, alas! were Balthazar of Padua and his

stripling clerk to be found?—and when found how would they be persuaded to return gifts which had cost their donors so dearly?

Bassanio groaned aloud.

But Gratiano, forgetful of gratitude, cursed the whim of a learned doctor's clerk.

CHAPTER XXXII

A SWEET CONFESSION

"**M**ADAM!"

Portia turned impatiently, a letter held in her hand, whilst she scarcely concealed the yawn of weary boredom as she stretched a free arm above her head.

"Well, Nerissa?" she demanded tartly.

Nerissa came to the side of the great carved chair in which her lady sat, facing the window. She was smiling slyly.

"Gratiano hath written to me, madam," she observed, half extending her hand which also held a letter, "and sent it by Stephano."

Portia laughed, sat up, and tossed a loosened coil of fair hair back from her forehead.

"My Lord Bassanio hath also written to me," she mimicked, "and sent it by Balthazar. I'll vow the pair of them are of a tale, Nerissa. Come! you shall tell me what thy Gratiano says?"

Nerissa flushed, whilst the dimples played merrily over her smooth, round cheeks.

"He complains, lady," said she, "that I should so falsely accuse him of having bestowed the ring he had of me on a woman. By every saint in Christendom he swears most solemnly that he gave the ring in question to the clerk of the young doctor who saved Signior Antonio's life He argues—as though he himself were a lawyer bred and born—that the gift was yielded at the lad's importunate request, whilst he, on the impulse of a moment, when joy at Antonio's salvation made him recklessly generous, found it impossible to refuse the plea. Yet now he is at pains to vilify the poor clerk whose whim has lost him his wife's favor."

Portia laughed heartily. Holding the key to the jest, they could afford to be amused, whilst the love of teasing kept them for the time to the sport of punishing these care-racked swains whom they would presently reward by full confession of most astounding truth.

"My Lord Bassanio," said the lady, resting her golden head back amongst silken cushions, "is as full of argument as I myself proved to be yesterday. By his honor he swears, Nerissa, aye, by his soul, that no woman had that ring of mine, but a civil doctor who refused three thousand ducats and begged the ring. 'The which I did deny him,' writes Bassanio very truly, 'and suffered him to go away displeased, even though he had saved the life of my dear friend.' Then come arguments which show what shame and discourtesy it· would have been not to relent and send the ring after this wise Balthazar, who had conceived so freakish a desire. And, after urging that I myself would not have permitted such base ingratitude, finally admits that the ring was offered and accepted—hence all this misunderstanding. Oh, Nerissa, my sides ached when I read the effusion."

"Why, so did mine on seeing Gratiano's, mistress. Yet I admit my heart ached too for his distress."

"Tra, la, la—they shall have comfort enough later. I think, for my own part, they deserve this lesson to teach them never to break oaths sworn to a woman. Did you answer your letter, Nerissa?"

"No, lady. I—I came to you."

"Who have answered for both. Poor souls! How they will fret, gnaw their lips, and vow vengeance on all false swearers and liars! You are curious, child? Well, this is the message I sent, namely, we had heard on indisputable authority, that in Venice two fair ladies openly boasted they had these selfsame rings given them but yesterday evening by their lovers."

Nerissa drew a deep breath.

"Madam! You said that!"

"Certainly—it is no more than truth."

"Gratiano will despair. Consider, lady—he—they—may do violence to themselves in their anguish."

"Tra, la, la. Not they. They will argue, Nerissa —trust a man for that! They'll champ and rage, swear great oaths, write many billets and in the end find that we were simply stating true and honest facts, which but for their masculine folly they would have read long since."

Nerissa smiled faintly. "Indeed, I think I should have come at the truth in part ere now, had I been they," she murmured.

"Of course, child. So we teach these husbands respect of us at the outset. But who comes here? Another messenger—did I not tell you so?"

"He carries no billet, lady."

Portia turned to where a page stood bashfully in the doorway, holding the silken curtain back with his right hand.

His mistress beckoned him.

"Come hither, pretty Gaspard, and tell me who sent you?"

The boy came forward, dropping on one knee by the lady's couch.

"The Lord Bassanio and his friend the Signior Gratiano send you their love and homage," he replied in a shrilly sweet treble, "and bid me acquaint your ladyship with the fact that within the hour they ride for Padua; nor will they return without a certain learned doctor you wot of, and his clerk, together with the rings they bestowed too hastily upon them. And in this the lords crave your patience, since, though they may be long absent in their search, they will await success."

Portia glanced softly to where her maid stood, glum and mumchance at the foot of the couch, and though her own pretty face clouded, she could not conceal a lurking dimple.

"Why," she murmured, "if they do wait to find Balthazar and his clerk anywhere than here I do not think we shall see our husbands again, Nerissa. What say you?"

"Lady, that we discover the truth to them. It were cruel to send them away."

"Faith, it is none of my sending! You shall—you shall tell the Lord Bassanio, little Gaspard—but no, who comes here?"

Another page was at the door; he looked scared at the sight of his lady's frown.

"Gracious Signora," he stammered, "it is the Signior Cainello, who is desirous of seeing you at once."

Portia rose slowly, a dainty figure in her blue gown of soft velvet and broideries.

"Antonio," she murmured. "Why, Nerissa, here is the very messenger for our need! Or shall we call him father confessor to naughty penitents? Or—there, there, run away Gaspard, there is no answer to your message; and you, Pietro, bid Signior Cainello in.

Nerissa, you shall wait there.   Now all is ready for the
peace-making."

She had folded her hands in mock humility as Antonio
Cainello entered.

The young merchant's face wore a troubled expression,
and he looked at Portia's laughing countenance with
some apprehension.

Truth to tell, he could not fathom her mood, having
expected to find her either in depths of woe or shaken by
tragic rage.   This merry, dimpling girl, whose air of
grand dignity had been laid aside, was disconcerting
enough to him.

"Lady," said he, "I have craved audience very boldly.
Yet in my unhappiness could do no less, since I grieve
to think I am the cause of all these quarrels."

The dimples faded from Portia's cheeks.   Impulsively
she stretched out a friendly hand.

"Nay, you shall not grieve, Messer Antonio," she
urged.

"Alas!" he sighed.   "How could it be otherwise,
since I see much melancholy on a dear friend's face?
Melancholy in place of such joy as rejoiced a friend's
heart to see.   He was so happy, lady, in returning to
you.   And now his gladness turns to grief by this sad
misinterpretation—for I do swear to you, by my honor,
that he who had the ring was he who saved my life when
its fate trembled on the balancing of a hair.   Nay, I
myself helped to persuade your husband to bestow the
gift, and for this cause the more urgently beseech your
forgiveness and faith to him, staking my soul on the vow
that he will never so transgress again."

Once more the lady laughed, gay and clearly as a bird
in springtime, whilst, coming nearer to the other's side,
she held out a ring.

"Then you shall be his surety," she replied. "Give him this ring—it is the same he gave the doctor from Padua, whilst Nerissa here would thank you for being messenger with hers for her Gratiano. You looked amazed, Signior. Is the riddle too hard for you?"

"Indeed, lady, it is so. My wit goes stumbling in such perplexities."

Portia laughed merrily. "You shall astonish our husbands more then, since you may tell them that they need seek no further than Belmont, aye, nor this house, for the young doctor and his clerk. Is it then so wonderful, Signior, that a woman has wit and can play the dissembler too with the best of men?"

"It is not possible, lady, that you——"

"Were young Balthazar who answered Shylock the Jew to his discomfiture? Come, sir, you shall believe me on proof. Sit here awhile and listen to the tale which you shall carry straightway to those poor fools in punishment yonder. Tell them it was their own fault, since my last command to them in Venice was to bid them know us when we met again."

Mystified, amazed, wondering, Antonio listened to the fantastic tale which Portia di Nerlini told, and when it was finished took the speaker's hands, kissing them with a gratitude which brought quick tears to her eyes.

"Lady," he murmured, "you saved my life in this sweet conspiracy. I thank you for it, since all other words fail me. I thank you, lady."

"Why, then," she cried, her blue eyes glistening, "I am repaid—though that I was before in helping to save so noble a friend to my husband, and making him my own, I hope, thereafter?"

Antonio rose. He was thinking of how Bassanio
still waited without in the garden on the brink of a
forlorn journey.

"Your friendship with his, lady," he said with emotion, "will make the happiness of Antonio's life. Indeed,
'tis strange how closely knit are tragedy and laughter.
Yesterday I was a ruined man and like to die a cruel
death. To-day I am restored to all my best estate
with another noble friendship to seal and cement a
former."

"Yet your wealth——" hesitated Portia.

The other smiled. "Fortune is lavish with her
favor," said he. "Last night as we sat down to dine,
a messenger came in haste from the Rialto bringing me
the intelligence that three of my lost argosies, driven by
fierce winds out of their course, had weathered the
storm and safely come to port. I am rich in all to-day,
lady—but chiefest in my friendships."

"I think," quoth Portia softly, "Bassanio is very
fortunate in such a friend. I am glad of your happiness,
Messer Antonio."

Yet as she looked into the young man's handsome
face and dark, mournful eyes, shadowed even in laughter,
she guessed the secret Bassanio had never learned
throughout long years of friendship, and knew that
Antonio Cainello had learned both the meaning of
love and loss.

And the knowledge quickened the friendship which
she too offered her husband's friend that day.

"We will come," she whispered softly, "after you.
But you, our friend, shall tell the story to our lords."

So Antonio went, to heal a fancied breach and bring
amazement, love and laughter to those who grieved
yonder amidst the flowers and trees of the palace gardens.

Was it possible this tale were true? asked one of the other, and then their eyes being opened, they fell to mocking their own folly that they had never guessed so patent a truth before.

Had not memory played her game of will-o'-the-wisp with both Bassanio and his friend as they stood yesterday in court? The Paduan doctor's voice, the trick of poising his head—his clerk's pert chin and dark eyes. Where had their own eyes been, poor dupes and fools? Yet there was not sufficient time for their own tongues to scourge them, since their ladies were even now coming to them across the sunlit lawns.

Portia had stopped, meeting Lorenzo and Jessica upon the way, too kind of heart to raise her own brimming cup of happiness to her lips ere quenching others' thirsts.

So she waited to tell this anxious pair how the law gave wealth to them from the hoards of the rich Jew's coffers, and that so without fear or care they might go whither they would, escaping dread of vengeance to enjoy the happiness which love assured them of.

Jessica wept for very joy at such news, whilst with Lorenzo's arm about her she wandered off down some shady path, painting with him a pleasant picture of the future, rose-lit by a kind hand.

As for Nerissa, she had already found her Gratiano, and was scolding him too, since he was fain to show his admiration, repentance and devotion by kisses when she was all for chatter and teasing, listening to ardent vows or the making of shy confessions Portia had crossed the lawn to where Bassanio stood, halting there, watching his lady as she came to him in all her gracious beauty.

The birds sang their sweetest melodies in the myrtle bushes near. The sunshine poured its welcome warmth on everything, crowning the golden glory of Portia's shining tresses. She was coming! And he loved her. How the birds sang! How filled with happiness was the whole wide world!

Love held royal sway that day in the gardens of the Palazzo Nerlini. And if Antonio Cainello walked alone he too thanked God for all the joy around. Was he not happy too, rejoicing in the joy of his friends?

"Portia."

"Bassanio."

With hands locked fast they stood beside the plashing fountain, which formed sweet accompaniment for whispered vows—as old as the hills, yet eternally new to youth and trusting faith.

"And is it possible you were that wise doctor who saved Antonio's life?" whispered Bassanio, as he bent to look closer into his wife's smiling eyes. "How can I praise you, bravest and sweetest of lawyers? How can I reproach you for not betraying your secret before to one who suffered so just now?"

But his wife only laughed as she raised rosy lips to meet his eager kiss.

"You deserved far worse, Bassanio," she vowed, "since you looked into your Portia's eyes—and did not know them. Yet I will forgive you—shall I say for your friend's sake or your own?"

"So you forgive me I care not at all," he answered with all a lover's fondness, "for there is still one thing that with all your wit, dear doctor and healer of men's hearts and lives, you cannot argue away."

"And that?" she asked, blue eyes like stars, as she

looked into those gray ones above her which told their own tale.

"My love," answered Bassanio, very softly.

THE END

Lightning Source UK Ltd.
Milton Keynes UK
UKHW012126061118
331891UK00009B/572/P